1/17

DISCARD

Black Lotus

Black Lotus

A WOMAN'S SEARCH
FOR RACIAL IDENTITY

Sil Lai Abrams

HUNTER

Gallery Books · Karen Hunter Publishing

New York London Toronto Sydney New Delhi

G

Gallery Books
An Imprint of Simon & Schuster, Inc.
1230 Avenue of the Americas
New York, NY 10020

HUNTER

Karen Hunter Publishing
A Division of Suitt-Hunter Enterprises, LLC
P.O. Box 632
South Orange, NJ 07079

First Karen Hunter Publishing/Gallery Books hardcover edition August 2016

GALLERY and colophon are registered trademarks of Simon & Schuster, Inc.

For information about special discounts for bulk purchases,
please contact Simon & Schuster Special Sales at 1-866-506-1949
or business@simonandschuster.com.

The Simon & Schuster Speakers Bureau can bring authors to your live event.
For more information or to book an event, contact the Simon & Schuster Speakers
Bureau at 1-866-248-3049 or visit our website at www.simonspeakers.com.

Manufactured in the United States of America

10 9 8 7 6 5 4 3 2 1

Library of Congress Cataloging-in-Publication Data is available.

ISBN 978-1-4516-8846-7
ISBN 978-1-4516-8848-1 (ebook)

For Amanda

DISCARD

All you are ever told in this country about being black is that it is a terrible, terrible thing to be. Now, in order to survive this, you have to really dig down into yourself and recreate yourself, really, according to no image which yet exists in America. You have to impose, in fact—this may sound very strange— you have to *decide* who you are, and force the world to deal with you, not with its *idea* of you.

—JAMES BALDWIN

Prologue

AFTER A COUPLE OF MINUTES OF SMALL TALK, I KNEW. I KNEW IT
was going to happen, tonight. I was about to cross the threshold
from just a girl to a girl with sexual appeal.

I was on the verge of my first French kiss and I had absolutely
no idea how the hell to do it. Matt began to lean in toward me.
Everything was moving in slow motion as our faces came together
with expectant tension. My mind raced over how I was going to
execute this foreign dance of tongues, when he suddenly pulled
back to a comfortable distance and said:

"You aren't black, are you?"

"No!" I said in a loud stammer. "I'm not black!"

"Okay, cool."

He leaned back in and pressed his mouth against mine. Instinctively, I opened my mouth and allowed his tongue to slip
between my lips. My mind was buzzing with fear that he would
scratch up against my braces. Holding my breath, I did my best
to follow his lead. His tongue entered my mouth, then mine his
seven times, then capped off with a peck on the lips. I literally
counted each stroke of his tongue, and with each touch wished
that it would end. The uncertainty of my technique was kill-

ing me, and I didn't want him telling everyone that I was bad kisser.

As our bodies moved apart, I felt an instantaneous disconnect from the boy I had fantasized for months about kissing. With the sexual tension gone, we were once again two relative strangers facing each other in the shadows of the skating rink. After a moment of uncomfortable silence, Matt said, "Well, I gotta go. I'll see you around."

"Yeah, see you" was my quiet reaction. I watched as he walked away and reconnected with his best friend and fellow skater boy Robbie, who had just emerged from the back of the rink with his latest sexual conquest. Rushing to the building entrance, I waited for my friends Marideth and Wendi to come outside so we could catch a ride home together.

I saw them smiling and waving as they exited the rink. Their faces were a relief. "Where did you go, Sil Lai?" Wendi asked. I hesitated for a moment, then told them both what had happened between Matt and me. Leaving out his question about my race, of course.

"Good for you! You finally had your first kiss! Did you like it? Was he a good kisser?"

I didn't know if Matt was a good kisser or not. After all, I had no frame of reference. But I laughed and said, "Yeah, he was good," as we watched my mom pull up in our family's eight-passenger van.

I didn't say much during the brief ten-minute ride home. Once we pulled up into our driveway, I hugged the girls goodbye and ran into my house. After brushing my teeth and washing my face, I went to my room and lay on my bed. Doing as I had done so many times before, I stared up at the ceiling in the dark.

My mood was disturbed. A first kiss is supposed to be a happy teenage moment, or at the very least, a triumphant one. Yet mine was overshadowed by the fact that I had to lie about who I was in order to achieve it. Had Matt asked me the question about my race three weeks earlier, it would have been an honest answer. As far as I knew up until that point, I was Chinese, white, and Hawaiian. But I had just found out the truth about my racial identity and paternity, so what I had told him was a conscious lie. It sullied our already awkward interaction with shame. My takeaway from my first kiss wasn't sexual. It was social. I learned that if I ever expected any boy to touch me, I would have to lie about who I was.

"Passing" describes the choice to identify as a member of another racial group rather than face social prejudice. Passing has been practiced in other cultures, such as Jews seeking to avoid persecution from Nazis during World War II who passed as non-Jews in order to survive. But today the term is used almost exclusively to describe black people who consciously adopt a white identity.

The origin of this practice stems largely from slavery and Jim Crow: the systematic economic, educational, and social degradation forced on blacks in America by law. The system of Jim Crow, which legislated segregation, enabled the disenfranchisement of black people, and institutionalized white superiority led a significant number of light-skinned brothers and sisters to assimilate into white society. Civil rights activist and NAACP leader Walter White wrote in his *Saturday Evening Post* feature "Why I Remain a Negro" that approximately 12,000 blacks vanished into white society on an annual basis. This article was written in 1947, but the message of white supremacy and anti-blackness has been perpetuated for centuries. Fear, shame, and the desire to escape the burden of blackness continues to lead some black people to pass today.

In late 2010, I gave a lecture at Tuskegee University on the subject of colorism, which is the discrimination between members of the same race based upon the color of one's skin. During the question and answer session following this discussion, many students shared views sadly showing how these ideas persist, even among young people who were among the descendants of those who actively participated in the Civil Rights and Black Power movements.

Some may wonder how people of all races would continue to buy into the soul-shattering, body-breaking, and life-taking message that black is inferior. The internalization of the belief that one's value increases in our dominant culture—white society—simply by changing the texture of your hair by wearing long, silky weaves, bleaching your skin, or having cosmetic surgery to "un-Africanize" your features. Sources of this message are numerous. It's disseminated on internet search engines and in the magazines we read. The advertising we consume. The media we watch, the music we listen to, the films and television programming we see. The myth of black inferiority is rife in popular entertainment stereotypes, which often depict black people as ignorant and savage. It's promoted by the way mainstream media covers our lives, or in most cases, erases our humanity. Four hundred years after Africans were enslaved and forcibly brought to the United States in order to provide free labor for white slave owners, many of us are still enslaved. Mentally enslaved, since our social hierarchy is based upon white supremacy. Anyone who is "other" than white has to intentionally create their own counter narrative to the repetitive message that black is dirty. Coarse. Violent. Hypersexual. Irresponsible. Ugly. There is also the counternarrative that black is beautiful and brilliant. However, this message is generally drowned out by the persistent message that to be black is to be inferior. But if many of us were honest with ourselves—people of all races—we would also realize that within our own homes the effects of the "white is all right" mentality are still being passed down from generation to generation.

Sandra Laing is a black South African who was born to two white parents during apartheid. Prior to her birth, they didn't realize there was African blood in their genealogy. Sandra lived as a white child, despite her darker skin and kinky hair inherited from her parents' recessive genes. But at the age of ten she was expelled from her all-white school after being reclassified as Coloured by the government. Fearful of the social impact this would have on Sandra, her apartheid-supporting parents fought to have her reclassified as white.

Her amazing story has been told in a documentary, feature film, and countless articles. But this practice of choosing a child's race based upon denial, fear, or convenience is not as uncommon as one might believe. Eight thousand miles away in America, "benevolent" racial reassignment by one's parents happened to me. Just like Sandra, I was born into a white family and raised in a white community, with great measures taken to eliminate my black heritage—before I had a choice.

As Sandra matured, she came to see their "well-meaning" racial reassignment as an alignment with the white supremacist power structure. It was also a negation of who she really was. This is a revelation I would eventually have as well.

This is my story of how I grew up believing I was ethnically white, Chinese, and Hawaiian while being raised in a racially and culturally white world. This book is my journey of a woman who as a child initially "passed" in complete innocence and then later intentionally—and my rocky transition to embracing my blackness, both ethnically and culturally, as an adult.

Me with Daisy and Dad in Maui, 1970.

CHAPTER ONE

$\mathscr{I}$N ALMOST EVERY FAMILY THERE IS SOMEONE WHO FOR WHATEVER reason just doesn't fit in. In the Baber family, I drew the short straw. My outsider status wasn't because I was moody and defiant. It wasn't because I was always failing at school, and a blackout drunk by the age of fourteen. Both my mother and father were runaways and high school dropouts who had long-term relationships with the bottle. Unlike in other clans, it wasn't juvenile delinquency, mental instability, or addiction that pushed me to the fringes. Unfortunately, in my family these issues were not an aberration. My dysfunction, if anything, was an expression of solidarity.

Like those omnipresent cobwebs hanging from the ceiling that you never see until you're ready to sweep them away, my differentness was based upon something that was hiding in plain sight. I was the black sheep, both figuratively and literally, for I am the only black person in my family.

Looking back on old family photographs today, I have to laugh at the brazenness of Dad's lie and my naïve acceptance of it. We look nothing alike. I had warm pecan skin and curly hair. While swarthy, Dad was clearly white, with the type of thick, wavy black hair common to Mediterranean men. Despite the obvious physical differences between us, I believed him when he said he was my biological father. He's the only dad I've ever known, and he is white. But not "white white." He was Italian and English and his physical appearance heavily favored his Italian heritage. Dad spent a lot of time working outdoors, so most of the year he had a "farmer's tan." It was dark enough for the brown hair on his arms to seemingly blend into his ruddy, sun-weathered skin. The fact that he was capable of acquiring a deep tan made his lie somehow more plausible. Even though when our family was together in public spaces, people stopped and did a double take at me, the one brown body in our clan.

But I guess what was so obvious to the world wasn't to me because that's the way my dad wanted it. When I was born he "adopted" me as his own child the moment he signed his name on my birth certificate. Legally, George Baber is my "real" father. However, as I would come to learn after years of his lies, my biological father is really a black man whom I've never met and doesn't even know I exist.

Yet, as much as he tried to erase the truth, the question of my paternity was always there. Lingering. Like a persistent, unpleasant odor, the source of which you can never quite discern. My nagging suspicion is what led us to have an annual paternity Q&A that went something like this:

"Dad, are you sure you're *really, really* my dad?"

Chuckling, he would smile with his mouth and not his eyes, and say: "Of course I am."

"But why am I brown, and May Lai and Dan are your color?"

"Sil Lai, your skin is brown because you were born in Hawaii, and Hawaiians have brown skin."

"Dad, are you really, really, *really* sure? May Lai and Dan were born in California, but that doesn't make them Californians, right?"

"Stop asking so many questions!"

And for a time his answers placated me.

I'd seen photos of Hawaiians in the National Geographic magazines that Dad's mother, my Grandma Lou, kept stacked like kindling on the low bookshelf near her front door. While my hips were narrower and hair was much wavier, I thought a hula skirt *could* look quite natural on me once I hit puberty.

As I grew older, something about his explanation didn't sit quite right, but I knew better than to debate him. My capacity for argument at the age of seven was still relatively unformed, and he had twenty-six years of living on me. Even though I desperately wanted to press the issue, I'd leave it alone until the next time he was in a receptive state of mind, which wasn't very often.

I always thought I favored Dad, but as I grew older I was told on more than one occasion that I was a larger-framed version of my mother, Daisy Lui. She was a waifishly built Chinese woman with a five-foot-eight build reminiscent of an Upper East Side Manhattan society wife, and although it might sound like a stereotype, her facial features truly were as delicate as bone china. Her eyes were large, wide-set almonds framed with short, dense eyelashes, accented with salmon-pink rosebud lips. Daisy's jet black hair fell halfway down her back like a cape, which she often wore pulled behind her ears, showing off her elegant collarbone and swanlike neck. My mother's movements were refined, betraying her upper-middle class upbringing in the Kowloon district of Hong Kong. Like many Chinese, she kept her emotions hidden under a façade of agreeability, until you pissed her off.

Then you'd better duck, for she was known to throw the closest thing to her.

Daisy and Dad were roughly the same height, but that's where their similarities ended. His olive skin contrasted sharply with her paleness and their personalities clashed as much as their features. Dad was brutish and loud; Daisy was reserved and wary. Looking back at photos of the three of us together when I was a baby, I strain to see how I could have been so misguided as to believe that I was Dad's biological child. But my sun-kissed, caramel skin and wispy, wavy dark hair appeared to be a fusion of the two adults in the photographs. In the mind of a three-year-old, I believed I was George Baber's blood-related daughter.

Dad's features were inherited from his mother Lucy (Lou) Nicastro, an industrious and fiery-tempered Italian-by-way-of-Hammonton, New Jersey, a town known as "The Blueberry Capital of the World." In her prime, Grandma Lou resembled a more ethnic version of the legendary 1940s American movie star Rita Hayworth. She was noted for her independent spirit, grueling work ethic (a result of a childhood spent laboring in the blueberry fields), her indisputable culinary skills, and the ability to stretch a dollar. She was really something.

Equally renowned were her sharp-tongued criticisms of her two children—my dad and his younger sister, Doni—as well as their father, her ex-husband Ralph Baber. Although I didn't realize it at the time, Grandma was the first woman with quasi-feminist leanings I ever encountered. Her beliefs shaped much of my early, personal philosophies around gender.

Despite her feminist tendencies, Grandma still favored Dad over Doni. My aunt attributed it to the Italian culture's reverence for their sons and the fact that out of her two children, Dad was the one most like her. He was the physical embodiment of Grandma Lou's bloodline—a true Nicastro man. To her dismay, his sister took after their father, both physically and temperamentally. Both had patrician features and a taciturn personality that was as subtle as their gray eyes.

Grandma's obvious favoritism of her firstborn created a complicated relationship between her and her children. Doni resented being marginalized by her mother, and spent much of her life trying to gain approval that never came. Dad and his sister had a combative way of interacting with each other due to the rivalry that naturally developed as a result of Grandma Lou's behavior. But it wasn't Doni who lashed out at Dad as would be expected. Instead, he would assert his dominance in ways that could be outrageous. For example, when I was around nine years old, we took a family trip to pick oranges at a local California grove. It was a lighthearted, family-oriented day that ended in tears when Dad decided to "play" rough with his sister on our front lawn. We were all tossing oranges at each other when Dad hauled off and threw one at his sister with such force that it made her cry out with pain. "George! What are you doing?!" Doni asked, tears running down her face. I could see the large red mark on her pale thigh that would turn into a dark purple bruise by day's end.

"Oh for Christ's sake, Doni, stop being such a baby!" He laughed, oblivious to her pain.

"You know how easily I bruise! Why would you do this?" she demanded.

"You know what, fuck you, Doni. You're always so god-damned sensitive. Suck it up!" he shouted as he stalked away into the house.

Dad's resentment of his mother and sister was perplexing given his golden child status. However, in retrospect, I could see why he could be angry—at least at his mother. Grandma Lou was highly opinionated and rarely hesitated to share her views and unsolicited advice with Dad. More than likely, her decades-old resentment of Grandpa provided additional fuel for his emotional rejection of her. Instead of completely removing himself from her life, he accepted his mother's occasional financial support, while limiting her access to him and his family. It wasn't until I was an adult that I could perceive the complex facets of this woman who could simultaneously attract and repel not only her own children, but also her extended family and friends.

When I was a teen, I learned the root of her hatred from one of my paternal great-aunts. Aunt Thelma was married to Grandpa's brother, Glen, another quiet, unassuming man. Thelma—whom Dad wasn't very fond of—("she's got Glen's balls in her pocket")—had shared their sordid story with me during one of her visits. Grandma Lou and Grandpa's miserable marriage ended in a disastrous divorce during the 1950s, around the time Dad was twelve or thirteen. The issue wasn't just that they had divorced, but also that my grandmother had lost custody of her children in the process. In the 1950s Grandpa had done what was unthinkable—been granted sole physical custody of their children. This was during a time when paternal custody decisions in divorce cases were about as rare as four-leaf clovers.

Grandma Lou lost custody of her children because she was deemed mentally unfit by the judge presiding over the case. The reason for his decision was pretty basic and rock solid: in what would be one of their last arguments, she had grabbed a long knife in the kitchen and attacked Grandpa. No one knows if she had intended to murder or simply maim him; however, in the fray she managed to slice through the tendons in his hand, nearly severing his thumb. This part of the story Aunt Thelma had left out, but Grandpa shared it with me during one of my many inquisitions about our family history.

As far as he saw it, losing custody was a beneficent act on the judge's part: "She was lucky she wasn't sent to prison. Instead, she went away [meaning "was sent away"] to a mental hospital." Grandpa would show me his hand. There, ever so faintly, I could see the thin, silvery scar on the webbing between his thumb and forefinger.

The idea that Grandma Lou, a woman I knew as an incredibly loving, affectionate, and generous woman, could be a violent, potentially murderous harpy was unresolvable. As much as I didn't want to acknowledge it, I knew the story was true. Grandpa wasn't a dishonest man and the story had later been corroborated by Uncle Glen and Aunt Doni. Still, it was incredible to comprehend. The grandma we knew was devoted and caring, albeit a little smothering at times, and completely and unequivocally dedicated to her grandchildren. When we spent weekends at her tiny efficiency apartment in Long Beach, California, she would cook huge Italian feasts in a kitchen so small you could barely turn around. She sent us cards for birthdays, money when we would lose a tooth, Christmas gifts, Easter cards, valentines, and even St. Patrick's Day cards.

Grandma Lou did for us the things my parents were either unable or unwilling to do, such as taking us for outings to the San Diego Zoo, Sea World, the Pike in Long Beach, and the *Queen Mary*, which was docked at the Long Beach pier. Grandma was my idol, a woman who worked for years as a clerk in the Long Beach family court building and was able to modestly retire with a small pension, savings, and social security benefits. She was fiercely independent, emotionally tender, and endlessly encouraging. In her presence, I never felt anything but loved. I'd never seen her lose her temper. It was unfathomable that she'd be capable of violently attacking anyone, let alone her husband, with a knife.

Years later as a young adult I would ask Grandma Lou if the story Grandpa had told me was true. She admitted it was, saying, "It was a horrible marriage, Sil Lai. Grandpa wasn't abusive, but he was completely unavailable. He was like a ghost. A man completely shut down, who simply lived in our house and went to work. There was no communication. No money. Nothing. It was like we didn't exist." She added, "I was just happy to have found someone who would love me and help me with the burden of caring for my younger sister. When my dad died, I was fourteen years old and had to help raise my younger siblings. I couldn't go to college because my family needed me. When Ralph came along, I thought my prayers were answered." She snorted. "What a joke! I was so much younger than he was and didn't know it. Grandpa lied to me about how old he was when we got together. When I asked him his age, he said, 'How old do you think I am?' I answered something along the lines of him being in his early thirties and he let me think that. I only found out his real age when World War II started and he wasn't drafted. When George was born, I was twenty-six and Grandpa was forty-eight!"

When I pressed her to tell me her version of what happened after their divorce, Grandma Lou's eyes welled up. "After I got out of the hospital, I still couldn't see my children. The judge had given Grandpa the right to decide when and if I was ever going to see them again. Back then, women didn't have the same rights as their husbands, unlike today. But I wouldn't let him or a judge stop me from seeing George and Doni. I would go and stand down the street and watch them play in the front yard from a distance. For almost a year I watched but couldn't speak to them or let them know that I was there. Finally, Grandpa agreed to let me start visiting them. Not long afterward George started running away from home. My relationship with your dad and Aunt Doni would never be the same."

Both of my grandparents were not what they seemed, or at least, hadn't been. The simple, honest man who I knew as my grandpa had in his younger years been a drifter, a ne'er-do-well who had hoodwinked a much younger woman into marrying him with the promise of a stable life after a youth spent chasing women. As is so often the case, people are much more complex than what they present. What happens between a couple is rarely what is seen by the world.

Perhaps it was Grandma Lou's controlling behavior and unintended emasculation of my father that planted the seeds of seething resentment and abandonment in future generations. "Repetition compulsion" is a psychological phenomenon in which a person re-creates past trauma as a way to try to rewrite their past. It's a defense mechanism that leads some to constantly choose the same type of partners, often those who share personality traits with their opposite sex parent. Like many survivors of childhood neglect who grow up in chaos, Dad had an unacknowledged need to bring a sense of order to his life. But youth and circumstances (like the Vietnam War) led him to select a partner with whom he would end up creating an even more volatile home environment than the one in which he was raised. A mate who, despite the differences in appearance, mirrored the emotional instability of his mother.

The Baber family, Yakima, WA, circa 1946.
(L to R) Grandma Lou, Dad, Aunt Doni, and Grandpa Ralph.

The Lui family, Hong Kong, circa mid-1950s.

CHAPTER TWO

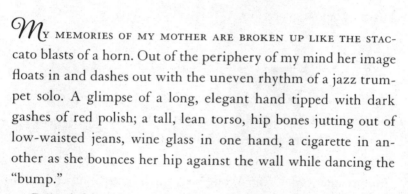

$\mathcal{M}$Y MEMORIES OF MY MOTHER ARE BROKEN UP LIKE THE STAC-cato blasts of a horn. Out of the periphery of my mind her image floats in and dashes out with the uneven rhythm of a jazz trumpet solo. A glimpse of a long, elegant hand tipped with dark gashes of red polish; a tall, lean torso, hip bones jutting out of low-waisted jeans, wine glass in one hand, a cigarette in another as she bounces her hip against the wall while dancing the "bump."

Daisy left our lives when I was around five. In her wake we were left with an emotional crater that I didn't recognize existed until decades later. This is not to say that if she had stayed that our lives would have been any better. In all likelihood, I'd probably be dead by now—if not physically, most definitely emotionally. Instead of death, what I've been left with are chronic sores that to this day are reopened by these splintered memories. A mother is the most important figure in a child's life. Or at least, she should be. But how does a girl learn to depend on a figure constructed from the fragments of a handful of conversations, peppered with the occasional dose of actual memory? She does it in the only way possible. By creating a psychological surrogate to live in the space where her mother *should* have existed. By doing this, Daisy became a larger-than-life archetype, ascribed virtues inconsistent with her true character by the five-year-old girl inside me who deified a very mortal and damaged person in order to emotionally survive. These treasured memories, frozen in time and nurtured over years, were of a woman who in fact had deemed me unworthy of her love. But this did not stop me from needing to fill in the gaps. To learn more about her so that I could understand not only who I was, but what was so wrong with either of us that she would choose to abandon me. Eventually my yearning to create a salve that would finally heal my wounds would bring me some answers, but no solace.

My mother was born in Kowloon, Hong Kong, on April 2, 1951, the year of the Metal Rabbit. Her birth name was Yau Lai Lui (or as it is written in Chinese, Lui Yau Lai). She was the third of four biological children born to my "Poh Poh" (Cantonese for maternal grandmother), Mei Ying Wong, and my "Gung Gung" (Cantonese for maternal grandfather), Cheung Siu Lui, a successful Kowloon businessman.

When Poh Poh met Gung Gung he already had a wife. He had married "First Wife," Kwei Fong Woo, back in his hometown of Shandong, but left her and their three children behind when he was stationed in Hong Kong during the Second World War. It was in Hong Kong that he met a woman with whom he would have a child, but never give the status of "wife," Po Fung Yung. Their daughter, my aunt Yau Choi Lu, also known as Shalina, was largely tolerated by Gung Gung, along with her mother, yet he still financially cared for them, albeit begrudgingly and sporadically.

In time, First Wife, Po Fung, and their children, along with Gung Gung's father, would all move in together in a small flat

in To Kwa Wan. But their stay in this town would be only temporary. They quickly moved again to another cramped flat in
Tsim Sha Tsui. Not all of his children with First Wife moved in,
as some by this time were already adults; in fact by the time my
grandmother entered the picture, all his children by First Wife
were out in the world, living their own lives.

Family legend has it that he met my poh poh one night at a
ballroom and soon thereafter moved her into this narrow flat with
his other "wives." Poh Poh already had a daughter, Yau Ling,
who was from a prior relationship. Like me, her true paternity
was hidden from her, and never discussed. Gung Gung "adopted" Yau Ling, and moved her in with his huge family, raising
her as his own. (Technically, only First Wife was his legal wife.
Both Po Fung and my poh poh were not legitimate wives—they
were in fact common-law wives, or as it is referred to in China,
concubines.)

Soon, Gung Gung's home would be overflowing with even
more people as he and Poh Poh's four biological children were
born in quick succession: my uncle Yau Kok in 1948; my aunt Yau
Gai in 1949; and my mother, Yau Lai, in 1951. My aunt Yau Wai
would be born five years later, in 1956. As was customary, all chose
English names that were used in lieu of their traditional Chinese
ones. Yau Ling, Poh Poh's daughter from a previous relationship,
was called Esther; Yau Gai became Judy; Yau Kok, Stephen; Yau
Wai decided on the name Lisa; and my mother chose Daisy.

The reasons why Gung Gung rented a one-bedroom shotgun
apartment that eventually housed ten people (plus the maid) are
up for debate. By now, the flat was so overflowing with people
that the balcony was used by family members who created two
make-shift sleeping areas separated by a partition. He was a
successful businessman who ostensibly had the means to acquire
larger accommodations for his family. However, there was a

severe housing crunch due to much of the stock having been destroyed during air raids, and the huge influx of people who relocated to Hong Kong after World War II.

To complicate matters further, according to multiple family sources, Gung Gung was an addict who spent much of his days lounging in opium dens, while his eldest sons ran his businesses. Addicts aren't particularly known for their fiscal management skills, or sound decision making. Despite this information, there is no way to know if this cramped living arrangement was the result of the housing shortage, a lack of cash flow, or a hazy, opium-influenced mind.

At the insistence of Poh Poh, Gung Gung left First Wife, his father, Po Fung, and their daughter Shalina behind, and took up residence with my grandmother in a roomier flat that would become their primary residence. While he still paid the bills, he had essentially deserted his other household and rarely visited, content in the new life he was building with Poh Poh.

Curiously, I was to learn years later that when Gung Gung and Poh Poh moved into their own apartment, they only took four of their five children (which included Esther; Lisa wasn't yet born). The child left behind? Daisy, who would live with Gung Gung's discarded family for a decade before she rejoined her parents.

Why they opted to leave her is not known.

But as I would come to learn from my personal experience decades later, familial abandonment and rejection provides fertile ground for seeds of rage.

✿

How Gung Gung went from internment camp guard to successful businessman in the aftermath of the Fall of Hong Kong during World War II is a plotline straight out of a Hollywood film. During the Japanese occupation, several thousand British internees lived under harsh conditions resulting from the lack of concern for the well-being of their prisoners. Malnutrition ravaged the captives' bodies. They subsisted on small daily rations of rice or congee unfit for human consumption, food that was often littered with cockroaches, cigarette butts, and dirt. While many of the guards ignored, or even abused the prisoners, Gung Gung took pity on those under his supervision, and did what he could to ease their suffering. If one wanted a cigarette or an extra food ration, he found a way to provide it. Two weeks after the Japanese surrendered, the British fleet arrived to take the internees home. Given that they were fleeing the country, several of his grateful charges bequeathed to Gung Gung the titles to their businesses. This is how an illiterate peasant from the Shandong province of China would become the proprietor of a blue jeans factory, antique shop, banquet hall, and a bar named the Red Lion Inn Pub.

As a child I always imagined the Red Lion to be a quiet, dark wood-paneled inn where nattily attired Englishmen played chess while sipping cognac out of crystal snifters, tapping out the heavy ash from their fragrant cigars into DuPont ashtrays. Elegant Chinese hostesses glided through the room, their slim figures draped in silk cheongsam dresses, Mandarin collars clinging to their pale, graceful necks, pouring drinks and bringing the patrons cigars or bar snacks. There, Gung Gung would stand at the top of the stairs overlooking his sophisticated establishment, thumbs hitched into the front pockets of his trousers, surveying the stately furnishings and moneyed clientele with smug satisfaction.

In reality, the Red Lion Inn was housed in a squat, three-story building in the Tsim Sha Tsui district of Kowloon. Its bright red-and-yellow neon sign flickered provocatively in the humid, heavy night air, a beacon to its largely merchant marine clientele. Instead of elegant wood paneling and crystal snifters, there were two-for-one drink specials and linoleum flooring. In lieu of elegant hostesses, there were barmaids, or "good time girls," who laughed loudly, threw back shots, and danced with patrons to the music blaring from the jukebox until the wee hours of the morning. It was in this rowdy, dank environment that my mother came of age, amidst the lecherous stares and propositions of drunken military men. And it was in this unromantic space that fate, for whatever inexplicable reason, would bring Daisy and my dad together into their macabre folie à deux.

Dad was a twenty-three-year-old artilleryman in the United States Army during the Vietnam War who'd wandered into the Red Lion Inn looking for a good time. Scarred from a troubled childhood and the war, he came in for a drink, an escape to his harsh reality, and found both in my mother. When his eyes fell upon Daisy working behind the bar, he was immediately captivated. Daisy was an exotic creature unlike any woman he had encountered back home in Yakima, Washington. At sixteen, she carried herself with the carefree and arrogant manner of those who've never questioned their place in the world. She was independent, fun loving, and passionate. A freewheeling and capricious sprite.

After an intense courtship, Dad asked Gung Gung for my mother's hand in marriage, to which he agreed, with one condition: Dad would have to pay for my mother to move to America. Gung Gung could have paid for the airfare, but for him it was a matter of pride and principle.

In his naïveté, it never occurred to Dad why a successful Chinese businessman would be willing to allow his eighteen-year-old daughter to marry a "*Gweilo*," or "white devil," high school dropout. The truth was the family was tired of tracking her down at parties, the constant arguing, rebellious behavior, and violent outbursts. Gung Gung was probably thanking his ancestors that someone had come along to take his problem child off of his hands.

Years later, I would ask Aunt Esther how the family responded to the news that Daisy was marrying a foreigner. "We were happy for her. But your mother, she always fighting with your Dad. One time they get into fight. She got mad and threw her engagement ring into the street. We spend hours looking for the ring in the dark. Fortunately, we find it for her and give it back."

Many other men would have been put off by her volatility, but not Dad. No, he failed to recognize that the passion between them was fueled by their mutual addiction to chaos and alcohol. Like many who grow up in dysfunctional homes, the emotional intensity between them was a bond that no rational thought could break.

Dad flew back to America and bussed tables until he had saved enough money to bring his true love home with him. It took many months for him to do so, but he arrived in Hong Kong during the fall of 1969 to claim his bride.

Wedding portrait of my mother Yau Lai Lui
to George Baber, Hong Kong, 1969.

CHAPTER THREE

DAD AND DAISY WERE MARRIED IN A SMALL CIVIL CEREMONY attended by only her immediate family. There was none of the pomp and circumstance that one would expect for the daughter of a successful Hong Kong businessman. In fact, the only formal part of the whole affair was their clothing.

The first time I saw their wedding day photograph I was thirteen. I was stunned. Who was this handsome, well-groomed man in the picture? The Dad I knew resembled John Goodman's character on the '80s television show *Roseanne*. He was unapologetically blue collar, from the tip of his paint-splattered work boots to the top of his unkempt hair. His belly hung over his pants, navel pulled taut over a stomach that had seen one too many cases of Budweiser. Dad's hands were always speckled with the residue of house paint that never completely washed out of the dark strands of his hair. In the middle-class, white-collar neighborhood where we lived, his appearance was a source of extreme embarrassment. As a young teenager, I wanted nothing more than for my father to fit in with the rest of the dads in the neighborhood. Men who wore business suits. Yet, here he was in this black-and-white portrait, looking like a heartthrob straight out of *American Bandstand*.

Dad was attractively attired in a sleek black suit with a slim black tie. A white carnation pinned to the lapel. Hair swept back from his face, he could've been an Italian version of one of the Everly Brothers. The only giveaway to the man I knew were the pant legs barely concealing his socks and the black, thick-soled loafers he wore instead of wingtips or oxfords. "His suit was a rental," Daisy would sniff years later when recalling the story.

My mother carried a small spray of white irises in her ruched white gloves. The tulle veil resting on the crown of her head was thrown back from her face, exposing her pearl jewelry. You'd never know she was already pregnant with me by the way her tiny 100-pound frame swam in her empire-waist floor-length white taffeta dress. Gung Gung's wild child looked so innocent. Eyeing the photograph for the first time, I laughed out loud thinking, *So much for the myth of the submissive Asian wife.*

Years later I'd ask Daisy why she left the financial security of her father's house to marry a poor man from the United States. "I wanted to get away from home. I wanted to be free. I didn't know your father was poor. I thought all Americans were rich. You know, like cliché—the streets in America were paved with gold." The word *love* never came up as part of her explanation, so I guessed she chose the closest thing: lust. "Your father was a very good-looking man," she said.

Instead of streets paved with gold, my father's dashing good looks and conditional discharge for going AWOL during his tour of duty netted them a small, second-floor apartment facing the Pacific Ocean at 845 Front Street in Lahaina, Maui. It was to this tired furnished efficiency that I was brought home from Maui Memorial Hospital after my birth in July of 1970.

I always imagined that my parents' early days of marriage were happy ones. And according to the way my dad tells it, they were. His eyes always lit up when he would tell his "when you were a baby" stories.

"When you were a baby you took a donut, dunked it in the sand, and then ate it!"

"When you were a baby you saw a cruise ship out the window of the restaurant we were eating in and yelled out, 'Boat! Ship!' Everyone stared at us. They thought you were yelling 'bullshit'!"

"When you were a baby, I would throw a quarter into the deep end of the pool and you would dive to the bottom and bring it back to me. You were just over a year old!" Beaming with obvious pride.

During their first year of marriage, Dad worked in a jewelry store, leaving his pregnant wife home alone. Years later Daisy would admit that she'd smoked and drank throughout her pregnancy. "I didn't see a doctor until my seventh month. I didn't know I was supposed to go."

Daisy and Dad didn't have a support system in place in Hawaii. Being young newlyweds, they still wanted to go out and partake in the bar scene they enjoyed with a passion. Since they couldn't afford a babysitter, I would be left home alone in the crib while they pub-crawled.

I would learn this truth years later about my "happy" infancy (at least as it was described by Dad) when Daisy shared a shocking story with me decades later. As the words fell off her tongue I was horrified, although I did my best to hide it from her. By then I was a mother myself and felt a sharp twinge of pain in my gut. *What kind of human being can feel comfortable leaving an infant alone while they go out partying?* My mind raced with images of infant-me awakening in the middle of the night, crying from hunger, or a soiled diaper, with nothing but the darkness answering my wails. I was sickened and fought back tears of shock. Tears I held back for the baby girl left alone to fend for herself twenty-seven years earlier.

Daisy shared the story very matter-of-factly and with no emotion. If I had the courage to admit such an act of neglect to my children, I would've been on my knees begging for their forgiveness. Not wanting to discourage her from sharing more stories from my childhood, I kept a neutral face as she spoke. It was only later that night when she left that I cried. Wondering how much their irresponsible actions had damaged me. If they had played a role in the formation of my own deep, emotional issues.

❧

Within a year following my birth, my parents left Hawaii for California, and settled in Huntington Beach in 1971. It was there in 1972 that my sister May Lai was born. Another move quickly followed, this time to Newport Beach, where my brother Daniel was born in 1974.

In appearance my younger siblings were a perfect blend of our parents and virtually indistinguishable from each other. Both had raven hair so straight that it could be mistaken for the synthetic strands on a doll, and their ivory skin tanned to a light wheat color in the sun. They were petite framed and sweetly natured, a stark contrast to me. My skin was significantly darker and for years I dwarfed my siblings by half a foot with my lanky and wiry build. While theirs were wide and open, my features were condensed into a small triangle in the center of my face, with small black eyes that perched neatly above what Dad affectionately called my "little button nose." In time my wisps of hair became a thick mass of black waves and eventual curls that were as unruly as my behavior. I was loud, rambunctious, and full of bounding energy that would eventually earn me the nickname "Spaz" in elementary school. The difference not only in appearance but temperament between my siblings and me was painfully obvious, but never openly discussed.

On the outside, we looked like a stable, progressive, young, multiracial Southern Californian family. But instead of beaches and blanket parties my parents were living a post-Vietnam nightmare: an uneducated vet coupled with a spoiled, emotionally unstable Chinese wife during a time when Americans were angry at anyone of Asian descent. Heavy drinkers raising three children under the age of five while subsisting on the limited income of an automobile mechanic. As the magnitude of their bleak reality began to seep into the fiber of their union, their fragile marriage began unraveling like thread flying off a sewing machine bobbin.

Still, they fought, clawed, and clung to each other with the tenacity of a drowning man to a capsized raft. They discovered there is something that can bond a couple together more tightly than love. Desperation and addiction. And together they sank rapidly into an abyss of economic instability, lashed together with the burden of young parenthood.

Each day Dad would leave us to work at the garage, entrusted in the care of our increasingly distracted mother. Daisy liked to pass the time playing music on the radio, lying on the couch absently smoking cigarettes, while May Lai and I would scamper around on our knees on the tan, matted carpet. "Play with us, play with us!" I would plead, grabbing and pulling on her arm. Irritated by the constant chirping, she'd banish us outside to play. "Go! Get out! You're too noisy!" she would hiss, pushing us out the door. There was the *click* of the lock and then silence.

Kicking the door with my bare feet, I'd call out, "Open up! Open the door!" Grabbing the knob, I'd jostle it quickly, bracing the entirety of my three-and-a-half-year-old body weight with one foot planted against the door as I tried to pull the knob off while May Lai sat off to the side of the stoop, absently playing with her hair. After a few minutes went by with no answer, I'd grab my sister's hand. "Let's go play with the roly-polys!" I'd say, more as a command than a suggestion, as she dutifully allowed me to lead her to the apartment complex's laundromat around the corner.

The laundromat was a low-ceilinged building with multiple air vents that forced warm, humid air out over a dirt trough bordered by the concrete pavement that led around the entire complex. There in the grit and dust of the soil beneath the vents, the damp air created a hospitable environment for the breeding of hundreds of pill bugs. We would pick them up and watch as they curled up into a tight ball on the small, soft skin of our palms. If we stood very still for a minute, the bugs would unfurl their bodies and begin an avid race off our hands. When we blocked their escape with a finger, the beleaguered bugs would ball themselves back up. Rolling them around in the small of our palms, we'd clasp our hands together, then shake them in our fists like dice. I was terrified of bugs like worms or roaches, but butterflies, roly-polys, and ladybugs were objects of sweet adoration.

We could entertain ourselves for hours with blades of grass, pieces of lint, or marching lines of ants. As the sun began to set and the cool, dry Southern California night air crept through the thin, cotton panels of our dresses, May Lai and I would huddle with our backs pressed up against the wall of the building. When the dryer closest to me would shut off, I'd move down the line of ducts until I found another vent to sit under that was still blowing warm air out into the night. "I'm hungry!" May Lai would whine. I was, too, and knew the solution. "C'mon. Let's go see Grandpa." Clasping each other's dirty hands, we'd wander past the swimming pool that sat in the heart of the complex, and make our way over to our dad's father's studio apartment. We'd tentatively climb the pebble stone steps that vibrated under our feet until we reached the top of the landing, where I'd ring his doorbell.

"Well, well. Look what we've got here," Grandpa would chuckle as he opened the door. Rushing past his legs in the doorway, I made my way immediately to his dinette table where there were always rolls of Lifesavers in a candy dish. "Can I have one?" I'd ask, fingers already wrapped around the roll. "Just one, Sil Lai. You give one to your sister, too." I'd peel back the silver wrapping that covered the sweets and look for a red or orange one. "Here," I'd say as I handed May Lai whichever color came first. Dutifully, she accepted.

We'd sit on the edge of Grandpa's mustard-brown-colored vinyl dinette chairs, legs swinging above the floor while he fried hot dogs for us to eat. When our humble meal was finished, we would sit on either side of him on his low, asparagus-green couch as he nodded off watching ABC's *Wide World of Sports*, or the nightly news. We would hang around his apartment until after dinnertime, when he would walk us back home to the other side of the apartment complex.

We loved spending time at Grandpa's, but at some point he began to turn us away.

"You hafta go home, Sil Lai."

"But Daisy won't let us in."

"Well, you can't come here every day. You've gotta go to your mother."

He would instruct us to sit on the couch while he made a brief phone call, and after a few minutes he'd come back and say, "Your dad is coming to get you."

"Nooooooo!" I'd wail.

Dad was always in a bad mood when he had to pick us up from Grandpa's apartment. When he arrived, he'd briefly pepper Grandpa with disgusted questions.

"How long have they been here?"

"Did you talk to Daisy?"

"She didn't answer the phone?"

"Jesus Christ, do I have to do everything around here?"

At the conclusion of the inquisition, he would finally end with a "Thanks, Dad." Swinging May Lai up on his hip, he'd grab my hand and dragged/walked us to our apartment. Once we entered the door, he would bark, "Go to your room!" As we scampered up the stairs I'd hear him shout at my mother. "Daisy! Goddammit! How many times do I have to tell you that you can't lock the girls outside?!"

As they fought, May Lai and I would huddle close. And then, the front door would slam. Jumping up, I raced to the window to see which of my parents had left, but it was too dark to make out a form. The sudden absence of tension in the home was disquieting. We knew better than to leave our room until told, so instead of satiating our curiosity, we'd jump up and down on the bed, even though it was forbidden, because it was the best use of our nervous energy.

The muffled sound of heavy footsteps on the carpeted hallway stairs would break the rhythm of our jumping. Not wanting to be spanked, we'd slide down off the polyester comforter and lean back against the side of the mattress. When I saw my dad's face in the doorway, I would be momentarily confused. "Where's Daisy?" I'd ask. Ignoring my question, Dad would reply, "Come on, girls. Let's get you ready for bed."

❀

Dad routinely rescued us from Daisy's neglect but he was not a true savior. He moved around our home like a caged bull, always looking for a target. As the "man of the house," it was his job to administer the more severe punishments for our misbehavior. It didn't take much to earn his wrath.

Once, Dad whipped me with a belt because I broke the heel off a new pair of play plastic heels given to me as a gift.

"I told you not to touch them and since you can't listen, you're gonna get the belt. Lean over the couch, Sil Lai!" he roared. Dad liked to heighten my anxiety by "cracking" his belt. Chuckling sinisterly, he grabbed the ends and folded the belt in half. Pushing the ends together in the center, he'd rapidly snap them apart so that the leather would pop like the crack of a whip. Dad would repeat this process three or four times before actually striking you, laughing sadistically as your panic increased.

Eyes darting around the room, I strained to see if there was any avenue for escape, but quickly gave up the idea. Even if I made it outside the door, where would I go? His voice boomed in my ear, snapping me out of my frantic assessment of the situation.

"I said bend your ass over the couch. *NOW!!*" I knew that whining only made his temper worse, but the words tumbled out of my throat faster than I could stop them.

"I'm sorry, Daddy. I'm sorrrrreeeeeeeeyyyy! I'm sorry. I'm sorry . . ." I wailed faster and faster, until my words blurred together like a rapid Buddhist chant.

"Goddammit, shut up!" he roared, raising his arm up in the air, leather belt hovering like a kite.

Eyes pleading as I looked back at him, I braced my body for the impact of the first blow. *Thwack!*

I cried out as the leather came down against the soft skin on the backs of my legs. Shrieking, I instinctively brought my hands up behind me, palms extended face-up over my backside.

"Move your hands!" he shouted. I paused, and he repeated, "I said move your hands, Sil Lai!" I tentatively slid them to my sides, and felt a searing white heat on my backside. Yelping like an injured puppy, I jumped down onto the floor and scooted on my behind up and down the carpet, desperately trying to transfer the sharp pain into the coarse fiber.

"Go to your room!" he yelled, as I tore up the stairs to the safety of the space I shared with my sister. I threw myself onto my bed. The welts on the backs of my legs chafed against the scratchy, baby-blue polyester comforter. My entire backside was on fire. Crying, I drifted off to sleep, wishing I'd never been given the toy shoes.

❀

At three years old, I began to notice that Daisy had her own way of interacting with me that was often different from other mothers I knew. This awareness spawned another feeling in me: envy. I *envied* the neighbor girl who lived next door. Periodically, we would end up exiting our apartments at the same time, running into each other on our shared front doorstep. I watched how she instinctively wrapped her arms around her mother's lower thigh, gripping tightly as her mom struggled to lock their front door. She buried her head in the folds of her mother's dress, peeking out at me when her mom bent down to scoop her up onto her hip as they left to run errands. I knew better than to reach out for comfort from my mother. Daisy was emotionally and physically distant, always finding a way to create space between us.

The more I grasped for her attention, the farther away she moved. For some reason she instructed me to call her by her first name instead of a maternal nickname. Until years later, it never really dawned on me that her distance and request that I call her by her first name could be due to her shame about my appearance. Me, the child who was a constant reminder of her dalliance with a black man. A child whose skin was like that of the peasant class in China, or worse, Filipino—those lowest on the Chinese social totem pole. By calling her Daisy, no one would mistake me for her child.

With my sister, she seemingly had no problem showing affection, or being called Mommy. I came to see the two of them as conjoined twins, locked in the reverie of love between mother and daughter, a love that I hungered for but didn't know how to extract. She was affectionate with her, and in our old photographs I noticed how it was always my dad holding me, never her. Instead, Daisy carried May Lai in her arms.

Maybe this was because May Lai's hair and skin tone was closer to her own. Or maybe it was because I was loud and always getting into things that I had been told not to. Whatever the reason was, Daisy didn't appreciate it when others chose to compliment me over my sister. Instead of pride, she would be visibly irritated.

"Your skin is such a beautiful shade of brown. Oh, what I would give to be able to get a tan like that!" cooed a middle-aged white woman in the supermarket in one poignant moment. Moving closer, she exclaimed, "You're so pretty. Do you know you're such a pretty girl?" Beaming broadly, I showed off the rows of my evenly spaced white teeth.

"Say thank you, See You Lai," Daisy instructed in her accented English, nudging my shoulder.

"Thank you," I parroted, grinning even wider. I looked up at Daisy, eyes shining, hoping to see my feelings of happiness reflected in her eyes. But instead, she kissed May Lai on top of her head, and avoided acknowledging the words from the kind stranger.

It's said that nature abhors a vacuum. A disconnect between a child and mother creates a void that will be filled with emotions other than affection. In our case, this detachment invited covert emotional and physical neglect that would transform into subtle acts of cruelty.

For example, during one uneventful afternoon, Daisy coaxed me to enter the dark hallway closet, and then slammed the door shut behind me with a roar of laughter.

"Let. Me. Out. Let. Me. Out!" I shouted, words muffled by the folds of the coats hanging around my head. I kicked the door, first with one foot, then alternating feet back and forth until I built up into a steady rhythm. "Let. Me. Ouuuuuuuuuuut!!!"

Throwing my body against the door, I felt her solid mass holding it fast in place. Hot tears began to tumble down my face, but my crying accomplished nothing. I sat down with my back against the door, bare feet finding an open space among the hard leather shoes littering the closet floor.

"I'm going to tell Daddy!"

"Tell him!"

I don't know how long I was in the closet. At some point I must have fallen asleep. The next thing I remembered was my dad opening the door and pulling me into his arms.

I began to watch my mother with wary eyes, waiting to see when her indifference would shift into menace. There was a quiet, pulsating sense of anticipation and unease that always throbbed beneath the surface of our relationship. Of contempt. But I couldn't identify what was wrong between us. To a child, it's unfathomable to think that your mother doesn't like you, and if she doesn't it's because of something you did—not who you are. Daisy was my mommy, even if she didn't allow me to call her that. Any shadow cast upon our relationship couldn't have been because *she* was somehow emotionally deficient. There had to be something was wrong with *me*. If I was the problem, then maybe I could fix it.

So over time I began a lifelong pattern of trying to change who

I was in order to be loved. Contorting myself into a thousand variations of what I thought she (or later "they") wanted me to be. I began to apologize for my presence in a million little ways. Barely perceptible gestures and slips of the tongue that signaled to the world that I wasn't quite certain why I was even here. I came to believe that if I could just be good enough, smart enough, pretty enough—if I could figure out the right combination of positive traits that I would be loved.

A rejected child never has a sense of certainty. Of belonging. Just the overriding, desperate ache of wanting to belong. At the tender age of three, I had begun to shoulder my pain and confusion alone, trusting neither my mother nor father.

If you're really fortunate, as you mature you will come to realize that nothing *you* do will ever change *them*.

Most of us aren't ever that lucky.

In 1973, Daisy managed to convince Dad to allow her to go home to Hong Kong to visit her family. And so along with my sister, the three of us boarded a plane and embarked upon what was to be a one-month trip. Our return was postponed once, then twice, then indefinitely, as Daisy enjoyed the freedom of living amongst her family, with no rent or food bills to worry about, and built-in childcare that enabled her to resume her unencumbered, pre-marriage lifestyle.

Concerned about her daughter's seemingly overall lack of interest in her motherly responsibilities, Poh Poh finally put her foot down and instructed her to return to the States and deal with her marriage. She also asked that I be left in Hong Kong to be raised by her, voicing concerns over how I would be treated by Dad given that I wasn't his biological daughter. Daisy declined Poh

Poh's offer, and returned to the States with both her daughters in tow. Another act of defiance to add to the laundry list of offenses toward her mother.

To this day I wonder how my life could've been different had I been allowed to grow up with my extended family. In Hong Kong I would've had the benefits of financial stability and strong family ties. Most importantly, I would've been chosen, my presence a result of someone's love and concern, not an unwanted child kept out of a sense of parental obligation or defiance.

After four months abroad, we returned to Dad and our hollow apartment. Whatever happened during our time back in Hong Kong disappeared from my memory. To this day I can vividly remember my childhood going back to the age of two or three, but something happened that caused me to black out this trip. Over forty years later, I still can't remember those months that were spent largely in the care of Daisy's extended family. Although I am an avid searcher for the truth, in this particular case it is probably better that these memories remain buried. Gut instinct tells me that some things are best left in the past.

❧

Now that we were back home I hoped things would be better between my parents. But they weren't. Something was seriously wrong, but I didn't know what *it* was. At nearly four years old, I was beginning to develop a consciousness that extended beyond my immediate wants and needs. I noticed how my parents no longer spoke to one another, and the constant bickering and sniping that now substituted for genuine communication.

Even though it was unclear to me, by now the truth of my paternity was an open secret among the adults in my family. On occasion, I would walk in on the tail end of their conversations.

"George, she has a right to know . . ."

"Dammit, she's my child and I decide what she should and shouldn't know . . ."

"She's gonna figure it out . . ."

"You're making it worse for her. You just don't know it yet."

Their heated exchanges would evaporate whenever I entered a room. I had a vague sense that these secret and heated conversations centered around me, but I couldn't prove it.

By now Daisy had all but abandoned her role as primary caregiver. In response, Dad's family members went out of their way to try and take care of her children while shielding me from her thinly veiled disgust. Grandma Lou and Aunt Doni especially coddled me with praise for my intellect and beauty, while showering me with affection. They placed more of an emphasis on me than May Lai—which didn't go unnoticed by both my parents and wasn't appreciated. "Stop showing Sil Lai so much favoritism!" Dad would demand. Nonplussed, they both continued this practice for years. Grandma Lou would tell me later that she loved all of us the same, but saw that out of her grandchildren, I was the one who needed her attention the most.

In spite of the strange energy that permeated every facet of our lives, I still managed to find many tiny joys around me. My greatest treasure was my younger sister. It was true that I resented May Lai because of our mother's obvious preference for her. Nevertheless, I adored her in spite of my acute pangs of jealousy. We were sisters and loved each other in that special way that only sisters can. She was my best friend and biggest rival for attention. Sadly, as the years went by, my sibling rivalry led me to engage in overtly emotionally abusive behavior toward her that would create a wall of distance between us as teenagers.

When we returned from Hong Kong, Dad had become edgier and kept a tighter grip on his family, becoming tyrannical in his behavior. After our prolonged absence, he wanted to make sure that we wouldn't leave again. So he began erasing anything that reminded him of Daisy's almost successful escape from their marriage.

One of the gifts that May Lai and I brought back with us from Hong Kong was a basic understanding of Cantonese. I loved that we shared something that no one else in the family, save Daisy, could understand. After our return, we had taken to chirping back and forth to each other almost exclusively in our newfound language. Most parents would be thrilled if their children learned a second language. Not Dad. He quickly put an end to our use of our mother's native tongue.

"In this house you speak English! You get it? English!" he shouted. Despondent, we reluctantly stopped speaking Cantonese rather than risk our father's anger.

Nevertheless, it didn't matter how assiduously he tried to eliminate my mother's ties to her homeland—nothing was going to stop her from eventually leaving him. The trip to Hong Kong did more than ease Daisy's homesickness. Unbeknownst to the family, it emboldened my mother to leave us all.

❀

Unfortunately for her, any immediate plans that Daisy had to divorce Dad were scuttled when she became pregnant after returning from Hong Kong. Although she was already emotionally gone, she was physically trapped, at least for the next nine months. After my brother Daniel was born in June of 1974, the fighting between my parents escalated, moving beyond verbal abuse and constant arguing to a physical denouement.

When I would look back in the years to come, the entirety of my early childhood would be summed up in one visceral memory.

This moment became a story that was a simultaneous indictment and question uttered to anyone who would listen. When I started telling this story as a little child, in the pauses and gaps in my sentences I hoped for some sort of conclusion, an answer from the person listening. For in this final, cataclysmic scuffle my family was knocked out from its wobbling orbit and hurtled, freely and without direction, into the never-ending universe of "what might have been."

Dad's work schedule followed a predictable pattern that allowed Daisy to quietly create a hidden social life. From time to time she would have visitors over at our apartment, guests that I knew shouldn't be there. She never told us not to say anything to Dad about her friends. It was something that was a given, a betrayal hidden in plain sight.

On this particular day, there were two strange men in our apartment. I didn't know anything about them, but I hated them. There was something dirty about the energy in the room when their midafternoon beers clinked together in a toast. I didn't realize I was picking up on the scent of sexual anticipation. Deception. Lust. These men with their shaggy haircuts, chain-smoking Pall Malls and wearing faded, tight blue jeans were interlopers in our family home. I was only four, but I knew they shouldn't be sitting on *my* dad's couch. Or dancing with *his* wife. Or attempting to play with *his* daughters.

One of the men paused from dancing with Daisy and picked up May Lai, placing her on his shoulders. I gaped, wide-eyed at the sight, but my sister just gleefully giggled. I defiantly demanded that he put her down. Laughing at my indignation, he ignored my order while his friend grabbed at me. I yanked away, but undeterred, he grasped at me again, gripping me tightly under his arm. Heading for the door, he braced my short torso against his ribcage as he carried me on my side, legs and arms dangling in front and back like the carcass of a deer splayed over the roof of a pickup truck.

Someone yelled, "Let's go to the pool!" My mother giddily nodded her head in assent. Laughing, smoking, drinking, stumbling, with my sister and me tangled up in these strange men's arms, we made our way over to the pool where their revelry continued for the remainder of the afternoon. My brother was left behind in the apartment, safely nestled in his crib on the second floor.

I sat off to the side in a pool chair, watching Daisy and my sister in disgust. No one needed to tell me that what was happening was wrong. How could they betray Dad like this? I shot dagger eyes at these dogs panting at my mother's legs, hoping that the intensity of my gaze would incinerate them into ash, annoyed that I was the only one bothered by what was going on.

The pale yellow sun started to dip beneath the rooftop of the apartment complex and the air began to chill. So the group returned to the apartment, where the revelry continued until the early evening. An afternoon of drinking caused Daisy to lose track of time, and she failed to realize her party was dangerously overlapping her husband's expected return.

At 7:30 p.m. on the dot, the front doorknob turned, and Dad walked through the door. The lighthearted camaraderie vanished in an instant as they faced Dad's all-too-sober reaction to the scene. I watched as he took in everything, a thundercloud growing over his face. Eyes narrowing into two dark slits, he half-snarled and spat out the words, "Who the fuck are you?" Muttering words I couldn't make out, Daisy's friends stumbled out the front door, miraculously without coming into direct contact with Dad's fists.

May Lai, Dan, and I were at the dinner table area eating. My sibling's backs were to the living room, but I could see what was happening between my parents from my angle. And even if I couldn't have seen them, I would have felt it. The air in our home was alive, crackling with my parents' anger.

The showdown began between them in earnest. Dad yelling in accusatory tones. Daisy shrieking back in her heavily accented English. I heard a loud, grunting noise and watched as Daisy picked a heavy, dark-green glass Buddha figurine off a shelf and chucked it in Dad's direction. Missing its target, the statue hurtled past his head, flying in a low arc into the dining area where it finally made contact with my sister's short, tan Tupperware cup of milk. I yelped as the liquid splattered on my face and over the table, jumping up from my chair instinctively as I watched the contents spill off onto the linoleum floor.

The entire scene, from the living room to dining area, was cacophonous. My brother was seated in his highchair, rocking his body back and forth as he banged his plastic bottle on the top of the table.

"Stop that!" I hissed, only to have him throw his head back in laughter at my milk-soaked clothes. May Lai pointed at me, laughing, encouraging Dan, "Look at Sil Lai, look at Sil Lai!" Embarrassed and scared at the same time, I ran over to May Lai's side, clapping my hands over her mouth.

"Shut up! I said, shut up!" She ripped her head back from my grasp and yelled out for Daisy.

I spun my head around, anticipating the slap that would usually result from me touching my sister, and instead saw my parents writhing in a bumping mass in the middle of the living room floor. Dad's knee was planted in the middle of Daisy's back, keeping her down as she struggled against his weight.

Snarling, she tried to move her head, but he held her face

down on the carpet, as she kicked and flailed helplessly underneath him.

I froze. I wanted to run over and pull my dad off her. But
I didn't want to have my face smushed into the carpet, too. In-
stead, I stood in the doorway and screamed as loud as I could. I
screamed again and again, vocal cords burning from the intensity.
It was the only thing I could think of that might cut through
Dad's frenzy.

What happened next was a blur. A thumping at the door. Two
uniformed police officers entering our home. Loud voices and
more accusatory tones. My mother gathering a small bag of clothing. Palpable tension as she left the apartment accompanied by the
police. Then finally, quiet.

Astrophysics states that one can't "see" a black hole; it is only recognized by the abnormal activity of the matter around it. Daisy's
departure left a black hole in our home, and our family struggled
to gain some sort of footing as a result of the void she left in her
wake. In the weeks and then months that followed that final
fight, Dad's family rallied around him and took over caring for
his brood while he was at work. Initially Daisy tried to visit us,
but Dad wouldn't allow it. In this confusing period, I stepped up
and tried to help out as much as I could. At four years old I could
expertly change my brother's diaper, and was already used to
keeping a watchful eye on my sister. I heard whispers of the word
divorce but didn't quite understand what it meant. All I knew was
that our mother was gone and I didn't know when she was coming back.

Like many children, I learned to gather information by hovering around the edges of the room where the adults talked. If

I didn't make my presence known, I got to hear the stories they deemed too "grown" for children's ears. This is how I learned that my mother had been convicted, at least in a moral sense, by my family of the heinous crimes of infidelity, abandonment, reckless endangerment, neglect, and emotional cruelty. As far as the Babers were concerned, she was dead to them.

I could hear my father's voice, indignant in its tone.

"And you know what, Doni? She didn't even show up today for the custody hearing."

Doni replied, "I can't believe it. I mean, what kind of a mother does that? To her own children?"

Dad then added, voice angry, "It's just as well. I'm not letting that bitch take away my kids."

I sat up straight, trying to take in everything that I had just heard. As my mind teemed, I began to formulate the final period at the end of the Big Fight sentence.

My mother and father were divorced.

Dad didn't know where Daisy was.

Daisy didn't love us. If she did, she would've shown up at court.

Daisy was never, ever, ever coming back.

The sudden disappearance of Daisy was both comforting and bewildering. A new stillness descended upon our apartment. (I don't use the term *home*, for there was never any of the safety or comfort in our family dwelling that's associated with the word.) Or probably more accurately—aching emptiness.

My siblings and me circa 1977, Anaheim, CA.

CHAPTER FOUR

In the absence of Daisy, Dad became the center of our world. We learned to stay out of his way, to speak only when spoken to, his affection buried under his gruff, coarse behavior. Our father's long hours at the filling station made his presence a bookend to our days spent playing outdoors. He lived with us but not amongst us, a man reeling from the aftershock of his ill-fated love affair with our mother. Thus began a style of relating between him and his children that would not change for decades.

After the divorce, Dad retreated into a lifestyle of stultifying solitude, creating a way of life that was simultaneously nihilistic and quixotic. The one place he found respite from this self-imposed isolation was in his faith. Dad was raised Catholic, but during his time in Hawaii he had immersed himself in the Baha'i faith.

This offshoot of Shiite Islam emphasizes the spiritual unity of humanity. Founded in the mid-nineteenth century, the Baha'i faith is a religion based on three core principles: the unity of God, of which there is only one, who created the universe; the unity of humanity and the belief that all people are created equal, that diversity and cultural differences are to be appreciated and embraced; and finally, the unity of religion, with the assurance that all major religions have the same spiritual origin, and essentially worship the same God.

But as with so many people, there was often a break between Dad's personal beliefs and his actual behavior. Baha'is are known for their racial tolerance and peaceful perspectives on life, which must have been crucial to his psychological survival post-war. Yet, while his religious conversion may have provided him with some internal peace, it did not translate into his behavior. He may have sworn like a Hell's Angel, drank beer like it was permanently on tap, and steamrolled over anyone in his path, but his tone would change whenever he spoke of his faith. And since it was the only thing that seemed to bring him peace, I wanted to embrace it as well, with the hope that this could bridge the gap between us.

I'd listen wide-eyed to Dad's stories about the beginning of the Baha'i faith and the background of its founders: the Bab, Baha'u'llah, and his son, Abdul Baha. He highly praised the love, tolerance, and respect that form the core tenets of the Faith. It was evidence to me later in life that despite his flaws, part of him sought a higher truth. While Dad's faith was oxymoronic to his actual lifestyle, it was the one thing in the world that he seemed to respect.

Dad told me I came screaming into this world on the first day of the Feast of the Kalimat on the Baha'i calendar. Out of his three children, I was the only one with either the maturity or desire to actually learn more about the religion. Part of this education included him reading to me from a Baha'i prayer book for children (a book that he eventually gave me as a gift when I was able to read). "Sil Lai, I want you to keep this book and memorize the prayers." I cherished this book and read it repeatedly in an effort to prove to him my commitment to the Faith. One of the prayers I even managed to learn by heart: "O God, guide me, protect me, illumine the lamp of my heart and make me a brilliant star. For thou art the Mighty and the Powerful!"

There was something magical to me about the words in this book. They transported me to another place. A space in the universe where mothers didn't leave their children behind and fathers didn't yell and threaten to beat you with a belt when you accidentally broke the heels off of toy shoes.

Between his grueling work schedule and fellowship with his fellow Baha'is, Dad did his best to cope. On the outside he appeared like many other blue-collar men with young families. But he was a loner who rarely socialized, preferring to tinker on his car while nursing a Budweiser. He would disappear at night from time to time, doing what, I have no idea. But as disconnected as he was from his children, he was also militantly resolved to provide for them, at least materially.

❧

There was a strange sense of detachment in May Lai and Daniel in reaction to such a cataclysmic shift in the makeup of our family. At the time, Daniel was just under a year old and had never bonded with Daisy nor she with him, so the desire for his mother's touch was unexpressed. While Daniel was not physically capable of communicating his thoughts and feelings around Daisy's absence, May Lai could. Yet she said nothing about it, which was odd considering the closeness between the pair. This character trait, of not discussing what most would, would stay with my sister until adulthood.

I, on the other hand, would bring my mother up to the adults in the family, but my queries were either redirected ("Go see if your brother is still sleeping"), or ignored. My curiosity festered, but I did my best to follow the cues of my extended family and not mention Daisy too often. Frustrated, my inquiries slowed down, submerging into a running inner monologue on the "what ifs" of Daisy. And like my sister's silence, this, too, became a behavioral pattern that stayed with me as I matured.

❀

I had grown accustomed to my mother's emotional absence long before her physical equivalent. Still, I yearned for a way to communicate my feelings of confusion and longing for Daisy. Without her intense presence, or anyone to speak to about her, our apartment became just another drab, lower-class town house. Life became routine. Dull. Flat.

In time we moved away from the site where my parents' marriage imploded into a neat, small concrete block house in Anaheim, California, free from the violent memories. Our new neighborhood was bracketed by Brookhurst Community Park, known affectionately by locals as "Moon Park" due to its sprawling landscape of concrete stalagmites, bridges, arches, and giant craters and the nearby Santa Ana Freeway. Unlike our old apartment complex, our new home didn't have a pool, but we had a good-sized fenced-in backyard that provided us with hours of contained entertainment. May Lai and I would spend hours inspecting every inch of land in that small, concrete-enclosed space while making ample use of the ancient swing set in the center of the area.

My father's sister, Doni, and their father shouldered as much of our care as possible, but it became clear that Dad was going to have to find someone who could step in and take care of us. Thus began a revolving door of nameless sitters who never lasted more than a couple of weeks. These young women were initially willing to work for the job's meager wages, yet somehow they never stuck around. I don't recall any of their faces or names, for they never paid much attention to us, nor we to them. There was no point in learning the name of a person who was going to leave, anyway.

❧

At the ages of three and five respectively, May Lai and I were free to roam our neighborhood unsupervised. I, a woman who years later wouldn't allow her five-year-old son to wait alone in our apartment building lobby for the school bus, had grown up with no one placing limits on my excursions into the world around me. My sister and I climbed and crawled all over the areas near our house without restriction, reveling in the warm summer sun as we raced about, hair unkempt, clothes dusty and stained from hours spent rolling around in the grass on our front lawn.

To the right of our home rose a man-made hill of dirt and stone that jutted into the clear blue sky like a butte. At the top was the freeway, where cars flew by at breakneck speed. Just below, on a slope of craggy dirt, were the train tracks. The saying "go play on the train tracks," or "in traffic," is typically a dismissive statement, and a subtle wish for harm to come to the recipient of these epithets; in our case it was our reality. This was one of our favorite pastimes.

Hearing the train whistle off in the distance, I'd beg Grandpa for a nickel or a penny. Chuckling, he would give us each whatever change he had in his pocket (but never a quarter), and then May Lai and I would race off. Hearts beating quickly, we would clamber up the hill, stumbling over the granite ballast covering the sides of the tracks. Finally, we'd reach the tracks themselves, where we'd carefully place the coins on the center of the gleaming steel, feeling the tracks begin to vibrate ever so slightly from the train moving steadily our way. As soon as it was in sight, we'd move away from the tracks, sliding down the hill to wait for the mass of iron and steel to pass.

As it came closer, the train's whistle would wail, signaling it would be crossing the intersection near our home. The sound of the machine was deafening, the distinctive *chug-a-chooga-chug-a-chooga* spinning into a whir of noise that enveloped us. As the sound reached a roar, the train would burst into sight as it rolled past us and over our coin. Hugging each other with delight, May Lai and I would jump up and down as it passed by. We were just two little girls, one brown, one white, with unkempt hair and raised hands, dancing to the beat of excitement in our hearts. After what seemed to be an eternity, the caboose would swing by before we watched the train recede from our sight. Only then would we rush back up to the tracks to eagerly search for our coin.

Laughing and whooping, we'd grab the now flattened circular bit of metal and then skid down the hill, racing back home to show Grandpa what we had done. Seeing the compacted metal, he'd smile and tell us how he used to do the same thing when he was a boy. It apparently never occurred to the adults in our lives that two little girls under the age of five shouldn't be playing near an active train track.

❁

I longed to be able to talk with Dad as freely as I'd seen other girls speak with their fathers. But the chance of getting close to him without possibly inciting an angry reaction was remote. Instead, I walked on eggshells and did my best to stay on his good side.

One day Dad brought home a new babysitter for us named Julie, whom he'd met when she brought her car to the gas station where he worked. Julie Delano was just shy of her eighteenth birthday and a student at a local community college, a tall and very slim woman with thick chestnut-brown hair that fell down to the small of her back. Her blue eyes were as wide open and innocent as her face, which was bare of any makeup.

Within a short amount of time, Julie began watching us steadily. After she turned eighteen, she began sleeping over at our house. She and Dad tried to be discreet, but even at the age of five, I could see that something was unfolding between them. Dad was thirteen years older than Julie. She was sheltered and naïve, the seventh of ten children born to a builder and his stay-at-home wife.

Julie's father died when she was fourteen, but due to some wise estate planning, she and her siblings had grown up in relative comfort in a well-manicured neighborhood in Garden Grove, not far from Anaheim. She had been raised in a grounded and disciplined environment that was a sharp contrast to my father's chaotic upbringing. Unlike Dad, she rarely raised her voice, and from the start she took a very active role in our education and training. Under her watchful eye May Lai, Daniel, and I experienced parenting that bore little resemblance to the care we'd received from Daisy and Dad. In short order our slightly haphazard existence took on a more solid, regimented form.

To my disappointment, May Lai and I were no longer allowed to run around the neighborhood with impunity. When we came rushing in the door with our flattened coins from the train tracks, the look on Julie's face let me know that our days of playing this game were over.

One day we learned that our babysitter Julie, at the tender age of twenty, was engaged to our father. Her siblings had advised her against marrying Dad, fearing that he was only using her as a caregiver for his kids. (Years later, his sister would admit that at one especially low point in his life prior to meeting Julie, Dad had considered placing us in foster care; however, his family talked him out of it.) When Julie came along, innocent, willing, and full of compassion, he had found a very workable solution to his immediate problem. Julie was too lovestruck and enamored with us to consider that Dad's intentions weren't purely motivated by affection and appreciation. That is what worried her family, particularly her older sisters, some of whom were the same age as Dad. Unlike Julie, they sensed the possibility of ulterior motives, which would make up part of the unexpressed hostility I would soon pick up from them.

As their relationship continued to progress, we began to spend more and more time around her family. She and her nine siblings shared a close bond that contrasted greatly with Dad's family, who could barely stand to be around each other on holidays. The Delano clan was the epitome of what one would expect of a slightly conservative, middle-class White Anglo-Saxon Protestant family in Southern California. They were polite, but I couldn't help but feel as though they didn't really want us around. There was a wariness in their behavior that I didn't understand, a distance that I was unaccustomed to in Dad's fellow Baha'is, who embraced us with open arms.

Dad didn't fit in with Julie's family, but admittedly he didn't quite fit in with anyone, which seemed to amuse him in some sort of perverse way. I watched as her sisters and their husbands recoiled from his coarse speech and off-color jokes. "Stuck up" is what he called them.

The Delanos liked to socialize and regularly held barbecues at different family members' homes. It was at one of these gatherings that it finally clicked in my head that something was seriously off between me and the family I was getting ready to inherit. I was just a few months shy of my eighth birthday. And like other children, I was beginning to understand that I had an identity outside of "Sil Lai, the individual." That I was part of a larger collective, which in this case looked nothing like me.

On that breezy, hot California day, I observed my soon-to-be cousins, aunts, and uncles mingling with my family, and noticed the uniformity of their skin color. For the first time in my life, I was able to actually admit to myself that I looked very different from both my new family and the one of my origin. As my eyes scanned the pool area, I saw nothing but the whiteness of everyone in attendance except for me. That, combined with their dismissive attitude toward me, led me to conclude something that was inconceivable before: that their distance was because of the color of my skin. It was the only obvious difference that made any logical sense. This day was the first time in my life that I felt truly ashamed to be me; to be conscious of the color of my skin and what that color potentially meant.

The shock stung me like the tip of the lash of a whip. It was jarring like that moment in the film *The Wizard of Oz* where it transitions from black-and-white to Technicolor. And just like Dorothy, I felt I was in a foreign land.

It was then that I realized that everything that I saw and heard was white. White music. White colloquialisms. White films. White TV shows. White neighborhoods. White little girls at my grade school. White family members. White. White. White.

I also became acutely aware of the presence of my color. I was angry that I could never fit in because I could not change the color of my skin.

At this point, the secret of my biological father's race was still hidden from me. I'd never heard anything overtly negative about black people from members of my family. (Although Julie's mother once told me that another word for prunes was "nigger toes.") It was almost as if they didn't exist. It was true that I had heard derogatory comments about people of Asian descent ("gooks"), and Mexicans ("beaners" or "wetbacks"). Every other ethnicity was apparently fair game for racist commentary, *except* black people.

Yet in spite of the lack of outward hostility and racial slurs, my family was dismissive of black people and ignored black culture. I could see it in the quick manner that Dad would change the radio station if a song by a black singer came on. Or the way the TV channel would automatically get switched from *The Jacksons* in favor of *Donny & Marie*, or from *Fat Albert* to *Speed Racer*, or *Soul Train* to *American Bandstand*.

It was in this subtle way that I came to believe that there was something worse than being Mexican or Vietnamese. At least they existed. They may have been derided, but they were acknowledged. Black people were so unimportant to the larger narrative of our lives that we didn't even recognize their existence, despite the fact that blacks lived in our cities, and neighboring communities. One *could* argue that this erasure (avoidance?) was simply a matter of taste, the way some people prefer stripes to polka dots, or Picasso to Monet. But there were countless incidents like this over the years, small blips that peppered the landscape of my experience, that subtly said that black was deficient. Inferior.

After my racial awakening, I saw evidence of my exclusion everywhere, even in toy stores. Like many little girls, I played with Barbies and baby dolls. But I never felt a sense of kinship with my dolls the way that my sister May Lai did. Sitting on our front stoop I would stare into the face of my Baby Alive, a doll that would simulate the noises and bodily functions of a human infant, and feel disconnected. Even ashamed. Holding it close to my chest, I noted the difference in our skin tones. I knew that if I had a baby, it wouldn't look like my doll. I was embarrassed by the obvious difference in our appearance, but didn't share it with anyone out of shame. I lived in fear that one of the neighbors would state the obvious by yelling out while driving by, "That's not your baby!"

Of course, I could have asked for one of the black dolls in the toy store. But those dolls were for black girls, and I wasn't black (yet). Breezing down the toy aisles, my eyes consciously shunned the darker dolls. Their dark eyes and smooth chocolate faces were foreign, a niche product for a niche group of people. I wanted a doll that looked like me, but none existed at that time. (It would be decades before the new multiracial category would debut on census forms, and by extension a blossoming market for multi-hued children's toys.)

This consciousness of my skin color buzzed around my mind, always whirring away. Whenever I asked my father about the discrepancy in our appearance he would tell me the same thing: "Sil Lai, your skin is brown because you were born in Hawaii."

Although his answer temporarily filled me with ease, I was unable to shake the feeling that he wasn't telling me the truth. Daisy was the one person I thought could help explain this difference, but I hadn't seen her in over two years. And then one day, an innocent question that I asked my father made it clear that it was unlikely I'd ever get a chance to ask her about my appearance.

❧

Dad was an avid model aircraft enthusiast who devoted countless hours each month to pursuing his passion. Since Daniel was two (too young to be of help), and May Lai was simply too girly (her passions were Barbies and baby dolls), I was his chosen assistant when it came to building his beloved airplanes. I enjoyed these times together; these were the few moments where we actually were able to spend time together that was unrelated to chores or meals. During these rare outings, I felt a sense of pride at having been chosen over everyone else to share his hobby. Not Julie. Not May Lai or Dan. Me.

Besides the utilitarian purpose I served on these trips, I truly enjoyed the process of building model planes. I mean, how many things in life are more fun than gluing your index finger and thumb together and then watching your skin stretch as you peel them apart? Together, Dad and I had assembled a plane for me to fly that was simpler than the radio-controlled aircraft he built for himself. My plane was connected to four-foot-long cords on the side of the wings. To fly it required my father to start the nose propeller while I held onto the small, red plastic handles attached to the cords. Once the propeller was whirring, I would slowly turn around in a circle as the buzzing and vibrating plane hummed in the air while tethered to my small hands. We flew our planes in the parking lot of Anaheim Stadium on Sunday afternoons, where we would join dozens of other model plane enthusiasts, competing to see whose plane was the fastest and could fly the highest.

Building planes requires a litany of materials that one could find by special order in the back of magazines devoted to the subject or at the local Hobby Shop store. One day we went to the store to buy some materials to repair my plane's wing. After making our purchase we headed home.

The sun shone brightly through the windshield onto the cracked black dashboard of our family car, a green AMC Gremlin with black vinyl seats that stuck to the back of your bare, sweaty legs anytime the temperature rose above 75 degrees.

In a vain attempt to beat the heat, I had chosen to wear cotton short shorts. Unfortunately, their length was successful only in allowing the skin on my narrow legs to burn underneath from the hot vinyl, and on top from the sunlight shining mercilessly through the windshield. I planted my forearms flat onto the front of my thighs so they would cover as much of my exposed skin as possible, which relieved some of the heat.

As we turned onto our street, my mind turned as it often did to Daisy.

Usually I kept my thoughts of her to myself, but our outing had given me a false sense of security and closeness. I felt safe to express myself freely to him as a result of our daddy-daughter time.

I casually asked him, "Dad, when is Daisy coming home?"

Our car abruptly came to a stop just shy of the entrance to our short driveway. We were now awkwardly sitting halfway between the faded black asphalt street that ran in front of our home and the motor-oil-stained concrete that led to the door of our garage.

The tension in the car was palpable. Instantly, I realized I had made a huge error in judgment. Just two minutes before, we were listening to Electric Light Orchestra's "Telephone Line" on the radio. Now the only thing I could hear inside the car was his silence.

Dad's fingers gripped the steering wheel so tightly that his veins bulged blue. He turned toward me and leaned in close enough for me to see the large pores on his nose glistening with sweat.

Opening his mouth so wide that I could see the silver fillings in his molars, he bellowed, "Don't you ever say her fucking name again! Do you hear me? Don't you EVER say her name!"

Mute with shock at his outburst, I nodded my head quickly up and down, fighting back my tears. He accelerated quickly, and then hit the brakes hard so that the car jerked to a stop. I jumped out and raced inside the house, into my room, as far from Dad as I could get.

May Lai was sitting quietly on the floor playing and she looked up at me, eyes questioning.

"What are you looking at?" I snarled, throwing myself onto my bed.

"I hate him."

"Who do you hate?" my sister asked.

"Nobody. Just leave me alone!" I barked, turning my back to her so that I could face the wall. I didn't want her to see the tears that were streaming out the sides of my eyes. From that point on, I honored his "request" and never said Daisy's name again around him, and my mother became my secret, spoken of only between my siblings and me in hushed tones far away from his hearing.

Wedding of my stepmother, Julie Delano,
to Dad, Garden Grove, CA.

CHAPTER FIVE

On May 7, 1978, Julie Delano became my official step-mother when she married my dad, George Baber, in an intimate garden wedding officiated by a Baha'i official. To us children, their wedding was not the merging of two loving people, but a formality that elevated Julie from babysitter to family member. Dad wore a rented sky-blue polyester tuxedo with black piping and a ruffled white dress shirt. His bride walked down the garden path in a homemade dress from a Butterick pattern. My brother Daniel served as ring bearer and wore a smaller version of Dad's suit, while May Lai and I wore matching cotton sundresses, which Julie had sewn as well.

After the ceremony Daniel, who was approximately two months away from his fourth birthday, stayed close to the adults while May Lai and I scampered around the garden. At the reception Dad's mother, Grandma Lou, steered clear of Grandpa. Although decades had passed since their divorce, Grandma Lou's bitterness toward her ex-husband was palpable. At the time I was unaware of the history between them and couldn't understand why she hated him so much. Grandpa was a quiet man. He would share stories about the time he served in World War I and his experiences as a chef ("a short-order cook" Grandma Lou would snort derisively whenever I brought this up). She continued, "We lived in poverty. We practically starved. I couldn't afford to go to the hospital; I gave birth to your aunt in the bedroom of the little shack in Yakima that we lived in."

Through their divorce, Grandma Lou had not only lost her social standing, her marriage, and for a time, her freedom—she had, most important, lost her children. Years later as an adult it would dawn upon me how eerily similar their marriage would be to Daisy and Dad's union, and even my relationship with my firstborn child's father.

❁

Not long after their wedding, we moved out of the three-bedroom concrete-block rental near the train tracks, and into a four-bedroom home a few miles away on Chateau Avenue in Anaheim that Dad had purchased. Our new home didn't have the same outdoor space, but it had something even better: a view of the nightly fireworks show at Disneyland, which was less than a mile away. Kneeling at the window in my bedroom, May Lai, Daniel, and I would gaze out into the night and watch the kaleidoscope of lights explode over the rooftops of the houses on the other side of the street.

Our new home was in an extremely diverse neighborhood, not just racially, but culturally as well. In the house to our left lived the Malakais, a family of Hawaiians, and to our right lived the Nyugens, a Vietnamese clan. Down the street on our walk to school were several homes filled with Mexican, or "Chicano," gang members. But at eight years old, I was too young to comprehend the potential danger. Despite not understanding, I listened to our new mom when she admonished me, "never walk on *that* side of the street when you're on your way to school."

May Lai and I attended Betsy Ross Elementary, a well-

regarded school just a short walk from our home. I was enrolled
in third grade and May Lai was in first grade.

As the middle-aged white school administrator was busying
herself with our paperwork, I couldn't help but notice the occasional stares at us from the other women in the school office. Here
was a young, blue-eyed white woman of twenty-one who looked
like she was seventeen, registering eight- and a six-year-old girls
for school while holding my little brother on her narrow hip. One
of the girls was brown and the other two children were clearly
Eurasian.

"So these are your children?" asked the secretary.

"Yes, they are," Mom answered simply. No defensiveness. Just
a simple statement of fact. In retrospect, I realize how courageous
a woman our new mom was in this regard. To hold her head high
in the face of constant questions about the children in her care is
more than I ever would have been able to do.

In character, our new mom was the antithesis to Daisy. She
ran our household with the precision of a military lieutenant.
Breakfast was every morning at 7:30. Lunch at 11:30. Snack at
2:30. Dinner at 5:30. Snack at 7:30. Bedtime at 9:00. Julie valued
education and purchased grade-appropriate teacher's manuals,
which she used to teach us in her own version of school Mondays
through Fridays in the summer, much to my consternation.

Julie was a true homebody who loved to crochet, sew, and
knit, making a point to teach May Lai and me the basics, gently
encouraging us in our clumsy first efforts and praising us on our
progress. She baked all of our cookies and cakes from scratch, and
allowed me to hover around her while she was working, answering all of my questions matter-of-factly as she moved with smooth
precision around the kitchen. Always the teacher, she allowed me
to help by giving me small tasks, like buttering the cookie sheets,
or cracking the eggs into the batter.

She and my dad's nickname for me was Motormouth. I was always asking questions about everything and anything that came to mind. It was almost like Tourette's, minus the cursing. If a thought popped into my mind it came out of my mouth. As draining as I must have been, Julie did her best to answer my constant questions.

A whole new world of consistency and maternal interest opened up to us, some of which was appreciated and other parts (like the ones that limited my freedom to stay up late watching television) that were not. And while I did my best to push as many boundaries as possible with Julie ("Sil Lai, the answer is NO. En. Oh. Quit while you're ahead!"), I was drawn to her like iron shavings to a horseshoe magnet.

Daisy was never affectionate; in fact, I can't remember one time in which she ever held me or gave me a hug. But with Julie, my years of desiring maternal contact led me to be a little clingy. I'd throw my long, bony, pecan-colored arms around her and give her unsolicited hugs, or grab onto her waist while we were walking in the park. I would beg her to let me brush her thick chestnut mane of hair for her at night, which she sometimes allowed me to do. Without any request or discussion on either side, my siblings and I took to calling Julie "Mom," for that was who she now was. Our mother.

As enamored as I was of her, Mom's steady presence didn't erase the memory of Daisy. There was a fondness that never abated, although the impact of her complete erasure from our lives seemed minimal at the time. As months turned into decades, I would eventually learn how pivotal Daisy's neglect and rejection were to my development in a myriad ways.

For example, I was eight years old when what might have been an everyday incident for a child who hadn't been rejected by her biological mother revealed what would eventually grow into a deep character flaw.

Mom was sitting in our bentwood rocking chair with Daniel asleep in her lap. May Lai and I had been playing outside when I came bursting in the front door. Running over to her, I threw my arms around her shoulders to give her a hug. I was just beginning to trust her, to let someone into the space Daisy had held. But instead of welcoming it, she pushed me away with one arm. "Stop it!" she hissed. She continued to rock in the chair and carry on her conversation with Aunt Doni, who had come over to visit, as if nothing had happened.

I can see now that Mom probably didn't want me to disturb my sleeping brother. But I took her action as a total rejection of me. The look of mild disgust on her face when she pushed me away burned into my brain as I walked back outside to play. It scalded me in the wake of Daisy's abandonment. To guard against ever feeling that pain again, I said to myself, "I will NEVER give her a hug! EVER!" True to my word, it wouldn't be until I was well into adulthood that I put my arms around her. Defensive behavior that eventually developed into aggression that would in time sever our bond.

Soon we received surprising news: our new mom was going to have a baby. I was fascinated by the changes in her slim body, watching in wonder as her belly expanded larger and larger until it seemed like she would topple forward from the weight of the growing child. And then on Father's Day in 1979, Mom went into labor at around 7:00 in the evening.

Mom called to my dad, "Honey, the Lamaze instructor said I should walk when labor starts . . . Will you come with me around the block?" I was surprised when Dad said yes and watched them slowly make their way down the street until they were finally out of view. About twenty minutes later, they were back inside the house.

I watched Dad pace around the living room for a little while, and then he made an announcement. "I need to get some air. I'm going over to Dave's house. I'll be back in about an hour."

The hours ticked by. May Lai and I did our best to help Mom as her labor pains intensified. From time to time I would hear her groan or pant, and I would rush over to see if she was okay, but she would shoosh me away.

"I'm okay. Just go play with your sister."

Dad still didn't return. Mom was beginning to worry and called Dave's house repeatedly. Eventually he picked up. Mom apologized for her barrage of calls and explained that she was in labor.

"Julie, I haven't seen George tonight. I don't know where he is," Dave said.

It wasn't until just after 11:00 that Dad strolled back into the house. By this point her contractions were hitting with the frequency of the slow beeps on a heart monitor. With almost no time to spare, Dad made a quick call and asked Grandpa to come over and watch us.

In the early hours of the following morning, Mom gave birth to a healthy baby girl, my sister Julia (who I was later to learn was biologically my stepsister). Although he could have done so, Dad opted not to be in the room when Julia was born because in his words, "It wouldn't be fair . . . I wasn't in the room when the other kids were born." Around mid-morning Dad came home and went straight to sleep.

While Mom was in the hospital, we were cared for by Grandpa, who listened to my constant questions.

"How big is the baby?"

"What color is the baby?"

"What's the baby's name?"

Mom never did get a straight answer from Dad about where he had disappeared for all those hours, but her joy over her newborn distracted her from pushing the issue.

My siblings and I were giddy with excitement to finally meet the baby who had been living inside Mom's belly for the past nine months. Dad captured the moment on his Polaroid camera. I still have this photo of May Lai, Daniel, and myself staring wide-eyed up at the camera as our new sibling lay on her side in the bright orange portable bassinet Mom had bought at a garage sale for a dollar.

As cute as baby Julia was, I soon found my wonder being replaced with disinterest. Now instead of being able to focus her attention exclusively on us, Mom was consumed with caring for her daughter. There was no more racing down the hallway. Mom might be carrying the baby, who could get hurt. There were no more midday cartoons during the summer. ("Sil Lai, May Lai. Go outside and play. You'll wake the baby.") So, *Scooby-Doo* was out and the front lawn became our living room. There, we would use anything we found to keep us occupied while the baby slept, or ate, or was bathed.

When we were thirsty, we drank from the garden hose. And when we were hungry, we were allowed into the kitchen for a brief lunch while Baby Doola (Dad's nickname for Julia) was awake, before being swept back outside to continue playing.

Sometimes we would head next door to our Vietnamese neighbor to see what we could get into at her house. To-Quyen's family had immigrated to Anaheim after the Vietnam War. I noticed the way the Nguyens kept to themselves in general. While my parents occasionally socialized with some of the other neighbors, Dad never acknowledged Mr. Nguyen beyond a nod of the head. As a matter of fact, nobody really interacted with them. It

was 1979, and it had only been six years since America had ended
its direct involvement in the Vietnam War. The anger felt over
the U.S. involvement in a war that many believed we had no business entering in the first place was still very present. During the
evening hours, while May Lai and I played at one end of the living
room, I could hear Walter Cronkite droning in the background.
Invariably, I'd hear the word *Vietnam* pop up, though I never
paid any attention to what was actually being said. But the lingering scent of anger directed at the Vietnamese who had settled in
America was impossible to miss, even for me as a child. Being part
Chinese, my siblings and I would occasionally be asked if we were
Viet Cong by some of the more obnoxious children at school. But
by and large we were left alone by those we lived among. It was
when we went out into the world beyond our street that I felt a
discomfort around us that I would eventually be able to recognize
as racism. Strangers staring so hard that it felt like their eyes were
boring holes into us. The way they either looked past us as if we
didn't exist or worse, the direct glare of mild contempt at my parents and their rainbow tribe of children.

Yet, there were three things that were never discussed in our
home: Daisy, the Vietnam War, and race. How two white adults
were able to completely ignore the latter issue, which was as ob-
trusive as a boulder in the middle of our living room, escapes me.
Perhaps it was because of Dad's Baha'i beliefs, which promoted
racial tolerance. Or maybe it was because he didn't want to discuss
something that he didn't entirely understand himself. Mom was
a woman who shied away from controversy in general, so it was
more a matter of not wanting to be impolitic.

Still, despite having four children of various racial composi-
tions and skin colors living under one roof, three of whom were
half Chinese, there was no mention of race or our Chinese heritage. That would have led down the inevitable path of the ver-

boten subject of Daisy. The Chinese blood that ran through our veins and stamped our physical appearance was eliminated just as Daisy was from our existence. I soon discovered Dad had one more hand to play toward his goal of erasing any reminders of his first wife.

One Saturday morning I was awakened to the sound of an unusual amount of activity in our garage. Curious, I threw on some clothes and walked outside. And there were our things, laid out in two narrow aisles framing our oil-stained driveway.

"Why are you selling our stuff?" I asked my dad.

"We're moving to Florida."

It was in this off-handed way that I learned we were leaving California. Dad's manner of communication was like a dog dropping a dead bird at your feet. We didn't live in a home where things like "context" or "emotional preparation" were considered. This was his world, and our role was to go along with any decision he made without question.

The move itself didn't come as a surprise—I knew that Dad was looking for a new home. After he had left his job as mechanic at the 76 filling station, he had gotten involved in the newspaper circulation business, and assembled a small team of teenage boys that he would drop off in a neighborhood to sell subscriptions to the *Los Angeles Herald Examiner*. Business was going pretty well, as we had recently gone house hunting in a few more upscale neighborhoods.

Still, we had just moved into our current home less than a year before, and relocating to Florida was an entirely different matter altogether. Stunned, my eyes took in the inventory of what Dad was selling in anticipation of our move. I noticed an array of beautiful silk cheongsam dresses near the garage door. They were Daisy's.

I didn't know we still had anything of hers. But there they

were. A shimmering rainbow of pretty frocks. Seeing her clothes hit me ten times as hard as the news about the move. What woman leaves behind that much in a divorce? Women who either have the financial resources to replace them (she didn't), were fleeing for their lives, or whose ex-husbands had confiscated their effects as a form of retaliation. I would eventually figure out which of the three applied.

Now four years after their divorce, seeing her clothing glimmering in the sunlight meant Dad had transported her personal effects through two major moves. Why was he finally unloading them? The first thing that came to mind was our new mom, so I ran over to her and blurted out, "Why are we selling Daisy's clothes?"

"Because we're moving."

"But I want them. Pleeeease? Can I please have her dresses?"

"Go talk to your father."

I asked the same question.

"No. We're selling them."

"But Dad," I whined, "I really, really want them. Can I please keep one? Just one?"

"*No!* I told you no, so stop bugging me about it!" he said, voice slightly elevated.

"But Daddddyyyyy" (I only called him Daddy when I really wanted something). "Please, please, please let me have one. I'll work for it. I can clean the house, or do the dishes . . ."

I knew it was unwise for me to continue, but I was in a panic. These dresses were the only physical link that I had to my biological mother, and I wasn't going to give up easily. I had to—no, *needed* to—have at least one dress.

"If you don't get the fuck out of the garage and leave me alone, I'm going to whip your ass. Now get out of here before you get the belt!"

Tears streaming down my face, I ran to my room and sat on

the edge of the bed. May Lai looked up from the Barbies she was playing with on the rug and asked, "Why are you crying?"

"Dad has some of Daisy's clothes and they're selling them at the garage sale. I asked for one, only one, and they won't give it to me!" I wailed.

"But why do you want Daisy's dress?" she asked innocently.

I was frustrated by her inability to see why the dress was important to me. Yes, she was only seven years old, but Daisy was her mother, too. Why didn't Daisy mean anything to her?

"God, you're so stupid sometimes, May Lai. Just play with your dolls and LEAVE ME ALONE!" I gave a swift kick to the wall with my bare foot, then quickly checked to make sure that it didn't leave a mark. I'd get the belt for sure for that.

I flipped over on my stomach and buried my face in the pillow so May Lai couldn't see my face as my body was wracked with sobs. My feelings were overwhelming. So many thoughts to process and I had no recourse from my parents' decision. I was unhinged, inconsolable, my mind racing as it jumped between my memories of Daisy and Dad's total lack of concern for my need to stay connected to my biological mother. His decision to finally get rid of his ex-wife's belongings a testimony to his devotion to his new partner.

An icy thought that penetrated my mind: *I will never forgive them for this.*

I felt empowered by this silent resentment. That I could smile in their face while I harbored anger in my heart was something I hadn't fathomed before. The more my fantasy around the concept grew, the more I wanted to someday show them what it meant to be powerless.

My parents wiped her out of our lives, but they couldn't stop me from thinking about Daisy. Despite threats, I still spoke about her to my sister, whispering little stories to May Lai when my

parents weren't around. I thought of her often, nursing my memories. Carefully and repeatedly reconstructing every single thing I
could recall so that I would never forget her.

❀

While the decision to move out of state seemed to come out of nowhere, the time between the announcement and the actual move
itself couldn't have been more than two months. In a matter of
weeks my parents had packed up our entire house, piling everything into my dad's white Chevy work van and a U-Haul hitched
to the back of our wood paneled AMC Pacer. Our destination: Orlando, Florida. What made Dad choose this city out of all of Florida was beyond me. The only thing I knew about Orlando was
that it had the East Coast equivalent of Disneyland: Disney World.

Everyone on both sides of our family was blindsided by Dad's
sudden decision to move across the country to a city in which he
had zero relationships. It required Dad to completely abandon a
thriving business and our extended family. Mom, in particular,
was extremely upset to leave her close-knit clan behind. And
Grandma Lou was inconsolable at the prospect of losing proximity to her son and grandchildren.

Dad's decision seemed hastily made, and I was later to learn it
was likely not only a hasty one, but driven by a sense of urgency.
According to Mom, one day she received a phone call from an extremely upset mother of one of the teenage boys who worked on
Dad's newspaper delivery crew. As she recalled, this woman ac-
cused Dad of having an "inappropriate relationship" with her son.
Listening to her tell the story to me years later, I strove to wrap
my head around its implications.

"Mom, when you say 'inappropriate,' do you think she meant

that Dad was doing something stupid like smoking weed with the boy? Or do you think it was something else?"

"No, the way she said it didn't seem like he was doing drugs with the boy. I honestly don't know what she meant."

As the words swirled around my mind, I felt the air empty from my lungs. It was then, thirty years later, that I realized our expedited move *may* have had a hidden motive. Mom didn't know the details and, as was her nature, never forced the issue. Dad wouldn't tell her the truth anyway and his intimidation ensured that she never felt comfortable enough to ask him about anything. All we knew was that very shortly after this occurrence our house was on the market, sold, and we had moved across the country within the span of three months. Maybe what Dad had done was something unspeakable; however, like many things he did, we never would know what really happened.

The trip across the country took nine days, a few cheap hotels, and two campsites, but our family of six made it to Florida without incident. For the first few days we stayed in a hotel until Dad found a rental home just around the block from the house that he was purchasing. The closing took two months. When it was all over and done we had moved into a four-bedroom, two-bathroom house with a small, kidney-shaped in-ground pool. I thought the address was so cool: 5432 Nicholson Drive. Little did I know how different Orlando was going to be from Anaheim, and how much its culture (or lack thereof) would end up changing the entire direction of my life.

Pool party in Winter Park, FL, circa 1980.

CHAPTER SIX

Eventually, I learned that we actually didn't move to Orlando, but a small town on its outskirts called Goldenrod. Our neighborhood lay smack-dab in the middle of Seminole County (the same one where Trayvon Martin would be gunned down decades later by vigilante George Zimmerman).

During the late 1970s, Winter Park was best known as the home of Rollins College, a small private liberal arts school that was a popular safety choice for the scions of wealthy Northerners. Winter Park proper was the home to mainly upper-middle-class white families: Rollins professors and administrators, snowbirds from the North enjoying their retirement, and white-collar professionals. A zoning change to the area soon after our arrival gave us the prestige of a Winter Park address while residing in a lower- to middle-income subdivision. Over on our side the occupations were less prestigious: police officers, mechanics, newspaper route owners, and the occasional teacher.

Winter Park was and remains to this day a predominantly white community. In Old Winter Park, kids wore Izod Lacoste shirts and drove their parents' BMWs, while silently looking down their noses at those who weren't as well off. Over on our side, the one with the misappropriated Winter Park zip code, many of the kids wore the same clothes as our wealthier neighbors; however, our wardrobes were much more limited. The standard first car for a teen in our neighborhood was an almost-ready-for-the-junk-pile-but-still-drivable early '70s Volkswagen Beetle whose upgraded sound system often cost more than the car itself. Unlike in Old Winter Park, where issues like class and race were not discussed (at least publicly), our less-sophisticated inhabitants encouraged blatant racism and verbal attacks against anyone who looked different from their White Anglo-Saxon Protestant ideal. It may have been the early '80s, but there were still some who wore their red-and-white-painted Confederate belt buckles with pride while dipping Skoal and Redman chewing tobacco. Racial epithets were spat like conjunctions in a sentence. The majority of their vitriol was directed at blacks; however, anyone whose family had emigrated from a country of non–Northern European ancestry was a target for hatred. According to these holdovers from the Jim Crow era, "knee-gras," as they were politely called ("niggers" when they weren't feeling so politically correct), landed somewhere on the evolutionary scale between apes and humans.

In between Orlando and Winter Park lay the town of Eatonville. Eatonville has a rich history. Famed writer and anthropologist Zora Neale Hurston claimed Eatonville as her birthplace (despite having been actually been born in Notasulga, Alabama), having spent her formative years here. Not only is the town the setting for her most famous work, *Their Eyes Were Watching God*, Eatonville also has the distinction of being one of the nation's first incorporated black townships after the Emancipation Proclamation. Hurston described the town as "a utopia where black Americans could live independent of the prejudices of white society." Perhaps that was the case during the early twentieth century, but by the latter part of the century in the '80s, Eatonville provided local whites with a centralized geographic location for their racism. I witnessed this firsthand in high school when white students, fueled up on beer and marijuana, "entertained" themselves by speeding down Kennedy Boulevard, the main thoroughfare that cut through the town, shrieking from their car windows, "NIGGER! Nigger, nigger, nigger! . . ." to anyone unlucky enough to be outdoors at night. I was horrified by their behavior. Having lived in Orange County, California, I was used to people of all races and ethnicities living peacefully in close proximity to each other. Orlando was extremely segregated by comparison; however, I soon just accepted this as the way things were in Florida.

During the first week that we had moved into our new home, our doorbell rang. "Sil Lai, can you get that?" Mom called out from the kitchen, where she was preparing our lunch. Peeking out through the four-by-eight-inch glass pane in the center of the door, I saw three white girls who looked to be around my age smiling at me. Opening the door so that only my face and part of my body was visible, I tentatively said, "Hello," spoken more like a question than a statement.

Almost in unison, the girls said, "Hey!" The largest girl stepped forward and continued, "I'm Marideth Windsor, and this is my sister, Wendi, and our stepsister, Leslie. We live across the street there." She turned her head and motioned with a nod to the home with the perfectly manicured lawn that was perpendicular to ours on the right side across the street.

"We just wanted to welcome you to the neighborhood and introduce ourselves. We should hang out sometime!" she said perkily, adding, "Maybe we can come over for a swim?" I was stunned by her brashness and immediately mistrustful of this bright-eyed welcome wagon. There was something too forward, too friendly, too nice about them. I just couldn't believe that there were people my age in this world so confident that they would ring a stranger's bell and essentially invite themselves to be her friend and to spend time at her home.

"Uhh, okay," I replied, hoping not too warily.

"Well, great! Like I said, we just wanted to say hi. We'll see you later, 'kay?" Flashing a big smile, Marideth and her sisters turned and briskly walked across the street to their home.

I closed the door behind me, mind still perplexed over what had just happened, and headed back to the living room to return to the book I had been reading. I especially didn't like the way they had not-so-subtly invited themselves over to swim in our pool. (I knew that they didn't have one.) Despite being the new kid on the block, I wasn't in such a rush to make friends that I was willing to trade swim privileges for "friendship." After a few minutes of ruminating, I pushed them and our entire interaction out of my mind.

❦

Our move took place in May of 1980, with less than three weeks left in the school year—time I used primarily as an opportunity to acclimate to my new school, Eastbrook Elementary. To say that I experienced culture shock would be an understatement. It was as if I had landed in the middle of a different country, complete with a different ethnic makeup, customs, manner of dress, way of speaking, and cultural values. It was such a departure from my experience in California that coping consumed all of my attention, leaving very little mental energy for me to focus on my actual schoolwork.

In California my classmates were diverse in every way, and these differences united us into a patchwork quilt of ethnic, racial, and cultural identities. Anaheim was an eclectic, comfortable environment where you were judged more for your behavior than your appearance. At Eastbrook, I discovered the children had a robotic outlook on life that manifested itself in conservative uniformity. In California, kids wore pretty much what they wanted. At Eastbrook, you didn't wear any sneaker other than Nike Cortez and ankle socks, which for the girls included a small pom-pom on the heel. Shirts were either Lightning Bolt or Ocean Pacific tees, Izod-emblazoned polos, tank tops, or for the truly cool, a Ron Jon T-shirt. (One of the primary ways to show that you were hip was to proudly wear a shirt from this popular local surf shop in Cocoa Beach.) Although Winter Park was an hour from the beach, that didn't stop the kids from emulating beach culture. It didn't matter that these kids were too young to ride a board. Just the fact that you would wear a white Ron Jon painter cap and tee instantly associated you with Floridian cool.

When I first walked into class, with my floral-print dress, purple knee socks, and fake Vans sneakers, I was met with curious, blatant stares. Surveying the room, I noticed the homogeneity in hair color, skin tone, and clothing. This isn't to say that there weren't kids from other races and backgrounds, but there were so few that I barely noticed them. That was how I saw kids from other racial and ethnic backgrounds—as "other." I didn't identify with them because my entire experience up until that point in time was simply as George Baber's "Hawaiian" daughter. When I looked at row after row of little white boys and girls in my classroom, I counted at most three students from other races or ethnicities. But in my mind I wasn't like *them*. They had darker skin, but they also had cultural experiences that matched their appearance. I too had a deeper skin tone, but my cultural experience was white. To rectify this dissonance, I made a simple decision to follow Baha'i teachings and thought of myself as simply a human being. This was how I rationalized that my appearance didn't align with the school's "ethnic" students.

It very quickly became clear that the white students dominated our school. They were cruel and obnoxious, arrogant and brazen in the way they treated those they deemed inferior. Anyone that looked different was ignored, or terrorized. As the new kid, I stayed mostly to myself and found one or two kids in my class whom I could spend time with on the playground. After school, I'd rush to the safety of our home.

It was during my fourth-grade year that I developed my first crush on a tall, lean, brown-skinned Puerto Rican boy named Chris Lopez. His thick, jet-black wavy hair, Ocean Pacific T-shirts, and Goody comb that stuck defiantly out of the back pocket of his Levi 501s were a comforting sight, reminding me of the skateboarding California boys I had left behind in Anaheim. Chris was an underperforming student, but his cool, self-assured swagger combined with his neat, small features sparked my prepubescent adoration. In retrospect, we looked similar, both being the same shade of brown, which may have been another reason for my attraction. I admired the way he had somehow managed to escape being bullied by the white kids despite his skin color. Chris was, as they say, a badass.

Although I'd never tell him I was attracted to him, I did share my thoughts with a female classmate.

"You like Chris *Lo-pez*?" this classmate said, lingering on the *zzzzz*. "Ewww . . . he's a spic!"

"A spic?"

"Yeah, a spic, a Puerto Rican?" she said in a questioning tone. *Like, hello?*

Ten seconds before, I didn't know there was anything "wrong" with Puerto Ricans, much less that there was a derogatory term used to describe them. The ease with which the words flew out of her mouth was troubling. Instead of asking her why his ethnicity was so unacceptable, I chose to save face and go along with her racist comment. There was apparently a racial hierarchy here that I was unaware of, and I needed to understand the code before I found myself at the bottom.

"I was just kidding . . ." I said chuckling, and was relieved when her eyes lit up at my "joke" and she joined me in laughter. There was a smile on my face, but I secretly worried that she and the others might think the same thing about me. After all, Chris and I had the same skin coloring.

Still, the kids in my neighborhood knew that my parents were white and that I had white siblings who attended the same school. This invariably led to questions about my race (usually framed as "What are you?"). I always answered that I was Hawaiian, like my father had told me. "Oh really? Cool!" was their uniform response. My answer made sense to my nine-year-old peers, even if it didn't completely make sense to me. I was beginning to realize that it wasn't the geographic location of my birth that caused me to look so different from my siblings. My ability to reason was growing, and knew there was only one reason why I could look so different from my brother and sisters: Dad couldn't be my biological father. Why else was my skin brown and hair curly while my siblings had light skin and straight hair? Even more curious, my baby sister Julia had blond, curly hair and blue eyes.

Intuitively I began to sense that what wasn't making sense to me wasn't working with the adults in our neighborhood, although none of them directly said anything to me about my "Hawaiian" heritage. They didn't have to. The fact that our neighbors barely acknowledged my presence spoke volumes. When I would amble down the street, I noticed how they ignored me, but spoke to my brother and sister. One of the boys that my brother played with was named Christopher. His father, Dave, was a sergeant in the

Seminole County Sheriff's Department. A cold, arrogant, author-
itarian man, he spent his days when he wasn't working standing
near his open garage, drinking beer and shooting the breeze with
his next-door neighbor.

Whenever Mom asked me to fetch Dan from Christopher's,
I was greeted with an iciness that made me uncomfortable to
step onto their lawn, let alone ring their doorbell. At the time,
I thought the reason why his dad was so dismissive of me was
because I was a tomboy. Given that my parents never taught
us about American history, I didn't think anything of the large
Confederate flag that covered the back wall of his garage. Had I
known its brutal, racist history, I would have realized that Christopher's father wasn't just a jerk, but a racist jerk whose treatment
of me was to be expected by a man who would proudly display a
symbol of treason, white supremacy, and segregation in America.

But I didn't know anything about the history of racism in
America, since this was something that Dad had ensured we
didn't discuss. Racism wasn't a subject that was taught in our
school textbooks; most of the era was mimimized or erased the
United States history of violence against black people.

Since race was a "nonissue" in our home and in my classrooms,
it never occurred to me that the reason the neighbors were so
aloof was the color of my skin. It didn't make sense to me. What
was wrong with being Hawaiian? I mean seriously, what was the
problem with being born on an island paradise that was the home
of two of the most popular television shows at the time, *Hawaii
Five-O* and *Magnum, P.I.*? I would eventually come to realize, as
my level of awareness of my environment grew, that the chilly
response from my peers and their parents wasn't because I was
tall and skinny. It wasn't because my dad was unapologetically
blue collar in a white-collar neighborhood. And it wasn't because
Mom looked better in her shorts than 99 percent of the women

on the block. No, in time I was to learn that the main reason for their hurtful treatment was because I was brown in a world where being anything other than white was an abomination.

School ended in early June, and during that first summer in Florida I devoted my time to investigating the area around our neighborhood and the people who lived in it. Dad was busy building Super Clean, his truck-mounted carpet cleaning business, which he ran out of our home. His work schedule kept him busy and Dad was rarely around, but when he was he would tinker around the garage or lean against our car in the driveway, beer in hand. He would stand there, observing the happenings in the neighborhood, occasionally chatting with one of the men with whom he was cordial. However, just like in California, he largely kept to himself.

Although I had developed a few friendships (surprisingly with Marideth, Wendi, and Leslie of the infamous "welcome committee"), I spent a lot of time alone, because they preferred to watch soap operas or play with Barbies, which I had no interest in. I enjoyed more physical activities, which didn't require a companion such as bike riding, swimming, rollerskating, and skateboarding. Due to the sweltering heat, May Lai didn't want to join me on my outdoor activities, which was actually a blessing in disguise, since it was becoming harder and harder for her to keep up with me. And when the rainstorms came, which in a Floridian summer was nearly every day, I sat on the bench on our wide porch and watched the lizards scamper across the pavement, or disappeared into the quiet of my room where I would read for hours.

Something was happening to me during this time as well that I didn't understand. Not long after my tenth birthday, I began lashing out verbally at my family and my moods began to swing. There were afternoons when I would lie on the rust-colored carpet of my bedroom, door closed, and wail like a baby. These crying spells weren't necessarily instigated by anything. Some-times they would start out as frustration at my parents when they thwarted me from doing what I wanted to do. But more often, a mood would come across me like a flash flood. I would cry and cry and cry, flopping myself on my bed and burying my face in my pillows. Or, I would crawl under my bed and hide in the cool, enclosed darkness, tears streaming out the sides of my eyes and forming wet spots on the rough, synthetic strands of the carpet.

My mood swings were terrifying. I felt disconnected from my family and what I perceived as their superficial interactions with each other. I desperately wanted to be sheltered from this thing that was happening in my mind and couldn't articulate, but I didn't trust my dad or mom to comfort me. Besides, they were too wrapped up in the running of a household of four children and start-up business in an entirely new city, three thousand miles away from all of their support systems.

My emotional pain was searing. It tore at my spirit daily like a vulture picking over carrion. At ten years old, this was the first time I had the thought: *I wish I were dead.* In the beginning, it was a concept I kept to myself. Eventually I would take action to try to make it happen.

My emotional plunges into despondency could fade away as quickly as they came. Neither of my parents ever said anything to me about my crying spells, though I was certain, based upon the volume of my voice, that it would have been impossible for any-one within a hundred feet to not hear me. In the midst of a spell, Mom would knock on my door—"Sil Lai, dinnertime"—and continue around the house to bring the rest of the family to our daily communal meal. Even at the age of ten, I thought there was something very odd about the fact that she never acknowledged my despair. Mom never came in and sat down next to me to ask,

"What's wrong?" In the midst of my wailing, everything carried on like business as usual in the Baber household.

The fact that I could sit and cry for hours without anyone ever trying to learn what was wrong wreaked havoc on my concept of family. Most of what I learned about how the world *should* be was through television. I watched *Diff'rent Strokes* and *The Brady Bunch* on television religiously. Mr. Drummond and Mr. and Mrs. Brady would never have ignored their children's pain. There was always a teachable moment in which an adult would notice if something was wrong with one of their kids, and by the end of the episode a loving resolution was always found. Inherently, I knew something was seriously wrong with our family dynamics, even if no one else could see it at the time.

In late summer of 1980 I began fifth grade. It was during my fifth-grade year that Grandpa moved from California to stay with us. The reason stated was that it would keep him close to his son as he was aging—a gesture of filial support. But there was also a more practical motivation for Dad moving his father in with us: his monthly social security check. Grandpa shared a bedroom with my brother, and in exchange paid room and board that helped offset the monthly household expenses.

By now the other students at Eastbrook realized that I didn't have any older siblings or cousins to protect me, and they swooped in like a pack of rabid coyotes, attacking me daily with name-calling and intimidation. My skin tone and long, skinny frame placed a huge bull's-eye on my back for their bullying. The effects of the abuse began to take its toll. My grades began to suffer. Academics, an area where I'd always taken significant pride, became less and less important. My focus shifted to avoiding bullies, finding a sense of belonging at home or school, and escaping from my mood swings. My parents and teachers were frustrated with my behavior, constantly admonishing me to "do better" and "fulfill my potential." To them, it appeared that I was willfully ignoring their rules and sabotaging their efforts to help me. I tried, but I simply wasn't capable of getting back on track. Why should I care about what my teachers thought of me when they ignored the abusive behavior of my peers? Why should I care about my parents' disappointment when they didn't care about my pain, only my grades and whether or not I did my chores? Unbeknownst to anyone, I was spiraling into a full-fledged depression.

After completing fifth grade, the students at my elementary school transferred to Tuskawilla Middle School. This is where we would attend sixth through eighth grades. In middle school I hoped for a clean start with the students from two other schools that made up our population. Instead things were worse. What began as social ostracizing was soon replaced with aggressive and vicious bullying that focused on two things: my name and the color of my skin.

Sil Lai is actually a misspelled version of the Cantonese name Siu Lai. *Siu* (pronounced "see-you") means "little" and *Lai* (pronounced "lie") means "beauty." Siu Lai is a very common Cantonese name for firstborn daughters, as *Siu* also means "junior." My birth mother's Chinese name is Yau Lai; thus Siu Lai literally means Yau Lai, Jr., or "Little Yau Lai." To the Westerner, the word *Siu* doesn't linguistically exist. So when Daisy told Dad my name, he spelled it on my birth certificate in the closest way possible to what he heard, Sil Lai, which is pronounced by most Americans as "Suh-Lai." Add the letters *va* to the end of the American pronunciation and you've got weapons-grade artillery for 'tween social terrorists.

The vast majority of my new classmates had common names

like John, Wendy, Lindsay, and Angela. My unusual name was an affront to their white American sensibilities, and they were all too willing to let me know exactly what they thought about it. There were more days than I can count when a small group of my male classmates would stand on the periphery of the gym, or outdoors near the track for our hourly gym class. They would wait for me to wander far enough away from any adult monitor or teacher on the playground who might intervene, and then move in toward me quickly and tightly like a pack of dogs to launch their attack.

Slowly dragging out the syllables, they would call out, "Suh Lie Vaaaahhh!"

Upon getting no response, they would speak louder, "Hey, Saliva!"

I remained silent, even though I wanted to tell them to shut up. Mom had told me to ignore them, which I did. Truthfully, I really wanted to punch them all in the face.

Getting louder, they would move in closer. "Spit! Hey, Spit! Aren't you gonna say something, Spit? Can't you hear us, Spit?"

There was always one who felt the need to show off his exceptional skills with his salivary glands. Face scowling, he would slowly, loudly, and exaggeratedly suck the air through his nose, mucus pulling and dragging into the base of his throat. With a forceful heave that would project his body forward, he'd let out a guttural rattle and *splat!*, the loogie would land on the ground before me or worse, on me. The bystanders would laugh appreciatively at the boy's sophomoric humor, egging my tormentor on. In an effort to avoid my bullies, I began to stay close to the monitors during gym so there was less opportunity for them to torture me. Most of the time they would just follow me down the hall as we switched classes, pushing or bumping me in the hall, or calling me names as I walked by. I was eventually able to cut down on the number of daily assaults by taking shortcuts through the library to my next class.

Riding the school bus was an entirely different matter. It wasn't anything like what I had seen in movies or on television. School bus culture is unique unto itself; little things like where you sat served as a serious barometer of your social standing. The "freaks" (as the local potheads and druggies called themselves), jocks, and bullies sat in the back of the bus so their shenanigans could be acted out without detection by the bus driver. Average, nondescript kids dominated the central seating area, while the geeks and nerds clustered up front. In selecting your seat, you always had to weigh your need for physical safety against the sociopolitical ramifications of sitting in the front near the watchful eye of the only adult in the vehicle. I opted to sit four rows from the bus driver—close enough for protection while ostensibly maintaining my dignity.

The bus driver could protect you from physical abuse, but all bets were off for verbal. My parents had drilled into us that the only acceptable way to handle teasing was to ignore it and that any physical retaliation on my part would result in severe punishment. This wasn't because my father was a pacifist. His reasons were much more practical. Like a lot of working poor, my family couldn't afford health insurance. One of his biggest fears was that his children would injure another child or be injured themselves in a fight. The potential financial and legal consequences would be disastrous to a man who supported his family paycheck to paycheck. To ensure we didn't, my father told us that if we ever got in a fight, *he'd* "beat our ass." There was no way I wanted to be on the receiving end of one of my dad's whippings, so I did my best to ignore the taunts and prayed they would somehow stop on their own.

"Hey, nigger! I'm talking to you, nigger! Why won't you turn around and look at me, nigger?"

I'd pretend not to hear them while burying my head in the book in my possession. Face burning with shame, I silently counted down the minutes until we would reach the bus stop and I could rush away from the mob of young racists.

"Saliva! Hey, Spit . . . I'm talking to you!"

The clearing of a throat signaled the onset of a barrage of spitballs. If you were lucky, the gooey wetness would hit you in the hair, where the saliva-and-paper wad wouldn't touch your skin. Those you could subtly shake out while keeping your eyes averted to the floor so no one could see your embarrassment. The ones that hit your face were the worst. Loud whoops of laughter and the high-fiving of hands always followed the successful landing of a facial spitball. No matter how low you hung your head, you couldn't avoid feeling the stares of everyone on the bus as R. J., the King of the Bullies of the Tangerine Avenue bus stop's saliva dried on your face.

With every passing day a little bit of my soul was chipped away. I hated the kids on the bus. I hated the kids in my school. But most of all, I hated my skin color. *It* was the root of my pain and suffering, in and out of my home. And in spite of having skin that was (depending on the time of year) often darker than that of the "real" black kids in school, I clung to the secret pride of believing that I wasn't *really* black, even if the kids around me didn't believe it.

❋

Despite his religious conversion to a faith that embodied everything that he didn't receive as a child, Dad was never healed from the scars of his childhood and stint in the Vietnam War. Thus, like many children raised in emotionally or physically violent homes, I learned to scan the atmosphere in our home for his constant anger hidden just beneath the surface of our every interaction.

I unconsciously began to look for behavioral patterns in the people around me, trying to anticipate their next move. For it was my belief that if I could foresee the violence, I could avoid it. The inherent flaw in my paradigm was that it presupposed that there was an actual pattern to observe. Bullies can be notoriously unpredictable.

By contrast, Mom was emotionally neutral. She was most interested in molding our characters to exemplify solid middle-class values. She sought to teach us the basic differences between right and wrong, how to grow squash, or bake oatmeal cookies from scratch. Mom also worked to ensure that during traditions such as birthday and Christmas celebrations we received gifts by taking on a part-time babysitting job with a young boy whose family lived down the street. Dad didn't care about things like birthdays or holidays and made it clear that the only way we would receive presents was if someone else paid for them. His job was to pay our basic household bills—and nothing more—so Mom scrimped and saved her paltry pay to ensure that we had "normal" Christmases like the rest of the kids on our block.

She would also dole out light discipline in order to rein in our behavior. Well, especially my behavior. May Lai and Dan were pretty tame and tended to fall out of line only when I was leading them. As troublesome as I was to them (to another set of parents I might have been considered "spirited"), Dad and Mom were equally troublesome to me. Somehow I had found myself living in a home with people who offered no warmth or connection. That didn't stop me from wishing things were different, from praying to God that I would become, as my favorite Baha'i prayer said, "a brilliant star." Yet my prayers landed flat at the feet of what I perceived to be an unmerciful God, which in our home was Dad.

The unanswered prayers of a child never go away. They recede into hidden compartments in their heart. Calcifying, layer by layer, with each failed intervention from a kinder, forgiving life force. Slowly the innocence begins to drain out of the child's soul. Smiling eyes become distrustful. Warmth is replaced with coolness. Faith is transformed into fear as the optimistic child becomes a wary skeptic.

While we lived in California, Dad was fairly active in the local Baha'i community. Upon our arrival in Florida, Dad made sure to plug into the one in Orlando. Out of all his kids, I was the only one who had the faintest knowledge of Baha'i teachings. By now I was eleven years old, May Lai was nine, and Dan seven. Julia was only two, and was barely forming words, let alone understanding spiritual doctrine. Still, despite no one in the house but me having the most remote interest in the faith, Dad spent about a year trying to get everyone on board with his spiritual practice.

There are Baha'i temples in seven locations around the world; the most well known in Haifa, Israel. These buildings weren't constructed just for followers of the Faith—they are open to everyone. Unlike in other religions, Baha'i temples don't have congregations. In a sense, they're almost like pilgrimage locations. If they don't live near one of the seven temples, Baha'is gather at local centers or, as was the case in Winter Park, in individual members' homes. Baha'u'llah, the Faith's founder, believed that a separate class of clergy wasn't necessary since the teachings were what led the faith, not individuals. So, each member was considered to be his or her own pastor or imam—minus the congregation, of course.

Dad would pile us into the family car to go with him to the "feasts," as the monthly gatherings in various members' homes

are called. Sometimes Mom would take us to the Feasts when
Dad was too busy to attend. But since she wasn't a member of
the Faith, she wasn't allowed to participate. Years later she would
tell me how much she had tolerated in the name of Dad's faith.
"When your dad wasn't able to go, he would tell me to take you
guys and wait for you. Sometimes I would be sitting in the hot car
for hours. Being an obedient wife, I did as I was told." To this day,
I don't know how she managed to suppress her dignity for the
sake of a religious gathering. This didn't happen often. Usually, it
was Dad who facilitated the trips. He'd warn us as we pulled up
to the host's house, "You better not act up or else you'll get the belt
when we get home!", his threat hovering in the air. Hair combed,
Kmart clothes pressed, we'd march single file into the home, drift-
ing on the perimeter of the meetings, hungrily waiting for dinner
to be served.

My siblings and I largely tuned out everything that was said
during the group prayers. Our focus was on the spread of food
that always accompanied these gatherings (hence the name, feast).
Our eyes would widen at the potluck dinner placed temptingly on
the dining table off the living room. Stomach rumbling, I'd day-
dream while the adults spoke and was the first child at the table to
get my plate when it was time to eat.

I loved the members of the Faith and was honestly puzzled as
to why Dad didn't have the same peaceful vibe about him as the
others. Everyone else seemed so authentically happy and kind.
Over time I grew to loathe attending the meetings. Every peaceful interaction was a reminder of how absolutely defective my
family life was at home. Plus, it drove home what I was starting
to suspect about Dad: he was not a loyal adherent to the Faith.
Not only was he not peaceful, I learned that there were very
foundational Baha'i tenets that Dad chose to ignore, such as not
drinking alcohol or smoking. Physical punishment of children is

also forbidden. I was old enough to know that at best my dad was a superficial practitioner and at worst a misanthropic hypocrite. What was the point of following a faith when your father, the supposed spiritual leader of the home, couldn't even get the basics right? And since the Faith was something that Dad claimed to love, I decided to reject it. Which was fortunate for me in terms of timing, as the Faith gives children the right to choose whether or not to continue as members when they turn thirteen. In spite of its beautiful philosophy and loving members, I was most definitely *not* going to follow in my father's footsteps.

Slowly, a rage was building inside me, bubbling and popping just beneath the surface of my skin. But I learned how to shove it down into my gut. By now I knew that kids in other families didn't scatter like leaves when their father walked in the door from work. I was scared and resentful of my dad and fairly indifferent to Mom, except when it came to her highly regimented parenting style. With that, I was becoming increasingly furious.

As docile as she outwardly appeared, Mom could be quietly maniacal in her need for control. Every aspect of our lives was micromanaged, beginning with the simple things most children endure, such as the type of clothing we wore, the time we went to bed, and when and what we ate. Cursing was absolutely forbidden, although Dad swore with impunity. We weren't allowed to use words like "ain't" ("*Ain't* ain't a word, Sil Lai"), and she would have us go lick a bar of soap every time we swore, or said "shut up." Mom had a very simple approach to raising us, with the cornerstone of her parenting philosophy revolving around several non-negotiable rules: Don't talk back, don't curse, don't lie, and don't hit. Do your schoolwork, do your chores, and do your best to get along with your siblings. And I was violating all of them by this time. Unapologetically. The majority of my seventh and eighth-grade years were a blur of verbal fights between the two of us.

Exasperated, she began to employ methods that teachers use to discipline students, like having me write sentences. In the midst of one of my many back-talking incidents, she exclaimed, "Sil Lai, I'm not arguing with you anymore. Since you're not listening to me, go write a hundred times: 'I will not talk back.' And don't come out of your room until they're done."

I stormed off to my room and slammed the door. Did she really expect me to sit in my room writing sentences like I was a second grader? While whatever issue we were having was unresolved? Trying to silence my voice and redirect it into tedious, rote, meaningless words on a piece of notebook paper? This was too much of an affront to my sense of fairness. I decided I would not capitulate to her demand for obedience.

When dinnertime came and I sat down at the table with the rest of the family, Mom asked how things were going with my sentences. "They're not" was my reply.

"Okay. That's your choice. But if you don't finish them today, I'm going to double them tomorrow."

Rolling my eyes, I said nothing, stalked back to my room after eating, then spent the rest of my waking hours staring up at the ceiling.

Mind racing, I was consumed with indignation and rage.

Who the hell does she think she is?

She's such a bitch. She can't make me do this.

I kicked the wall next to my bed with all my might, bare foot contacting the drywall with enough force to create a heel-shaped indentation. I kicked it again and again until the space on the wall caved in like a small sinkhole.

I observed my handiwork with smug pride.

Wait till she sees this hole. She's gonna be pissed. How many sentences is she gonna give me for this?

Satisfied with my defiant destruction, I flipped over and went to sleep.

The next morning, Mom awakened me with a knock on the door.

"Yeah?" I called out.

"Unlock your door. You know you're not allowed to lock it!" she ordered.

I opened it and stared into her eyes. By this time I was now equal to her in height—five feet eight inches. "What?" I snapped.

"Did you finish your sentences?"

"Nope."

"Fine. Now it's two hundred. Don't leave your room until they're done," she said, walking away.

I slammed the door shut and flopped back on my bed. My eye spied the hole in the wall I had kicked in the day before. I kicked it again for good measure.

I can't believe she's really trying to make me do this, I thought to myself. *Well, we'll see about that. She's not the only one who can be a bitch.*

The day passed and I spent my time reading books and plucking my eyebrows. Putting on my training bra and trying to determine whether stuffing it with Kleenex or ankle socks would create a more realistic bust. I came out of my room only for meals or to use the bathroom. My day passed away, with me stonewalling Mom defiantly from behind my closed door.

The next morning, she knocked on my door and asked me the same question. "Did you write your sentences?"

"Nope" was my bland response.

"Fine. Now they're four hundred."

This went on for a total of five days, until finally I hit 1,600 sentences. By this point I was tired of being caged up. It was hot, I had run out of books to read, and I knew that accruing 3,200 sentences the following day could keep me locked up for another week. So, begrudgingly, I wrote those 1,600 sentences. And with every period at the end of all 1,600 sentences I meditated on the words *I hate her.* On the sixth morning of our standoff, I handed over the sheets of notebook paper with *her* sentences on them. Smiling, she said, "Thank you," and continued about her chores.

I raced out the front door and into the outside world. Back to my constant companions, Marideth and Wendi. When they asked me where I'd been, I bitterly ranted about the sentences. "Wow. That's crazy" was their reply. I agreed. It was crazy. But my parents hadn't even begun to know what crazy would look like.

❧

Summer. 1983. I was now thirteen years old and every interaction between my overworked parents and me began to turn into a battle. Mom was relentless in her pursuit to domesticate me. Dad essentially abandoned all of us to his treadmill of never-ending work. When he was home, he shied away from spending time with his family—even during our meals. While we all ate at the same time, Dad sat alone on the edge of the bed in my parents' bedroom. Their room was right off the kitchen and we watched him eat in solitude while the rest of us sat together at our dining table, no more than eight feet away. After a long day at work, Dad preferred the sound droning from his television set to a conversation with his family.

While alienated from Dad, I still felt some sort of connection to my mom. And then it happened. The moment when she crossed the line between being my mother to becoming my warden. From caretaker to enemy. It's interesting that sometimes the smallest things can make your feelings about a person snap. Incidents seemingly so minor that in that moment, neither you nor anyone else recognizes their potential impact.

I was under one of my never-ending restrictions, confined to my bedroom where I would stare longingly at our pool. While I was on this particular stint of restriction, I was also coincidentally involved in a fight with my best friends, Marideth and Wendi (Leslie and I never really clicked).

Our pool was a playground that required only a swimsuit. It didn't matter to me if I had any companions. During the summer months and on weekends, I could climb in at 11:00 a.m. and swim, splash, and float for hours until dinner was served at 5:30 p.m., only to go back out and swim until 9:00 p.m. Swimming endless laps back and forth under the water, testing to see how many I could do without taking a gulp of air. Rolling over and doing backward somersaults, body revolving like a water mill. I'd travel the length of the pool until the water became so shallow that my face barely avoided scraping against the bottom surface, and then turn around and do it all over again. When I grew tired, I would lie in the sun on the wet concrete until the heat evaporated the water on my skin, at which time I'd roll over like a log back into the pool.

In the midst of the fighting, arguing, confusion, and overwhelming sense of isolation, I had found a respite. Our family pool was *my* safe haven, and not being allowed to revel in it while on restriction was maddening.

Sitting in the sweltering heat of my room, I heard the doorbell ring. My bedroom door opened to a straight path to the front door, and I could see that Mom was speaking with Marideth and Wendi. And then the door closed.

That's odd, I thought to myself. *What the hell do they want?*

Given that I was on restriction, I was also not speaking to Mom, so I didn't ask her why they had come by.

About twenty minutes later, our doorbell rang again. This time I didn't bother to look. I was too focused on getting a reprieve from the heat by lying on my bedroom carpet directly under the breeze generated by the whirring blades of the ceiling fan.

Suddenly, I heard voices emanating from the backyard. I looked out my sliding glass doors and saw *them*. My best friends, whom I hadn't spoken to in a week, scampering across the concrete of our patio. Clad in swimsuits, with their brightly colored towels wrapped around their bodies like pig-in-blanket hors d'oeuvres. I heard them giggling and laughing, then a splashing sound as they jumped into *my* pool.

The sense of betrayal was overwhelming. I felt like I was in the movie *Carrie*, in the scene where the pig's blood was dumped over her head. Only I wasn't the prom queen, but a thirteen-year-old girl stuck in her room, without any agency. And my tormentors weren't the "cool" kids but my best friends, who were invading my territory and worse, my safe haven. Showing me through their laughing and splashing that they didn't give a damn about our friendship or my feelings.

My indignation erupted with an emotional frenzy that bordered on pathological. Trapped in my room, I was unable to defend myself from this blatant encroachment on my personal space by my frenemies.

So I did the only thing I could at the time, which was to stew and plot my revenge. After a half hour or so, I saw Mom open the kitchen door that led to the patio. Leaning partially out the doorway, she called out, "Are you girls okay?"

"Yes, Mrs. Baber," they happily replied in unison.

"Okay, just checking on you! Have fun!" she said.

As Mom began to close the door our eyes met, and that's when

I saw it. Emanating from her blue orbs like radio waves, I saw a smile crinkling the corners of her eyes that spread to her mouth as it slowly curved into the slightest grin.

In that instant, I realized that Mom had intentionally let my friends swim in our pool *knowing* that we were in an argument. She wasn't naïve; she knew exactly what she was doing. Mom had let my friends play in our pool while I was on restriction to punish me for my insolence. To further drive home the fact that *she* was the boss, not me.

As the awareness of her power play slowly began to sink in, a new, larger thought began to drown out the gleeful sounds of my "friends" splashing in my pool. Mom could also be motivated by malice, or at the very least, *the need to win*. When our eyes connected I saw her smugness and triumph.

Realizing that Mom was capable of willfully inflicting emotional harm on me irreversibly changed our relationship. And the fact that she would use my friends to do it was unforgivable. On that hot summer day in 1983, Mom became my enemy. Someone to be destroyed, lest I be destroyed.

It wasn't just my parents who became the enemy. It was the entire, cursed world that I lived in. I realized how powerless I was over everything in my life. The claustrophobic, smothering home in which I lived. The alienating neighborhood just outside my front door. The classmates at school who made it their mission to try to psychologically dismantle me with the racist bile that spewed out of their mouths and crawled up into my mind like a centipede in the darkness.

❦

That year I had caught an unexpected lucky break that coincided with my increasing rebelliousness. The bullies on my school bus had moved on to high school, which meant I was no longer subject to their tyranny. My rage began to spill out of me, uncontained. I became so brash and loud-talking that somehow I had managed to work my way to the back of the bus. There were still some boys in the neighborhood who could have bullied me, but this group had been stopped by a prior incident that put them on warning.

It was 7:00 in the morning and the kids in my neighborhood were waiting for the bus to take us to school. As usual, Jon Shultz and his younger brother, Doug, began teasing me. It was their daily ritual, which provided entertainment for the rest of the kids at the bus stop. Doug had snatched something away from me and I began to chase him, wildly flailing my arms to snatch it back. As I rounded the pack assembled at the bus stop, Jon stuck his foot out and tripped me. I landed squarely on my left arm, which had been injured slightly the week before when Jackie Ivester (a shapely and large-boned classmate known for her large breasts and perfect Scandinavian-blond feathered hair) and I collided into each other on the outdoor concrete basketball court during gym class. We were both around the same height, but she carried thirty pounds more on her frame. During practice she fell smack on top of me with her full body weight, landing on my arm and skinning it across the pavement. I had sustained a slight sprain and a long, nasty scab as a result of the fall. When Jon tripped me, I fell to the ground on the same arm. My sprain went from minor to severe, and I ended up having to go to the local health clinic with my dad. He was furious over the unexpected expense of X-rays and an office visit. That $150 might as well have been $3,000 to him.

Dad didn't have extra money to waste on an avoidable medical bill. So he walked me with my arm in the cloth sling around the corner to the Shultzs' house to confront Jon and Doug's father. He rang the doorbell and Mr. Shultz answered the door. He was a bespectacled, middle-aged, midlevel corporate executive, the complete antithesis of Dad.

"Look at what your boys did to my daughter!" Dad shouted, pointing to my arm in the sling. I stood by his side mutely, looking at the grass at my feet. *Gawd!* I thought to myself. *Where is a sinkhole when you need one to swallow you up?*

"You have no proof that my sons have done anything to your daughter. And if you don't get off of my property, I'm going to call the police."

I waited to see what Dad would do. The anger was radiating off of him. Was he gonna punch Mr. Shultz?

"I'll see your ass in court!" was Dad's retort. Storming off, he yelled back at me, "Come on!"

Calling out from his front door, Mr. Shultz replied, "Sure thing, George. Looking forward to it."

Dad and I went home, where he grabbed a beer and sulked in the garage near his workbench. I sat in a daze in my room, humiliated. There were so many ways he could have addressed the situation that didn't involve throwing a temper tantrum on a neighbor's front lawn in full view of anyone passing by.

In the end, Dad never filed suit. That would have required even more money in attorney's fees to fight for $150. The only good thing to come out of the situation was that the Shultz boys and their cronies left me alone. Without the fear of their aggression, I was free to begin pushing the boundaries of how far I could assert myself with my peers. Eighth grade was heavenly, for it was the first time in three years that I wasn't cowering in fear from the older bullies.

The only blip that year was when I had braces put on my teeth. Grandma Lou was still doting on me and offered to pay for them since my parents couldn't afford their cost. I would end up wearing them for a year before the orthodontist said I was ready to transition to a retainer. Unfortunately, I lost it the day after my braces came off, and Dad refused to replace the retainer in an effort to teach me a lesson about responsibility. His "lesson" essentially wasted Grandma's $1,000 investment in my smile. My teeth ended up partially shifting back into their original position because Dad had to make a $150 point.

❃

My tenuous emotional connection to my parents, to my friends, or to anyone for that matter, snapped that summer between my eighth and ninth-grade years. People became either good or bad. Light or dark. For you or against you. Psychologists call this "splitting." It's a defense mechanism that helps keep you safe from your mental bogeyman, from the cognitive dissonance you can't resolve. But I no longer felt confused. I believed I had discovered the truth: my parents and my peers were intent on destroying my spirit. And I was not going to allow it.

Of course, this attempt to squash my internal conflict with my parents' authority was maladaptive. The problem in my new position, of course, was that very few people are all anything, myself included. And my increasing inability to recognize this made me emotionally color-blind, with just as much potential to harm. If you can't tell the difference between red and green, for example, you're likely to run a traffic light and crash. The same metaphor applied to the way I would begin to interpret other people's emotional signals. For how can you have compassion, or connect emotionally to another human being, or see the value of a different perspective, when you don't have the ability to see all the nuances of a person's personality or behavior?

The tiny corner of the world in which I lived had no idea what was heading their way.

Lake Howell High School cafeteria, 1986.

CHAPTER SEVEN

𝒮UMMER 1984. THIS THREE-MONTH SPAN THAT BRIDGED MY eighth and ninth-grade school years was the point in time when I slid down my own personal rabbit hole like Alice in Wonderland. Alice, who spied a small bottle tagged "Drink me," slugged it down without any serious thought to the consequences, and subsequently grew so uncomfortably large for her surroundings that she wept tears of self-pity. It is an apt metaphor for what happened to me when I took my first drink of alcohol at the age of thirteen, just shy of my fourteenth birthday. I, too, didn't give any thought to what might happen to me if I drank the forbidden liquid. Unlike Alice, it wasn't my physical form that grew so large that it caused me to suffer. Alcohol served as a Miracle-Gro fertilizer for my character defects. My latent self-hatred, the anger at my parents and the society I was forced to live in, plus my emerging consciousness of my sexuality burst out of me like a racehorse at Belmont almost overnight.

Looking back, if there was one thing I could change about my life it would be the decision to take that first drink. For I, like so many others, didn't realize that I carried the alcoholic gene. Addiction ran rampant through my biological mother's family, although I didn't know it at the time—I only knew what my dad had told me about Daisy and her hard-drinking, irresponsible ways. But my naïveté, natural curiosity, and tendency toward risk-taking led me down a path that would eventually nearly kill me.

Even though I was a loud child, I was also painfully insecure and shy—a not-too-surprising combination for anyone with a basic understanding of the paradoxical nature of personality. Though I hid it well under my boisterous behavior, at my core I was suffering from severe social anxiety and depression. I envied the older kids in my neighborhood who hung out near their cars parked in their driveways with an arrogant air. Zipping by on my bicycle, I noticed how they cracked open bottles of beer and smoked cigarettes, seemingly without a care in the world. Mom had forbidden me from spending any time around the "druggies," her favorite term for these rebellious teens. She had nothing to worry about there. I was just the skinny little neighborhood "nigger" (as they would call me) on her ten-speed bike. They would never invite me to hang out with them.

My buddy and neighbor Marideth, on the other hand, was friendly with some of the Freaks, and so by proxy I was one degree of separation from an entirely new world of chemical emancipation. She was a year older than her sister Wendi and me, and had always been the cool one out of our little quartet, which usually included their stepsister Leslie. Over the years we became a tight-knit group of friends, despite our rocky beginning.

I idolized Marideth. She was everything that I wasn't. Blond-haired and blue-eyed, she was voluptuously built, with breasts sizable enough to rival a porn star's. That, combined with her highlighted Aqua Net–lacquered feathered hair, brash confidence, and small waist, made her a magnet for male attention, something the rest of us didn't receive.

Over the past year Marideth had been spending more time with some of the older kids in the neighborhood, leaving behind the less-desirable trio of Wendi, Leslie, and me. We were all dorky understudies to Marideth's leading-lady status in our small clique. Wendi was slightly overweight, but big-chested, and Leslie, who was a year younger, was beginning to fill out as well. And here I was, a flat-chested, tall, gangly "Hawaiian" girl with wavy hair that had over the course of the past few months morphed into dark, tight curls.

As the eldest of our quartet, Marideth also had a learner's permit, which meant she could drive without an adult in the car during daylight hours, and with one riding shotgun at night. When her parents upgraded one of their family vehicles to a customized luxury van, they gifted her with its predecessor: a battered forest-green Chevy Impala station wagon with a leaking oil tank that we affectionately referred to as "The Bomb." Cumbersome and unwieldy, it guzzled gasoline and motor oil, but it was transportation that didn't require one to pedal or skate.

It was through these chosen sisters that I was introduced to what would eventually become my lover and best friend for the next ten years: alcohol. When Marideth approached Wendi and me to take a ride to the local 7-11 convenience store, I was thrilled. She had been spending a lot of time with the Freaks and her invitation meant that she had finally decided we were cool enough to hang around with again.

"Hey!" Marideth called out to Wendi and me from her car. We were seated on my front porch bench, talking about the current heartthrobs who had taken over every square inch of my bedroom walls: Duran Duran. Our debates generally centered around why I loved the bassist, John Taylor, and why she preferred the keyboardist Nick Rhodes. Real deep conversations about adult male international superstars with whom we would never, ever in our lives be in the same room.

"Do y'all want to go to The Sev and get a Big Gulp?" We always referred to the 7-11 as "The Sev."

It was assumed that Wendi had permission since they were sisters, but I had to make sure I could go.

"Uh, sure. Just let me tell my mom I'm going and I'll meet you at your car."

"Okay, cool! Hurry up, though . . . I've got something to show you."

I found them both waiting by The Bomb, but it was going to take a couple of minutes for us to leave, for it was simply too hot to sit inside. We opened up the doors and waited for the overheated air to flow out and allow the "cooler" air to flow in, which was a joke. Central Floridian summers are brutal. It was probably 95 degrees Fahrenheit with the same percentage of humidity that day. The type of air that wraps itself around your body like a stifling, damp blanket.

Marideth had turned on the air conditioner as well to expedite the cooling-off period and after a few minutes, we slid onto the hot, avocado-green vinyl front seat and pulled our seat belts into place. I turned my head just in time to see her pull something out from down between her legs. I saw in her hand what she had hidden under her seat: a glistening bottle of rum. Its contents sloshed around in the half-empty container, amber liquid glowing in the bright sunlight.

I was giddy with excitement, but was also scared. I knew there would be serious consequences if my parents found out that I had disobeyed them—again.

While Dad was a heavy drinker, Mom hardly drank at all. She said she hated the taste of alcohol and imbibed only on special occasions. Even then, she would have one glass of wine and nothing more. Both were adamant that I not drink until I reached the legal drinking age—twenty-one.

"I don't know if I should do this . . . You know my parents will kill me if they ever find out."

"Don't be such a chicken! How are they gonna know?"

Marideth started to make squawking noises.

"Chicken . . . chicken . . . Bawk, bawk, bawk!"

Her display was embarrassing. And she had a point. While I was apprehensive about what could happen if I were caught by my parents, my fear of being exposed as a coward outweighed any other concerns.

Within seconds I gave in.

"Alright, alright! Let's do it!"

We drove to The Sev, and after buying a Big Gulp of Coca-Cola, Marideth promptly dumped out half its contents onto the black tar parking lot. Driving back toward our neighborhood, she ordered Wendi to fill the empty space in the container to the top with rum. This was not a small amount of alcohol . . . one-half of a regular Big Gulp made for sixteen pure ounces of booze.

Spying a remote section of our subdivision filled with houses still under construction, she parked her car.

Marideth had pulled out a pack of Marlboro Lights, so the car windows were rolled down while the air conditioning blasted in our faces, to ensure we didn't smell like we had spent time in a smoky bar. Smoking was another big no-no for our parents.

Frankie Goes to Hollywood's song "Relax" wafted tinnily from the car radio.

As she held her lit cigarette out the driver's-side window, Marideth downed a quarter of the concoction in seconds.

She then offered the container to Wendi, who took a few sips and choked, giggling. It was now my turn. I took the oversized paper cup from her hands and sipped tentatively from the straw. The liquid burned as it slid down the back of my throat into my gut, slowly radiating its warmth out to the tips of my fingers.

I was momentarily confused, surprised that something so cold could burn so hot in my stomach.

"Wow! You can't even taste the rum," I exclaimed, greedily sucking down half of what was left.

"Leave some for me!" Marideth cried.

As the alcohol began to make its way through my system, my insecurities flew out of the car window along with the smoke and strains of the music.

The bass line thumped with the lyrics: "Relax, don't do it . . . when you want go to it. Relax, don't do it . . . when you want to come!"

I was relaxed all right, with a wonderful feeling of elation that freed me from my insecurities and fear. For the first time in my short life I felt incredibly light. Free. Blissful. Another bonus: *everything was so damn funny.* We laughed hysterically at each other for nothing other than a sideways glance. It didn't matter how stupid the wisecrack, each of us practically slid onto the floorboards as our bodies were wracked with giggles. Together we screamed out the lyrics to the songs blasting from the car radio.

At that moment I thought I had found my life's panacea. Drinking was going to be my social salvation. And just like that, *voilà*!

Another alcoholic was born.

❋

During the summer of 1984 I reached what would ultimately be my adult height: five foot nine. By now I was operating on the assumption that Dad wasn't my biological father. After all, one doesn't have to be a rocket scientist to know that being born on an island doesn't make one ethnically indigenous. The larger question for me at this point was: Why did Dad continue to pretend that he was my biological father when it was clearly impossible? My mental maturity clashed with his ongoing attempts to quell my increasing insistence for the truth. But he refused to back down from his Hawaiian theory.

Up until this point I had accepted his ridiculous answer, never challenging him too much. But due to my increasing reliance upon alcohol, my personality was emboldened with a devil-may-care attitude that led me to become even more openly defiant and belligerent than I had been, challenging my parents on everything.

Maybe that's why one month before my fourteenth birthday, Dad finally told me the truth. After years of lies, he smashed it into my face like a brick.

The world as I knew it changed on a typical sunny day filled with too much humidity and too little excitement. Dad's meager income was just enough to cover the family expenses and rarely left anything over for formal summer activities. While many of my peers were away at camp, or visiting family in other cities, I was landlocked in our small neighborhood. May Lai and I were extremely restless, but we knew better than to whine about it. My parents addressed any complaints about our boredom with an automatic response of "I can think of something for you to do," which was their code phrase for housework, which of course was worse than doing nothing. So it was up to us to come up with creative and free ways to pass the time.

This afternoon happened to be one of the few times a year when Dad would "babysit" while Mom spent a few hours out alone at the mall with our neighbor Nancy. Mom cared for his brood of children 365 days a year with no complaint and zero support. In exchange for what was essentially indentured servitude, she was given two afternoons annually during which she was free to do as she pleased. Although these days were rare, they still were an extreme irritant to Dad, who much preferred refurbishing his Harley-Davidson Electra Glide motorcycle to managing four children.

As Dad distracted himself by working on his Harley, May Lai and I sat at the kitchen table just a few yards away from the door to the garage. I was the one who came up with the idea to amuse ourselves by reading out loud from a book entitled *Truly Tasteless Jokes*, a former *New York Times* bestseller that if published today would be attacked by the NAACP, GLAAD, PETA, the JDL, and every other civil liberties group quicker than you can say "First Amendment."

We'd already worked our way through the dead baby jokes and had moved on to the racist ones.

"Here's one! How do you stop a nigger from jumping on the bed?" my sister asked.

I bounced up and down on the wicker seat of the chair while waiting for the punch line.

"You put Velcro on the ceiling!"

Roaring with laughter, I grabbed the book from her hand, skimming the page for the next joke. Our glee was suddenly interrupted by the squeaky sound of *flip-flip, flip-flip* slapping across the lime-colored linoleum. We looked up just in time to see Dad come to an abrupt stop in the middle of the kitchen. *Uh-oh*, I thought to myself, glancing over at my sister, who looked just as confused as I was by the expression on his face.

His brows were furrowed, lips curled. It was clear he was pissed.

"I don't know why you're laughing, Sil Lai. You're one," he spat with contempt.

His words slapped me in the face and my laughter became clogged in my throat as it began to tighten with shock. Stunned, May Lai and I watched as he grabbed a can of Budweiser from the refrigerator and then *flip-flip-flip* flopped out to the garage without a backward glance.

And with those few words, my father stripped me of my identity and place in the world as his daughter.

For a few seconds, my sister and I just looked at each other as an uncomfortable silence descended upon us like a heavy fog. My face burned hotly with embarrassment, but what was worse was seeing the pity in her eyes.

Clearing the air of more than a decade of lies was liberating; however, just as quickly as I was freed, I was shackled again. For now, not only was I not his child, I was also black. An outcast in my home, I was now an outcast in society as well, as I had been taught to view it.

I was, as the kids at school said, a coon. A porch monkey. A jungle bunny. A tar baby.

A nigger.

I didn't know if I wanted to laugh or scream, or both. I could do neither, as my vocal cords were paralyzed.

A constellation of emotions washed over me. Rage at how callously my father told me the truth. Shame at the source of my skin color. Sadness, because the world as I had known it was forever changed.

I wasn't "Hawaiian" and Chinese anymore. Nor was I just the sibling who could get a super-dark tan due to Dad's Italian genes, or so I thought. I didn't want to be black. As ludicrous as it sounds, I wanted to stay a "Hawaiian." I wanted to rewind time and return to Dad's comforting cocoon of lies, but it was too late. I was now, by some cruel twist of fate by an unmerciful God, a black girl living in a white world. Dad and I hadn't been close for years, and the way he told me made me question whether or not he'd ever loved me. Was he harder on me than my siblings because I was the oldest, a common family dynamic? Did I get the lash of the belt more frequently than my siblings because of my personality, or was it due to his discomfort with the color of my skin? Or was it driven by the fact that I was a constant reminder of Daisy's bout with "jungle fever"? Or was it because he resented shouldering the financial burden of a child that wasn't biologically his?

My mind raced back to memories of Dad and Mom doing nothing when I came home crying in fifth or sixth grade after being called "nigger" and "porch monkey" by the kids at school. *That's why they didn't support me*, I thought. *They knew what the kids were saying was true!*

I had to get out of this house, away from my sister's pitying looks, away from Dad tinkering twenty feet away in our garage. There was only one person I could speak to about this: Wendi.

At her door, I rudely pressed the bell multiple times. I didn't care. I had to speak to someone before my head exploded.

Wendi's plump form filled the doorway as she approached the screen door.

"Hey! What's up?"

I blurted out, "I'm black! My dad just told me I'm black!"

Sitting down on the floral comforter on her bed, I tearfully recounted what had just happened. Her eyes were misty, and I could feel her compassion (or pity?) for my plight.

Pulling me close, she gave me a brief hug and said, "Don't worry about it, Sil Lai. *No one ever needs to know.*"

I was appreciative of her support, but at the same time I could feel the embarrassment burrowing deeper into my spirit. *No one ever needs to know.* That was the extent of the counseling and support I received for the attempted soul murder by my dad.

The last thing I wanted was to go home, but I had to return for dinner. As I embarked upon the fifty-foot walk back across the street, I felt dead. My "home" was a place where I was tolerated out of guilt or pity. I wasn't a true Baber. I was a black man's bastard.

I hated the way my dad had pulled the pin from our family's hidden emotional bomb and thrown it at me to catch. While he strolled off to finish his beer and polish the chrome of his motorcycle, I swallowed his grenade and it exploded in my gut. Destroying what little bond remained between us. He was no longer my dad. My parents were no longer my family.

In an effort to try and get some sympathy, I called Dad's sister Doni to tell her about Dad's "confession." After I relayed my story, she sighed with relief.

"I'm glad he finally told you. All of us, Grandma, Grandpa, and me, were against his decision to keep the truth from you," Aunt Doni said. She added, "Your dad lied because he didn't want you to feel different from the other kids. He loved Daisy and that meant loving everything that came with her, which included you. Plus, the Baha'is believe in racial unity. They encourage interracial marriages as a way to promote racial harmony. He didn't want you to be burdened by race. He loves you and just wanted you to be his daughter."

I responded, "Yeah? Well, he sure doesn't act like it! Doni, he's such a jerk! He doesn't love anyone but himself. He's so mean. Can't you see? Look at how he told me!"

But Doni wasn't swayed.

"Sil Lai, your dad loves you. You don't understand. I know my brother. He's got a good heart. But . . ." She paused as her voice cracked, then continued, "But you don't know how Vietnam changed him! George couldn't handle it. When he came back from the war, he was different. It broke him. George was a peaceful man. He never should have gone overseas, but he had no choice. He was drafted and wasn't in college. So he went." I listened, transfixed, as her story about Dad's life temporarily distracted me from my anger.

"Your dad would send messages home to Grandma on cassette

tapes. If you could have heard them! We lived to get those tapes and his letters. At least we knew he was still alive. But to hear his suffering broke our hearts. The war was destroying him. He wasn't emotionally built for it. That's why he went AWOL. He was lucky he wasn't court-martialed. So when he was sent home on a conditional discharge instead, Grandma didn't care. She threw him a party anyway. She contacted the local paper and they ran a story on his safe return home." By now, my aunt was sobbing.

For a moment, I felt sorry for Dad. Her story humanized this man who for years had done nothing but make me feel largely tolerated. I suddenly felt guilty.

"Sil Lai, I can't expect you to understand. But your dad loves you! He did what he did because he loves you! It was wrong. You have a right to be angry, but he's not a bad man."

But even as Aunt Doni continued to speak, my self-righteous indignation shoved aside her rationalizations about his behavior. He wasn't the only one suffering. I didn't really care that he used to be a sensitive man. What mattered was my current reality, not her sad stories about a man who ceased to exist before I was born.

After a while, our conversation ended and I was left with my thoughts. Her story explained a lot, but she didn't have to live with him. And she didn't have to deal with the emotional fallout of his lies. Over the years, and in spite of his supposed noble intent, his lie about my paternity had given me an identity built on shifting sand. Now, at the age of fourteen, I had been dropped into what W.E.B. Du Bois termed "double consciousness." To quote from Du Bois's article in the *Atlantic Monthly* entitled "Strivings of the Negro People":

It is a peculiar sensation, this double-consciousness, this sense of always looking at one's self through the eyes of others, of mea-

suring one's soul by the tape of a world that looks on in amused contempt and pity. One ever feels his two-ness,—an American, a Negro; two souls, two thoughts, two unreconciled strivings; two warring ideals in one dark body, whose dogged strength alone keeps it from being torn asunder.

Double consciousness was a term that I wouldn't come to know until later in life. When I did, it struck me like God's words to Moses on Mount Sinai. In the white world that I lived in, I had very little contact with black people and I wasn't personal friends with any. In spite of Dad's best intentions, I had been unconsciously struggling to reconcile two sides of my being my whole life. To be a part of a world that rejected me while trying "to be both a Negro and an American without being cursed and spit upon by [her] fellows." Little did I know that I had been in many ways living the black experience for much of my life—simply without a community or culture to protect me from being alone in the wilderness. What a difference it would have made for me to have grown up in a black home, with black people sharing with me the tools of how to navigate two worlds, a system of survival that is necessary even to this day. To be fourteen years old and to learn you are black—and then be provided with no cultural context—was cruel. It was the second time that Dad had stripped away my birthright. The first time it was Daisy, and now my identity.

There was no reason that I would understand or care about what it meant to be black or the struggles of a group of people that the society in which I was raised believed were genetically inferior. Like a lot of "white" kids, I had checked out during the seventh grade when we spent one semester studying black history during social studies. Of that time, I remember learning only a few things: black people were stolen by white people and enslaved against their will in the United States; Abraham Lincoln freed the slaves because he was good man; some black people were smart, like George Washington Carver, who cultivated the peanut. Harriet Tubman led a bunch of black people to freedom on something called the Underground Railroad. And a man named Martin Luther King, Jr., had died fighting for equal rights for black people. That was the gist of what I knew about black people from a historical perspective.

But from the environment in which I lived, I was told a much fuller, more emotionally complex story based on white supremacy. Most black people in America were the descendants of slaves, but over a hundred years after the Thirteenth Amendment to the U.S. Constitution, they remained as primitive as the drawings I saw in my history books and photos in *National Geographic* magazines. Black people were physically superior and mentally inferior to white people. Most were poor and uneducated, and the ones who weren't, like the teachers at my school, were an anomaly. Despite their "acceptabilty," these exceptions to the rule still spoke funny, smelled funny, and looked funny. Jheri curls were all the rage at the time and their hair, dripping with activator, seemed unnatural. Granted, white girls were perming their hair curly with equal popularity, but I couldn't see the hypocrisy of the belief that black permed hair was bad, while white people's permed hair was good.

Thanks to Dad's lie, I now had to completely reconcile my identity, not only as a member of the family, but also as a member of a race that I had no connection to at all and had been taught was inferior. I was completely unprepared for the task, and as my family would soon come to see, the price we would all pay for his lies would cause the foundation of my adolescent world to collapse, bringing the family down into the abyss with me.

❁

Within a week of this bombshell, my life resumed its usual routine. The summer continued with the usual activities of swimming, bike riding, and lounging around the house. But I now
had a secret escape that my parents didn't know about: drinking.
There was no reason for me to suffer when I could find escape in
a bottle. Alcohol was easy to get my hands on and provided hours
of entertainment on the weekends for the Windsor girls and myself when we went to our Friday night hangout spot, Semoran
Skateway.

Friday nights at the roller rink was the destination hub for
teenagers and adults from around the local area. It was a predominantly white crowd, of course, and I did my best to blend
in. There were small cliques of Latinos and blacks who came out
mainly to partake in the air-conditioned environment filled with
pulsating music and flashing lights. They didn't actually skate,
but spent the evening walking around the rink, looking like extras
out of the movie *Breakin'*. These groups of boys and their female
companions kept to themselves in a far corner of the rink, pop
locking and moonwalking, engrossed in their own private dance
party. They were left alone to do as they pleased, and occasionally
when the manager was feeling gracious, he would clear the skate
floor so the dancers could do an impromptu performance to "Jam
On It" by Newcleus, or "Rockit" by Herbie Hancock. While my
physical appearance clearly placed me in the category of black
or Puerto Rican, my mind was white. My friends were white.
My entire cultural identity was white. So I busied myself on the
skate floor with the other white kids, trying (and failing) to learn
to shuffle skate to the sounds of Shannon's "Let the Music Play"
and The Bar-Kays' "Freakshow on the Dance Floor." Wendi

and Marideth zipped around the rink, skates shuffling in perfect synchronization to the music. Every so often, the DJ would play AC/DC's "You Shook Me All Night Long," and the girls would disappear from the floor while the boys in speed skates took over the rink. Racing around and around, they were young white Central Floridian masculinity personified.

It was interesting, to say the least, to see kids who were so avowedly pro-white lose themselves into the sounds of urban music on the skating rink floor. Outside of the rink, they would never admit to listening to "black music," professing allegiance to white musicians and groups like Billy Squier, Journey, and Judas Priest. But the skating rink was its own world, with its own specific values that sometimes overrode the outside world's segregated views on race and culture.

It was at this skating rink that I had my first kiss, which had ended disastrously for me when I was vetted for my non-blackness by the blond-haired skater boy before he touched me. That experience exacerbated my fear and shame around my skin color. I was consumed with fantasies about how much better my life would be if I actually were white. But that wasn't who or what I was. Standing in front of the bathroom mirror, I would cry, wailing over my fate. Tears streaming, I bemoaned why God gave me this ugly brown face with a nose that didn't have a prominent bridge like my white friends. In utter frustration, I'd slap myself on my cheeks, hatred for my skin color fueling my self-flagellation. *Why me, God?* I would ask, over and over again. *Why do I have to be black? Why? Why? Why?*

Every message I had ever received about black people was negative. Why else would everyone spend so much time putting "them" down? Why else did the news feature so many of "them" being arrested? Why else did "they" live on the other side of the train tracks in areas like Eatonville, or in rental apartments dotting the area while the rest of us lived in homes our parents owned?

How in the world would I, with white parents of limited education, living in an all-white environment, even begin to understand how structural racism and the white supremacy that infiltrates every aspect of American life is the cause of the disproportionate rates of poverty among black people? How could I know about the true benefit of white privilege that prevents so many black people from rising up the economic and social ladder? There was one answer: I couldn't. And nobody in my neighborhood knew or cared to know. After all, why care about people you had already deemed worthless and detrimental to the fabric of our good country?

For years I had been unknowingly passing, but the summer of 1984 it became intentional. My beloved backyard pool was abandoned, as swimming meant that I would be exposed to the sun, which would make my skin darker. Instead, I stayed indoors and slathered large amounts of sunblock with an SPF of 48 on any exposed areas of my genealogically betraying skin. I not only had to change the way I looked, but the way I behaved. Forget about eating fried chicken, especially in public. Fried chicken was black people food. When my family gathered at the local parks and lakes for the rare outing and watermelon was served, I shied away from it, lest someone see it in my brown hands and think, *Of course Sil Lai likes watermelon, she's a nigger.* Now that I was getting older, my racial heritage was becoming more and more obvious. And with high school approaching, I had no idea what to expect.

❁

By the time I made it to my freshman year at Lake Howell High, home of the mighty Silver Hawks, I had shaken off most of my middle school tormentors. They had turned their attention away from bullying misfits like me and onto more important things, like getting laid and high. Lake Howell was an enormous school attended by over two thousand students, which made it an easy place to stay under the radar, if that's what you wanted. Even though it was a predominantly white high school, our principal, Mr. Evans, and vice-principal, Mr. Gaines, were, interestingly enough, black men—an irony that was not lost on our school population. In fact, Mr. Evans had been its principal since it opened in 1974 and would retire in 1993 as Seminole County's only black high school principal.

Wendi, Marideth, and Leslie had transferred out of the private school they had attended since kindergarten and were now students at Lake Howell. They comprised my initial core group of friends at school. Wendi's close friendship saved me from loner status, and Marideth, a bodacious and popular trash talker, served as my protector from the few girls who tried to intimidate me. Thanks to the Windsor sisters, I was no longer a solitary, friendless loser, and together we braved the awkward transition from middle school to high school.

It was during my freshman year that I discovered a subculture within the school that ultimately would transform my relationship with my family and my peers, allowing me to hide from myself further: punk rockers. This motley crew of loud and obnoxious upperclassmen were largely avoided by the general population at school. They were a spectacle of dark and ripped clothing, spikes, boots, studs, and eyeliner. Sporting bleached Mohawks standing six inches high that extended from their heads likes the spines of a sea urchin, shaved domes, or Cyndi Lauper–esque hair held firmly in place with cans of professional-grade hair spray, this group of approximately fifteen outcasts caused other students to walk around them in the hall and members of the school administration to roll their eyes and brace themselves when they passed by. Their clothing was eclectic and baroque, their hairstyles an insult to the sensibilities of our working-class environment—and I loved everything about them. Unlike me, they weren't ashamed of their actual or perceived uniqueness; instead they celebrated it. I marveled at their defiance of the status quo and envied their cool, unaffected swagger that mocked and attacked convention. With the exception of the Martinez brothers, Puerto Rican twins with shaved heads and flannel shirts, all were very white and very pale. I didn't care that I looked different from them on the outside (save the Martinez brothers). I completely identified with their hatred of authority and love of rebellion, and made it my goal to break into their clique.

Punk rock is not just about appearance, although this is the most noticeable element of the lifestyle. It is a state of mind that is manifested in the clothing, music, and way of life. For the past several years I had been developing an appreciation for British new wave bands such as Culture Club, Duran Duran, Frankie Goes to Hollywood, and ABC. It was not a stretch for me to push the boundaries of my musical taste beyond this to delve deeper into associated genres of music that had a message that was more aligned with my disenchanted state of mind. After years of being subjected to taunts and jeers for being different, I realized that this was the group I needed to belong to if I wanted to ensure that I wouldn't be abused for being "terminally unique." There was no question that I wanted to break in, but the question remained how I, a lowly freshman, would be able to do so.

The first step was to slowly modify my appearance so that I looked more punk than dork. I started wearing the color black from head to toe and shaved my hair off from the crown of my head down, leaving a cropped lawn of short curls on top that eventually spilled out into an eight-inch-long bleached bang that touched the bottom of my chin and completely obscured the vision in my left eye. Each morning before school I'd blow my bang straight and lacquer it into place with Aqua Net to keep it from curling up in the humidity. For some unknown reason, my middle-aged next-door neighbor offered to give me her collection of costume jewelry, so I now had the accessories to go along with the outfit. A collection of silver chains hanging down the front of my black clothes and multiple piercings in my left ear (seven, including the one at the top that earned me a month's restriction from my stepmother when I defied her instruction not to get it), black nail polish, and black-rimmed eyes and lips completed my physical transformation. In a little over three months I went from looking like the typical, Duran Duran loving and pastel wearing teen to the bastard child of Siouxsie Sioux and Prince. My parents were horrified and tried to get me to stop changing my appearance by banning me from participating in the annual family photo taken at the local mall's Sears Portrait Studio. Suffice it to say, their attempts to tame my appearance didn't work.

Now that my physical transformation was complete, I needed an in to the punk rockers' close-knit world. I was able to subtly infiltrate their group when Lance Bruce, a punk/new waver who lived in our neighborhood invited me to start riding to school with him and some of his other alternative music-loving friends. It was only a matter of time before I broke my way into the nucleus of their group, and by the end of my freshman year, Wendi Windsor and her sisters were out and the punks were in.

Wendi was furious that I had pushed her aside. We had been inseparable, to the point where we met between every class to give each other notes so we could stay in communication. Every weekend was spent together, sleeping in her twin bed, ankle to head. We knew each other well, both the light and the dark sides of our personalities.

We kept each other's secrets, like my attempted suicide at fourteen years old. At some point after one of my many arguments with Mom, I took a razor blade that I had stolen from my grandfather's stash in the bathroom and slashed at my left wrist. The cuts were superficial—deep enough to draw blood, but not to cut through a vein.

Grabbing my left forearm tightly, blood running down from the cuts and pooling around the top of my hand that was serving as a human tourniquet, I ran across the street to Wendi's house and rang the bell. She called for her mother, who tended to my physical wounds while admonishing me that to kill myself was a mortal sin that would condemn me to hell. She meant well, but I wasn't buying what she was selling. She didn't realize that as far as I was concerned, I already was in hell. I didn't care about what might happen to me when I was dead and gone. My concern was about how to end the pain *today*.

But for all of our emotional symbiosis, I felt stifled and controlled by our friendship. I was tired of the way she could manipulate me to do whatever she wanted, simply by withholding attention or picking a fight. And although she never asked me to do so, I was forever trying to ensure that I was her *real* best friend by various acts of self-abnegating service. I would volunteer to clean her bathroom so we could get permission from her mom to go out that night. I'd climb into her shower stall and scrub the tile from top to bottom with Ajax cleanser and polish the bathroom mirror, ending the task with scrubbing out her toilet.

My self-esteem was so low that when she snuck some older boys into her house during the summer, I "gave" my virginity to an eighteen-year-old I had just met for the first time that afternoon, simply to keep him company while Wendi played with his friend in the other room.

In the company of my new friends, I felt free. Something had been wrong for years in Wendi and my relationship, and my new friends were the opportunity I needed to break away from her hold over me. But Wendi wasn't having it. She first tried snubbing me for a few weeks, but when that didn't succeed in luring me back, she upped the ante to extortion. During an attempt to convince me to spend more time with her, she revealed exactly how far she was willing to go to get me back under her control.

"So you think you're so fucking cool now, huh? With your punk rock friends and their stupid fucking parties?" Wendi warned. "You think they care about you? No, Sil Lai. *I* care about you."

I didn't say a word.

"Fine. You want to go and be a fucking punk, then do it. But we'll see how many of the boys like you when I tell them that you're black." And with her ominous threat, she stalked away.

I breathed a sigh of relief. Although I didn't want anyone to know my racial identity, I had already figured out my countermove. If Wendi were to tell anyone, I would just deny it. After all, it would be her word against mine, and my friends loathed conformist, "trendy" girls like her who listened to more mainstream alternative music, and weren't willing to live the punk rock lifestyle. "Poseur" is what they called people who weren't committed to our way of life. And I knew Wendi's words would simply open her to a verbal attack by my new friends, who would defend me as one of their own.

Years later, as an adult, I would realize that my friendship with Wendi was a blueprint for many of my later relationships.

❖

As a fledgling punk rocker, I fully embraced the drinking and partying that went with it. Although I had begun drinking the summer before with the Windsor girls, within the confines of our close-knit world of rebels, I dove into my burgeoning addiction like a skinhead into a mosh pit. I wanted to escape from the ordinariness of everyday life and feel comfortable in my own skin. Alcohol provided me with the channel needed to unleash years of buried anger and resentment into the world. I began to act out in ways that would put the most troubled Hollywood starlets today to shame. Running away, skipping school, sleeping around, shoplifting, fighting. Had I been born ten years later, I would have been the perfect candidate for Bad Azz Kids boot camp on *The Jerry Springer Show*.

In retrospect, alcohol also served to distance me from the truth about who I was. By no choice of my own, I had the blood of the most hated racial group in the world coursing through my veins. It was alcohol and fear that kept my mouth shut about my ethnicity, and I turned a blind eye to my new friends' racism. I said nothing when we drove down I-4, the large freeway that intersects Orlando proper, and they drunkenly screamed racial epithets at the drivers around us whose only "mistake" was driving while black. I kept silent when the skinheads talked openly about the superiority of the white race, and did their "Sieg Heil" salutes. When Mike from LA (a petty thief who had recently moved to Orlando and resembled the Sex Pistols' lead singer, Johnny Rotten) told me that "Hawaiians are proof that the white man fucked the buffalo," I simply rolled my eyes and walked away. Even though I was really curious about what the big deal was around the film, I passed on going to see *Purple Rain*. I couldn't risk being spotted at the local mall coming out of a movie about a black and Puerto Rican singer—I was too afraid of being found guilty by association. I had found a group of friends who would embrace me, darker skin and all, but my silence was the price I paid for their acceptance. Drinking helped obliterate the truth from my mind and enabled me to keep up the charade that I was truly one of them in every way.

To reinforce my new badass persona, I began carrying a butterfly knife with me to school, which I flashed on a few occasions in various classes. I knew it was illegal to carry a weapon on school property, so I only did it on a couple of days. But the word spread throughout school, which helped curb any potential bully's thought that I might still be easy pickings for abuse. And in what I viewed as my pièce de résistance of rebranding, I took the razor I had been given to dissect a frog in Mr. Pagano's ninth-grade science class and used it instead to slice superficial cuts on the top of my forearm in full view of my classmates. This final gesture, combined with all of my other antics, created a safe space for me within the school. I was a misfit; a destructive, loud, and potentially violent one as well. Suffice it to say, bullying was now a nonissue.

By the time I started tenth grade, I was fully enmeshed in the hedonistic and nihilistic lifestyle of a punk. Even though I technically wasn't "hardcore," meaning I preferred the more melodious sounds of Siouxsie and the Banshees and The Cure to Suicidal Tendencies and the Dead Kennedys, I was more hardcore with my drinking than any of my friends. While they continued to attend class and limited their partying to the weekends, I enthusiastically expanded my previously "weekend warrior" party style to include around-the-clock drinking. As a sophomore, I had completely given up on making an ounce of effort to meet the minimum requirements of school attendance. So while I was physically present (mainly because my mom wouldn't let me stay home during school days, and I had nowhere else to go), I had completely mentally checked out.

In an effort to make the school day more bearable, I began sneaking booze into class, making sure to sit in the back so I could sip the vodka I had in my bag through a straw. I was fifteen and had no way to legally buy the alcohol, so I began stealing it from my employer. (At the time, I was working as an assistant to a retired fashion designer.) One Friday I was feeling especially daring, so I took a bottle to school with me and put it into my locker. Of course, the fact that this was a serious infraction of school policy didn't matter to me. The administration got wind of the presence of alcohol on school property when someone snitched on me. Fortunately, Lisa Sauls, one of my new punk friends, heard that my locker was going to be raided and moved the bottle out to her car, sparing me from suspension.

I played a game of chicken with the school administration for the first three weeks of tenth grade. Drinking in class. Showing up to school and leaving whenever I liked. Walking out of class to ostensibly use the ladies' room and never returning. Cursing at my teachers. Smoking cigarettes in the bathroom. By now the school realized they had a serious disciplinary problem on their hands. A bull's-eye was on my back and I knew it. The only reason I attended school was because I didn't have anything else to do and it provided me the opportunity to see my friends. But my days as a student at Lake Howell High were numbered.

Cigarette smoking was a rite of passage for many of the girls I grew up with. I had taken to smoking largely because I thought it made me look cool. In between classes, those of us who were either (a) bored, (b) defiant, or (c) addicted enough to risk a school suspension would gather in the girls' restroom to partake in our illegal habit. There was always the risk of a random raid, so one of us would stand lookout outside the restroom to give a heads-up on an approaching teacher or administrator, usually the vice principal, Mr. Gaines.

One morning in early October, I was smoking in the restroom along with seven or eight other girls when the warning cry was given by our lookout. "Mr. Gaines is coming!" That sent everyone scurrying about, flushing their cigarettes down the toilet, hiding their contraband in their bras, or dumping it in the trash bin. Some girl whose name I didn't know pulled a pipe filled with marijuana tar out of her handbag and asked, "Will you hold this for me?"

"Sure," I said, wanting to show her that I wasn't afraid of school authority. Mr. Gaines and a female teacher burst through the door and ordered everyone to empty their bags, which they did. He then turned to me and said, "Let me see what's in your pockets." Pulling out the pipe, I placed it into his hands.

"Ladies, I want you to clear the room. Except for you, Miss Baber. You stay here while I send for Deputy Starr."

Deputy Ken Starr was a friendly, kind, and extremely obese school safety officer whose presence was mainly ceremonial. As I waited for him to arrive, I knew the jig was up. I arrogantly stared down this tall, imposing black man and his teacher side-kick, thinking to myself: *Big deal. They'll suspend me and I'll be back in two weeks. Fuck them.*

When Deputy Starr showed up, Mr. Gaines pulled him aside and spoke in tones too low for me to hear. When they finished, Deputy Starr cleared his throat and said, "Miss Baber, you're under arrest for possession of drug paraphernalia. You have the right to remain silent . . ."

As I listened to him recite my Miranda rights, I cursed myself for being so stupid. How the hell could I let myself get arrested for carrying a pipe that didn't even belong to me? As I was led out of the bathroom, down the hall, and toward the school office, I held my head high and looked past the curious stares of my classmates.

"What the fuck you lookin' at?" I hissed at one of the members of the cheerleading squad whose eyes lingered too long on my face.

"Miss Baber, that's enough!" spat Mr. Gaines.

When we finally arrived at his office, I sat legs splayed, face scowling, in a chair outside the room while paperwork was filed and my parents were called. I had to wait there for an hour until they were able to reach my mom, who showed up angry, weary, and exasperated. She and Mr. Gaines had a brief conference in his office and when she exited, she simply said, "Let's go."

I looked at Mr. Gaines and asked, "So what's going to happen now?"

"You're being sent home, and we'll contact your parents to let them know what disciplinary action will be taken over your infraction." Mom said nothing to me on the way home, disgusted by my behavior.

A letter arrived approximately ten days later stating the school district's decision. Under other circumstances, a student caught with drug paraphernalia would receive a two-week suspension. However, my consistent history of disrespectful and rebellious behavior was untenable. This is why I was expelled from tenth grade after only three weeks.

❋

While the Seminole County School System had issued its decision on my drug paraphernalia charge, there was still the outstanding issue of the criminal case. The state was intent on pressing charges. However, the caseworker assigned to me pulled Mom aside and said, "If Sil Lai were to move out of town, the charges would be dropped since there wouldn't be any defendant to prosecute and this was a small, first-time offense." To avoid a trial and my potential incarceration, my parents enlisted the help of Dad's sister, Doni, who was now living in Seattle, Washington.

Doni was up for the task of trying to reform me. After a brief negotiation, she agreed to take me in at her small cottage on a hill on Lake Washington. I was elated. *Finally*, I thought to myself, *I'll be free of them*.

My stint in Seattle was cut short after four weeks, when I was sent back home for violating one of the two rules Doni had established as conditions for my living with her:

No drinking, and
No shoplifting

Shoplifting was a habit I had picked up during my freshman year of high school. When I started showing up with new clothes in my room that were inexplicably acquired (courtesy of my sticky fingers at my new job at the local mall), she promptly put me on a plane back home.

But my one-month sojourn wasn't a complete waste of time. During my brief stint in Seattle, I managed to get my GED. The state of Washington didn't have an age limit on when you could take the test, unlike in Florida, where you had to be either seventeen or eighteen. So I landed back in Winter Park with a high school equivalency diploma at the age of fifteen.

Without the need to attend high school, I was free to do the only other two things I could: work and party. Or I should say, work so that I could party. Thus began a pattern of my charming my way into menial jobs, like flipping burgers at McDonald's or Burger King, and working just long enough to get my first paycheck. As soon as I got the check I would quit, simply by not showing up again. Money in hand, I would use the cash to fund my drinking and carousing around town, a pattern that would continue unabated for years.

A few months after I came home from Seattle, I was picked up for shoplifting home accessories. My successful one-and-a-half-year run of jacking thousands of dollars' worth of clothing, makeup, and cassette tapes from the mall (I even lifted a strobe light once) was over. Following my arrest, I was placed into a holding cell at the local juvenile detention center. The tiny, modern room was claustrophobically small. Still, I remember the room being so quiet that it left you with nothing to do but stare at the walls and ponder your life. I wondered if I had what it took to spend the next year of my life locked up inside.

Mom was the one who received the call that I had been arrested. In a panic, she phoned around to the couple of bars she knew Dad frequented to let him know what had happened. She was finally able to get him on the phone long enough to tell him that he needed to go to the hearing in order for me to be released. Happy hour was Dad's sacred space, and he wasn't pleased to be interrupted by a frantic wife. After a few minutes of listening to her plead for him to bail me out, he hung up on her.

The next morning, Dad went to work and Mom, faced with the possibility of my having to wait in a juvenile facility until my trial, took matters into her own hands to get me out. Because she was not my custodial parent (she had never legally adopted me and my siblings), technically she had no right to seek my release. However, the judge didn't ask for proof of her parental rights, and released me into her custody.

Eventually I had my day in court and the judge ordered me to write a letter of apology to the store, banned me for life from entering it, had me pay restitution equal to the cost of the goods I had pilfered to the American Cancer Society, and made me attend one of those "Scared Straight" sessions where young delinquents tour an adult correctional facility while being intimidated with hard-knock stories by career criminals. While the other parts of my sentence were more of an annoyance than anything, the prison visit worked. I never shoplifted again.

By this point my parents had reached their limits. My constant lying, drinking, and coming and going as I pleased had created a tremendous amount of tension in our home.

The year before, in the ultimate test of their authority, I had begun running away from home. The first time that it happened, Mom tracked me down at a friend's house, and I was forced to return. In an attempt to drive home the message that they wouldn't tolerate my latest violation of their household rules, I was placed on restriction for twenty-six days. One day for every hour I was gone, with the warning that if I ran away again, I wouldn't be allowed back.

I was furious with their punishment, and chafed at the lack of logic. So six days later I ran away from home again. And then I did it again, and again, and again. There was absolutely nothing they could do to stop me. Threats of physical violence no longer worked. The last time Dad hit me, I told him that if he did it again I would call the police.

Their response to my repeated running away was to call the police and report me missing. This unfortunately led to low-priority searches of my adult friends' crash pads, where I would be picked up, then returned home in a police cruiser. My parents even tried to block my sneaking out of the house by drilling the window screens into place. I just bent them out of the window frame and slipped into the night and the waiting car of one of my friends.

❧

Nobody could understand why I was so angry at my parents. Perhaps I was, as Julie said, just too damaged from my early years with Daisy to appreciate the good things about my life. Taking things like food, shelter, and clothing for granted, as an entitlement, when in fact so many people don't even have the bare necessities.

Later, my brother would jokingly tease me when we were adults, saying I was "a rebel without a cause." And for someone more compliant (like Dan), or less observant, it could appear that there really wasn't just cause for my cantankerous personality.

But if people outside our family could have experienced our daily life, I think they would have seen things differently. It was a home where you received your basic necessities, but they were doled out in a prisonlike environment. As someone who hadn't signed up for incarceration, my teen-brain response was to stage what amounted to an ongoing prison riot.

For instance, to save money, Mom timed our showers. If you were in there longer than ten minutes you would be interrupted by a banging on the bathroom door that wouldn't stop until you turned off the water. (I learned to shampoo my hair first to make sure that I wouldn't be caught with a head full of soap when the banging started.) Every meal was portioned and rationed with precision. And there were no deviations from Mom's daily schedule. There was absolutely no eating in between meals outside those that she distributed like clockwork. It didn't matter if you were hungry. "Drink water. That will fill your stomach up" was her bland reply.

At a certain point, when I began stealing food from the kitchen at night to quell my hunger pangs, Dad brought home a used refrigerator that he retrieved from one of his worksites. He installed a lock on the door, and filled it with all the food from the main refrigerator that could be made into a meal. This was when I began going over to certain "friends'" homes simply to eat. Whether or not we had anything in common took a backseat to my need to fill my stomach.

Items like shampoo were a controlled substance. Mom began

to lock it up in her bathroom. When it was time for us to bathe, we had to go to her with a shallow Tupperware cup in hand into which she would squeeze a small portion. Bathing had to be timed accordingly, for if Mom wasn't home when I needed to wash my hair, it didn't happen.

Since Dad ran a home-based business out of our home, the phone line was used for business purposes only. He could have paid a little extra to add on the call waiting feature, but was unwilling to spend a few extra dollars a month. As a result, we could only make phone calls after work hours and on weekends. Otherwise, the rule was you had ten minutes per day that you could spend using the phone. It didn't matter if the call was outgoing or incoming. As soon as I dialed a number, Mom would set the timer on the microwave. When the call ended, she would announce how many minutes I had left for the day.

"You have three minutes of phone privileges left today, Sil Lai."

Heaven forbid if someone called for me that I didn't want to speak to . . . those minutes, ever so brief, still counted against my daily allowance. And if I got a call from someone I had been trying to reach all day, and I had run out of minutes? No chance of talking.

While Dad spent his days and many of his nights earning a living (or doing God knows what else and with whom), Mom had essentially been abandoned by him to run his home and raise his children. I only saw her challenge my dad once, when she chided him for yelling at Grandpa for grabbing the doorframes as he moved from room to room.

Grandpa used the frames as a way to balance himself as he turned a corner, but Dad didn't care. The only thing that mattered was Grandpa's dirty handprints marring the glossy white paint on the frames. The family was gathered in the kitchen for dinner one night when Mom said, "George! That's your father . . . it isn't a big deal." Dad responded, "Oh yeah? Well, FUCK YOU!" and then jumped on his motorcycle and peeled out of the driveway. Mom never contradicted anything he said again.

It was hard to watch him tear her down. She would later tell me that he had permanently stripped away her checking privileges when she bounced *one* check. At the time, I didn't know how far his controlling behavior went with our mom, but we all bore the consequences. It's like that cartoon where the husband gets yelled at by his boss, so he goes home and yells at his wife, who turns around and yells at the kids, who turn around and yell at the dog.

As a teenager, I didn't attribute Mom's actions to anything more than her being a watered-down version of Dad. Now I understand that her controlling behaviors were a way for her to feel less powerless. To some extent, I don't blame her anymore. After all, she most likely had Dad yelling at her over the cost of running the household. It must have been an incredibly painful and isolating time for her as well. Yet, she never showed it.

Mom just carried the burden of her emotionally abusive husband in silence. One way she tried to cope with the unmanageability of her life was rigidly watching every morsel of food she ate. At five-eight, she weighed 110 pounds, which was the perfect size for Dad. When we spoke about this time in her life later, she told me that she was so thin because of stress. It is said that people who hold their feelings in tend to have higher rates of cancer. Well, at thirty-two years old, Mom was diagnosed with stage four breast cancer. She would eventually beat the disease, but she paid a price as well for living in our loveless home. We all did.

In a last-ditch effort at trying to straighten me out, my parents began bringing me to see a counselor. Once a week, I would go to his office and sit in stony silence as he asked me questions about my background and probed into my simmering rage; however, I didn't trust him and refused to engage in any discussion about my problems in depth. Plus, I was utterly convinced that the entire family, not just me, needed to be in therapy. I intuitively knew that we were all sick; I was just the one who manifested the worst symptoms, which allowed my parents to focus their attention on what was wrong with me, instead of what was wrong with *us*. In psychology, this is called scapegoating: one member of the family is blamed for the majority of a family's problems. A friend's mother was a therapist and told me about this phenomenon at the time, so I knew that as troubled as I was, I wasn't the only one that needed help.

Nevertheless, for several months I attended these sessions alone. But two things happened that ended up terminating my brief foray into self-improvement.

The first was when my dad made the mistake of finally coming to a family session. He didn't want to go, but Mom convinced Dad that it would be useful for the therapist to observe our family dynamics firsthand. I was furious that Dad was invading what was supposed to be my "safe space" (even if I didn't treat it as such). I knew, even though the therapist didn't, that Dad was a liar and a hypocrite. My parents punished me for drinking and smoking pot, but I knew Dad did both. The drinking wasn't a secret in our household, but his weed habit was, until I found a joint he had hidden while snooping through his large Craftsman toolbox in the garage. I stared at the forbidden cigarette and pondered what to do: Leave it where I found it, or take it for my own consumption? After a few moments, I took the joint and hid it in my bra to smoke at another time. I figured it was unlikely that Dad would confront me on stealing his weed, for that would mean he would have to admit that he in fact "did drugs," as Mom would say. Which was something I knew he would never do. I thought my calculated risk-taking was brilliant and couldn't keep it to myself. So, I taunted my mom, saying, "I know something you don't know," knowing that she wouldn't ask me what I knew because it would force her to out her husband for his recreational pot smoking.

As Dad sat on the therapist's couch next to Mom, I glared at them both. The therapist began to ask Dad questions about his views on me and his own life and I sat quietly, waiting for an opportunity to pounce. "Do you drink or use drugs, Mr. Baber?" I could see Dad's momentary discomfort and was satisfied seeing him squirm. Was he going to tell the truth or lie? My bet was on him lying.

"Well, I drink beer. But not all the time" was his reply. I could feel Dad's irritation. He was not a man accustomed to answering to anyone.

I was sitting across from them in a chair, watching Mom's face to see what she would say. But her eyes were nowhere to be found, as her head was turned downward, staring at her fingers that she was nervously rubbing together. She wasn't going to speak the truth either; that I knew. There was no way she would go up against Dad on this one, even if it meant compromising my mental health.

As the therapist began to move on to another question, I projected my body halfway out of my seat. "You're such a liar!" I shouted at my dad. "He's a LIAR!" I screamed at the therapist, who was visibly taken aback by my outburst. "He smokes pot! I know it because I found it in the garage!" Dad just sat there with a blank expression while Mom was silent.

The therapist came out of his stunned silence to try and

smooth things over, saying, "Okay, Sil Lai. I hear you. Mr. Baber, is what she's saying true?"

By this point I had already tuned out, triumphant. For the first time in my life I had called out my oppressor in front of someone else. Someone other than my friends knew my dad was a liar. And that pleased me.

The final nail in the coffin of my "therapeutic intervention" came when I went out to the car to wait for my mom to drive me to another appointment. By now I had surrendered to the idea that I would have to attend these sessions, regardless of whether I thought they were beneficial. For some reason, I leaned my head down to look underneath the driver's seat and spied a spiral note-book. *That's odd*, I thought to myself, and being naturally curious (and completely uninterested in concepts such as "privacy"), I grabbed it and skimmed through the pages. Reading the words, I felt like I'd been sucker-punched. I couldn't breathe. Page after page was filled with notes Mom had taken on my behavior. Every time I acted out, every time I cursed or ran away, every time I de-fied her over the past year was written down, noted by date. And tucked in the back of the notebook was a letter on official statio-nery from my therapist.

> *"It is my recommendation that if the minor child, Sil Lai Baber, does not comply with therapy she be removed from the home. Her behavior is not only a threat to herself, but is an unhealthy influ-ence on her siblings . . ."*

It was then that I realized my suspicions about these therapy ses-sions were justified. This was proof they were willing to get rid of me rather than change our way of relating. Indelibly confirmed in blue ink on lined spiral-bound notebook pages.

When Mom got in the car, she turned her head and said, "Okay, I'm ready. Let's go before we're late."

I exploded.

"What the fuck is this?" I shouted, waving the notebook in my hands. "I knew it! This therapy thing is bullshit! I'm not fucking going to therapy today. I'm not going period. You're such a sneaky cunt!"

Mom grasped at the notebook, and I pulled it out of her reach. Disgusted, I threw it onto the dashboard console and bolted from the car. "Fuck you!" I yelled, and took off down the street. I don't know where I ended up that night, or when I eventually came home. But there was no more talk about therapy from either of my parents ever again.

The confirmation that my parents were seeking to have me removed from their home was as emotionally crippling as it was freeing. No more would I feel any sort of allegiance or affinity with them. When they asked me to do anything, the answer was an automatic no. Every interaction between us became a taunt on my side to *force* them to evict me.

For a few weeks, I waited for a state social worker to come and place me with a foster family. But the State of Florida Division of Child Protective Services never appeared. I would come to learn that while my behavior was outrageous, contemptible, and an all-around pain in the ass to my parents, it wasn't a priority for the state. A child whose offenses consisted of foul language, truancy, defiant behavior, underage drinking, and smoking pot didn't merit a taxpayer-funded intervention. To Mom and Dad's dismay.

My Florida driver's license, 1988.

CHAPTER EIGHT

❧

*F*OR THE REST OF MY FIFTEENTH AND SIXTEENTH YEARS I RE-
mained locked in a predictable, dysfunctional battle for power
with my parents. I kept partying with my friends at night and
spent my days wandering around the local malls, generally
while intoxicated. Those large air-conditioned spaces, combined
with public restrooms and food courts were perfect places for
us to kill time during the days until the night arrived, when we
could throw ourselves into our evening bacchanal. Although
by this time my skin had taken on a sallow, yellow tone due to
the copious amounts of sunscreen I was using and my tendency
to wear black clothing that covered me from head to toe, I still
feared that my secret racial identity would get out. Most of my
friends were overtly racist, so I would go out of my way from
time to time to show my solidarity with them by engaging in
cruel, racist behavior of my own.

One example of this to this day fills me with shame. My
friends and I were hanging out at the Altamonte Mall on a ramp
that connected the top level of the mall to the bottom one. Sitting
on the ledge midway between the two levels, I spied one of the
black boys from school, Darrell Starks, sauntering our way. Darrell was a tall, gangly member of our high school basketball team,
a congenial goof-off whose face always had a ready smile. He was

socially ensconced in the small group of twenty or so black kids out of 2,000 that attended Lake Howell High.

As our group of punks passed the black students in the hallways, or as we sat in our respective silos in the school cafeteria, we typically ignored each other. In retrospect, I realize that our general refusal to engage in overt acts of racism toward the black students at school was at least in part motivated by fear, as it was among most white students. The black girls at our school were legendary in their ability to lay on an ass-whipping, and no one, even the most outrageous white high school bully, was willing to take them on.

But another reason for our truce was our recognition that, while we were different, we were both alienated from mainstream society. Of course, it goes without saying that there is a huge difference between ostracization due to a choice in how you dressed and wore your hair, and being deemed socially unacceptable because of something that is not a choice—race. We were both outsiders, and would never be accepted by the society in which we lived. In a similar fashion to how Jews and blacks learned to live side by side in urban ghettos, we found a way to coexist out of a fundamental recognition of our "otherness." This didn't mean that we necessarily respected one another. But it did mean that we left each other alone.

Yet on this particular day, for some reason Darrell attempted to cross the invisible color and cultural line by engaging me in a public conversation. As he approached, our eyes connected and I knew he was coming our way to speak to me. Turning around so that my back faced his incoming direction, I continued to chat with my small group of friends.

"Hey!" he called out, jumping up and swatting me on my bare arm. Ignoring him, I heard him say my name, "Sil Lai!"

I was mortified. Spinning around, I gave him a glare.

"What!"

An ever-so-slight frown crossed his face. But he wasn't going to be deterred.

"What's going on?" he asked.

My friends were watching this scene with amusement. But I wasn't amused at all. Why was this black boy speaking to me? I had never given him any indication of a desire to communicate, and was completely bewildered as to why he was approaching me *here* of all places. The mall was *our* domain. I was a mall rat, and our presence was so constant and quizzical to the "normal" mall patrons that a local reporter from the *Orlando Sentinel* wrote a story on our subculture.

"What do you mean, 'What's going on?' That's none of your business," I snapped.

"Yo, chill. I was just trying to talk to you," he said, voice still confident. But I could see the confusion on his face. He had done nothing more than try to speak to me, and I was treating him with as much contempt as I showed my parents.

"Well, I'm not trying to talk to you, okay?" I retorted, turning my back on him.

I heard him chuckle and say, "A'ight. Later."

Out of the corner of my eye I watched him amble off into the mass of concrete and neon signs. Still, his departure wasn't enough. I didn't want my friends to think that I was a "nigger lover," and I had to make a point to show them this.

"Gawwwwwd!" I exclaimed. "I can't believe that nigger would talk to me. And he fucking touched me, too!" No one in the group had said anything to me about the interesting inter-action they had just observed, but I wanted to make sure that I made as big a distinction between me and *them* as possible.

"I gotta go to the bathroom and wash my arm. I can't believe he fucking touched me." Jumping up, I called out, "I'll be right back." I rushed to the bathroom with my friend Lisa, who needed to use the toilet. As she relieved herself in the stall, I made it a point to make a huge display of my displeasure and disgust at Darrell's behavior by washing my forearm with soap and water twice. Lisa exited the stall as I was drying my arm off with a paper towel. I waited for her while she washed her hands, still indignant at Darrell's offense.

We walked back over to our group and one of them said, "You ready to go?"

"Yeah, let's get out of here," I said. "Don't wanna run into Darrell again. Who the hell does he think he is?" My performance was over the top, and probably unnecessary as none of my friends had said anything about our exchange. As the Shakespearean quote goes, "The lady doth protest too much . . ." But I had to do everything in my power in that moment to disassociate myself from Darrell's blackness. I had finally found a milieu to call my own. A family where I belonged and was accepted with all of my contradictions and brokenness. And I wasn't going to let anyone cause me to be ousted or exiled.

❧

During this time my sister May Lai also began to act out. First by getting thrown out of middle school for truancy, then running away to spend time with the boys noticing her emerging beauty as she embarked upon her teen years.

Both of us were extremely sexually active with the constant parade of boys and, eventually, young men who were all too willing to take advantage of girls with self-esteem issues. My parents tried to stop me from acting out on my sexual impulses by shaming me and placing harsh restrictions on my freedom, but their actions were futile. Nothing could stop me from seeking a temporary respite from the overwhelming feeling that I was utterly alone and disconnected from the world. So I attempted to fill my aching sense of alienation in the only way I knew how: sex. For during that hour or so of an encounter, I discovered that I could momentarily feel connected to another human being, even if the basis of the connection was fleeting. Every tryst was a fix, a high, a momentary escape from the heartbreaking isolation that I felt at home and in school. It didn't matter that the boys didn't really care about me. Thirty minutes of passion gave me the feeling of being wanted, of being accepted, of being okay. It would be years before I learned that I had anything else to offer other than my body.

These boys were of course all white, and overwhelmingly blond. There was a special feeling that came with conquering (or being conquered by) a boy whose appearance epitomized the Aryan ideal. That simply by his willingness to touch me, I was being given the white man's stamp of approval. That in spite of being black (which of course I never divulged), I was sexually appealing. Of course, I had no idea that there have always been people who engage in the "taboo" sexual activity of sleeping with members of other races. It never occurred to me that while I was attempting to elevate my self-esteem, I was likely satisfying an urge for these boys seeking a taste of the "exotic." I clearly wasn't white. It must have been quite the thrill for them to engage in a behavior that was completely socially unacceptable in Central Florida.

Despite the fact that I would freely give my body away, that didn't stop one boy from forcing himself on me while I was passed out drunk. I woke up one night in a hotel room near Daytona Beach with him inside me. Digging my nails into his waist, I scratched at him until he finally climbed off. I freaked out and grabbed a knife in the kitchen, waking up our drunken hotel mates with my yelling. Eventually I calmed down, yet I was also asked to leave, not the boy who assaulted me. No one in the room believed me when I said that this boy had forced himself on me. He was too good looking and popular. It was a long time before I could actually say to another human being what had happened.

I was raped.

Like many victims of sexual violence, I blamed myself for getting drunk, and not waking up earlier. Writing these words now, I know what this phenomenon is called: rape culture. The acceptance on a social level of the idea that a woman's body can be violated in the most intimate way, and that it is usually "her fault."

Were these the types of experiences my parents were trying to protect me from? It didn't feel that way. If they were, it was never articulated to me that the world can be a very dangerous place, filled with all sorts of acts of violence that a naïve young girl could never imagine.

Between nocturnal escapes, I was banished to sleeping on the couch. As punishment for my continued disobedience, my parents had rented my bedroom out to one of my dad's friends. All of my belongings were placed in the front hall closet and I lived like a transient. If they wanted to make a buck off my space, so be it. I knew they were trying to send me a message, but I was nonplussed since I was never around anyway. According to my mom, during my sixteenth year I had spent more than 250 days away from home. To me, it didn't matter that I was now exiled within our house. I was too busy exercising my independence with as much impunity as possible. Whatever I wanted to do I would, with or without my parents' consent or cooperation.

At seventeen I decided to apply for my driver's license. I asked
Grandpa if he would take me, and pay the fees, which he did. As
he waited for me in the lobby, I went to fill out the forms, pausing
at the section where it asked for my race. Face burning hotly, I
looked around the room to see if anyone was watching, and then
quickly checked the "white" box. As I walked up to the counter
to apply for the permit, I felt queasy. Sliding my paperwork to
the clerk, I watched as she eyed the documents and entered the
information into the database. I held my breath as she typed,
waiting for her to call me out on my obvious lie about my race.
But she said nothing and handed back my paperwork without
any questions. Now, it was official, at least in the eyes of the Florida Department of Motor Vehicles. I was white, as indicated on
my driver's permit. Anyone looking at the photo on my license
and the listed race could see that there was an obvious distortion
of truth. But for whatever reason, the clerk didn't question the
veracity of my self-designation. I wondered as I left the building
that day, if Darrell Starks had applied for his license and marked
white, would the clerk have let it slide? I knew the answer: unequivocally no.

It was around this time that I began to disassemble my carefully cultivated punk rock persona and transition into one that
would give me more access to a wider range of young men: the
vixen. I eschewed my former shaved hairstyle and grew it out
into a curly bob. My weight had begun to fluctuate due to my
long nights of drinking and binge eating, so I started working out
on a daily basis to get myself back down from 140 pounds to my
pre-drinking weight of 125. My weight loss was also augmented
by massive amounts of laxatives and diuretics, which I began taking after making a connection between the speed with which food
exited my system and weight loss. The faster it went through me,
the fewer calories would be absorbed by my body. I cut my food

down to a meager 1,000 calories a day, carefully tallying my diet in a notebook. But I was still struggling to keep my weight down due to my nightly drinking. I was consuming over 2,500 calories a day when I included the alcohol, so my size kept yo-yo'ing.

One day I happened to tune into *The Oprah Winfrey Show* and my approach toward eating was totally changed—for the worse. On the episode a young white woman was discussing her struggle with bulimia, an eating disorder in which a person gorges on huge amounts of food, and then purges through induced vomiting and/or the use of laxatives and diuretics.

It was clearly apparent that this woman was in excruciating emotional pain over her disorder. She wept and cringed while describing her suffering and the hold that bulimia had over her life. But I skipped over her anguish and focused only on the benefits one could derive from purging food by vomiting. The *intent* of the episode was to shine a light on bulimia as a serious emotional disorder with far-reaching physical consequences. But all I heard was a solution to my never-ending battle with the bulge. A path that would enable me to stop starving myself, eat as much food as I wanted without having any of the consequential weight gain that was a lot more effective than just using laxatives.

Later that day I gorged on ice cream, grilled cheese sandwiches, potato chips, and Coca-Cola until my stomach was distended like a hunger victim's. Heading to the bathroom, I closed the door and pushed the lock in place. Turning on the faucet so that the running water would cover any sounds, I stuck my finger down my throat and threw up the 4,000 calories I had eaten in one sitting. I shoved my finger down my throat repeatedly until my stomach was empty and I felt the hollowness inside.

Getting up off my knees, I washed my hands and rinsed away any flecks of food left around my mouth. Gazing into the mirror I felt a wave of relief, even triumph. For I had found a way to have it both ways: eat everything I wanted and not gain a pound. Oprah's show was intended to spread awareness and educate her audience on the horrors of bulimia. But I had unwittingly been given information that provided me instead with a self-destructive method of manifesting my emotional instability and self-loathing under the guise of as "weight maintenance." A sickness that I would end up battling throughout the next ten years of my life. (It abated only when I aged out of the behavior.)

Despite having been told that I was pretty by adults as a child, I'd never believed any of them. Now, with my new appearance, I wanted to test their statement. And maybe if what they were saying was true, I could find a way to earn money that didn't entail flipping burgers or ringing cash registers.

On a whim, I walked into the leading Orlando modeling agency at the time, the Cassandra Agency. Its owner, Cassandra Carrigan, was a former model in her late forties from the Orlando area who had worked in New York City in her heyday.

During our initial meeting, I couldn't stop staring at her. Not only was she stunningly beautiful and impeccably dressed; she exuded the confidence, power, and grace of women who up until that point I had only seen on television shows like *Dynasty*. A woman who stood in the fullness of her being and was unapologetically independent and proud. A businesswoman. A BOSS. She was nothing like any of the women I was raised around. There is a word used to describe her quality, one I wouldn't learn the importance of until many decades later: empowered. Despite not knowing the existence of this word and all that it entailed, I was mesmerized and hoped someday to be like her.

After taking a look at some of my snapshots, she signed me on the spot, and asked me to meet with one of her clients. After they took a Polaroid, I headed home.

I drove down Aloma Avenue, the main artery back to my neighborhood, as if in a trance. I, Sil Lai Baber, was now officially a model. Someone like Cassandra Carrigan thought I was pretty enough to make money off my appearance. It was a transcendent moment. For years I had been psychologically tortured by those who frequently said I was "just a nigger." And like black women everywhere, I had internalized the constant barrage of media messaging that told me I was unattractive because I wasn't white. Yet somehow, I was now doing something that none of the popular, pretty *white* girls in my school could. I was going to be paid for the same appearance many of them despised.

About an hour after I returned home, I received a call from Cassandra.

"Great news, Sil Lai. They booked you for the commercial. It's a three-day shoot at a rate of $150 a day. You need to show up tomorrow morning at 6:00 a.m. at the following address . . ." I jotted down the information and hung up the phone. Jumping up and down in place, I yelped with laughter. I was going to make more money in three days than I would working full-time at a fast-food restaurant for three weeks.

The next day I showed up at the shoot, which took place in some swampy location in Ocala, a city located about an hour away. The day was a whirlwind of activity and attention. We zoomed in speedboats on the murky, algae-covered water, following the commercial's script that directed us to "find" treasure in the swamp—in this case, our Italian client's ice cream product.

After a long day, we wrapped our first shoot and returned to a local shacklike restaurant in the middle of nowhere. The cast of models and crew all indulged in a hearty banquet of food that included alligator tail, which I found to be delicately flavored and, as the cliché goes, tasted like chicken. The alcohol was being freely served, and I jumped in and drank more than my share. The three other models selected were also my age, but I could tell that they were straight-laced. Not wild like me. The others had at most one drink, but I proceeded to get hammered. By the time I left the restaurant, I was so drunk I could barely stand, but that didn't stop me from driving home. Miraculously, I made it back in one piece and collapsed into my bed, blacking out as I did most nights of the week.

The next morning, I groggily opened my eyes and looked over at my clock. The gently glowing digital numbers said 10:26 a.m. I popped up in my bed like a piece of bread in a toaster.

Damn! Damn! Damn!

I had somehow slept through my alarm, missing the 6:00 a.m. call time. I ran to the phone and called the agency to tell them what happened. Cassandra got on the phone and was curt. "There is no need for you to go today, Sil Lai. As a matter of fact, you won't be finishing the shoot. They've moved on without you."

Hanging up, I felt a wave of shame. Partying had cost me a lot over the years, but none of the consequences had ever really mattered to me before. This was something different. I knew I had royally screwed up and would have to make it up to Cassandra. Not only had I behaved unprofessionally, but I was now out $300.

Cassandra never mentioned the incident to me again and still sent me out to castings, which I began to regularly book. Apparently she wasn't going to question the hard-partying antics of a seventeen-year-old underage drinker. Whenever a client asked about my ethnic background, I always responded with: "Hawaiian." In a few months' time, I had gone from a random blackout-drinking party girl to an up-and-coming model who appeared on the cover of *Orlando* magazine and the *Orlando Sentinel* Style section.

Modeling ended up saving my life. It would be my path out of a place where I would never belong, to a space where I could safely begin to embrace my true racial identity—to live honestly and most importantly—free from shame of the color of my skin.

Before my eventual escape, our family would end up losing the glue that held us together—Mom.

❋

It was an uneventful morning that followed my nightly blackouts. The renter had left our home and I was once again sleeping in my bedroom. I came out of my room to find a flurry of activity happening in the house. Mom was rushing around, grabbing photos from the wall, helped by Sherri, one of her few friends. She was married to Dad's friend Patrick and used to attend our occasional barbecues.

Sherri was helping her lift the television out of the living room, grunting as they carried it toward the front door to Mom's van, then rushing back to continue pilfering random items.

I couldn't believe what I was seeing.

"What are you doing?" I asked, already knowing the answer.

"I'm leaving your father, Sil Lai. I've wanted to go for years, but I didn't want to leave you kids alone. But you're all old enough now that I can do this. I can't stay married to him anymore."

After years of arguing and battling her, I thought I would feel happy, relieved that she was leaving. Instead I was overwhelmed with a cluster of conflicting feelings.

"But why? Why now?"

"Sil Lai, I'm not going to get into it except to say that your father has done things that I cannot forgive. If you want to know what those things are, you can ask him. But I want you to know something." She paused and stepped closer to where I was standing.

"No matter what he tells you, I am not leaving him because of you. Don't let him put this on you. I'm leaving because of *him*."

I wondered what had been her breaking point. After thirteen years together, what made her leave? Decades later, she told me that a young man had shown up one night at our house swinging a baseball bat and threatening to "beat Dad's ass." Allegedly, Dad had been "messing around" with this man's sister, a teenager who lived in a neighboring housing development. Somehow Dad managed to talk the man down and avoid ending up in the hospital. But it would take Mom at least another year to leave him.

It was then that a horrible realization clicked in my mind. Dad married Daisy when she was eighteen years old, but had begun a relationship with her when she was sixteen and he was twenty-three. His next wife was a young woman who he began pursuing when she was just shy of her eighteenth birthday. He was then thirty-one years old. I remembered the accusation from the teenage boy's mother in California. And now here was the story of a teenage girl that Dad had allegedly engaged in some sort of sexual relationship when he was in his early forties. When I learned this latest story about the man with the bat, it seemed to confirm what I had always suspected about my dad: that he was more than a bully. He was someone who had a lifelong pattern of exploitative behavior with women, both consciously known and speculated.

But for now, I only knew that Dad had done something unspeakable and Mom was finally heading out the door. About a half hour later she was gone, fleeing with my stepsister Julia, making one brief stop at the elementary school around the corner to say goodbye to my brother Daniel. In the span of less than two hours, a mother had disappeared. Again.

I sat down on the couch in a daze. I thought I hated her, that there was nothing left between us. Things had gotten so bad that at one point we had a physical scuffle in the kitchen. Although she was my sworn enemy, I also felt pity for her. She'd lived under Dad's oppressive regime like the rest of us, but unlike us, I felt she had a choice. In fact, I had grown to loathe what I felt was her cowardice for allowing herself to be subjugated by a husband who controlled her every move. During one of our many epic arguments, I hissed at her, "You make me sick. When I grow up you're the last kind of woman I ever want to be. I'm never going to live your kind of pathetic life with an asshole for a husband!"

For years I'd dreamt of this moment. Yet Mom's leaving brought no sense of satisfaction. It kicked up a constellation of emotions around being abandoned again that I hadn't expected. Like Daisy had done years earlier, Mom chose to flee Dad, leaving May Lai, Daniel, and me behind. I went to my bedroom and cried.

A few hours later Dad came in the door around midday for lunch. As he entered the living room, he yelled out, "Sil Lai, where's the television?"

"It's gone. Mom took it. She's gone, Dad. She's left you."

Dad froze. Standing across the room from him, I watched the stunned expression take root on his face. Turning on his heel, he rushed out the door, jumped into his truck, and peeled out of the driveway.

She really did it, I thought to myself. In spite of our turbulent relationship, I was proud of her. Dad never showed Mom any kindness or appreciation for the sacrifices she made to take care of his kids. For thirteen years she toiled, receiving in exchange his indifference, infidelity, and insolence.

Sitting alone in the house, filled with emotion, I couldn't stay put. I had to tell someone what had happened. I had to get to May

Lai, who was by this time enrolled at my old high school. After stealing a neighbor's bike and riding it the three miles to school, I pestered Mr. Gaines, the vice principal who had expelled me, to allow me to break the news to my sister. He agreed under one condition: he would have to stay in the room with us. Given my prior behavior I didn't blame him for doubting my reasons for interrupting my sister's school day.

"May Lai, Mom is gone," I told her in Mr. Gaines's office. "She asked me to tell you that she said goodbye and would try to reach you soon. She would've come to tell you herself, but she was too afraid that Dad might catch her here."

My sister's slight shoulders heaved rapidly up and down, and she began sobbing into her palms. I felt helpless and was horrified for coming to the school to tell her this. But my heart was breaking and I needed to know that I wasn't alone. And I wanted May Lai to know that she wasn't, either.

As we had so many times before in the face of tremendous emotional upheaval, May Lai and I sat in silence. She sobbed for a few minutes, and then stopped.

"Are you okay?" I asked, knowing that no matter what she said, she was not okay.

"I'm fine. I'm going back to class," she announced, standing up.

I too stood, and then reached over, pulling her close to me and squeezing her tightly with my arms. Turning my head into the hair covering her ears, I whispered, "Everything is going to be okay. I promise."

She nodded her head up and down and pulled away, embarrassed by my unexpected display of affection.

Mr. Gaines cleared his throat and said, "Okay, ladies. I'm going to have to ask you to wrap this up now."

"I love you, May Lai. I'll see you later, okay?"

Nodding, she walked out of the office and headed back to

class. I thanked Mr. Gaines for accommodating my request and then dialed up my friend Lisa, who had already graduated and had a car.

"Hey, Leese. It's me, Sil Lai. It's a long story, but can you pick me up at Lake Howell?"

After a half hour or so Lisa pulled up into the circular driveway that ran in front of the school. I slid into her car and hurriedly told her about my mom's departure earlier that morning.

"Wow. That's crazy" was all that she said. Mainly, she listened as I spoke in a rapid-fire, stream-of-consciousness style, barely pausing for breath.

The only thing I had on my mind was to find a way to escape my feelings. I desperately wanted to get drunk, and it was a little on the early side, even for me. Still, now that Mom was gone there was no one that could stop me from drinking, so I asked Grandpa for some money, and Lisa and I made a quick run to the 7-11 for some Bartles & Jaymes wine coolers that I purchased with a fake ID I had borrowed from a friend I'd made at one of the local nightclubs I had begun frequenting.

We hung around my living room for a while until she had to head back home and get ready for her shift at a Little Caesars pizzeria. By this time Dan had come home from school. His tall, lanky body looked small in the door frame to the family room, where I was now drunkenly lounging on the couch.

"You okay?" I asked. He stared blankly at me as I continued, "Mom said that she was going by the school today to tell you goodbye. Did you see her?" He nodded his head and paused for a moment as if he were going to say something, then stopped. My brother was always the quiet one of the group. He was so reserved, so introverted, that at one point I remember Aunt Doni asking if he should be tested for Asperger's syndrome.

Dan hesitated and then rushed off to the bedroom he shared with Grandpa. May Lai didn't come home that day from school, or the next day either. Eventually she showed up, but it was only to grab clothes and head back out to stay over with a new friend she had made who lived in an apartment complex near our home. This "friend" was in his early twenties and May Lai was only fifteen.

Dad continued his workaholic pattern, and we saw him at the usual times. Early in the morning, when he left for work at around 7:30. In the early part of the afternoon, when he stopped by the house in the middle of his workday, ostensibly to check in on us. And then around dinnertime, when he came home to eat a meal I had prepared, before heading back out for the night at around 7:00.

Mom, as much as I hated to admit it, had been the hub that kept our dysfunctional brood somewhat together. Now that she was gone, there was a yawning gap in the center of our home that I, at seventeen, tried to fill. I was working part-time at a deli in the nearby shopping center, but had most of my time free. Modeling in Orlando, especially for a girl of color, meant sporadic work. So outside of partying at night with my friends, I was home. So for the next few months, I did my best to take over Mom's former duties.

I'd make May Lai and Dan's brown-paper-bag lunches for them to take to school, lining them up next to the refrigerator just like Mom had done. Granted, May Lai wasn't attending school much by this point, as the majority of her time was spent partying at her new boyfriend's apartment. I, unlike my dad, was appalled by her increasing disappearances, and thus began my search-and-rescue missions for her that took place every three weeks like clockwork.

It usually went like this: May Lai and Dad would have an argument. May Lai would take off and disappear for days. I would call around to her friends until I located her, and then drive over in Grandpa's car and plead with her to come back home. I'd convince her that Dad was sorry and would back off, and that I would run interference between them. The only condition was she needed to attend school. Warily, she'd agree to my terms and come home, only to end up fighting with Dad again about her constant partying and truancy. After a few days of this she'd disappear again and I'd be back on the streets searching for her.

Dad was completely disconnected from what was happening with his kids, which wasn't unusual. But I could tell that Mom's absence had an impact on him, though not in the way that you'd think after losing his partner of thirteen years. It was his ego that had taken the biggest hit. Mom had humiliated him by leaving and taking his daughter Julia. She'd escaped from his control, showing that—on top of the rebellious behavior of his daughters—he no longer held the power he'd been wielding for years over anybody.

Without her steady presence, our home became just a house filled with strangers who came and went about their lives while living under the same roof. We lived with each other but didn't *see* each other, at least not in the emotional sense. We were all too walled off in our own suffering to help each other shoulder the pain of abandonment.

But soon I would have a way out. About two months after Mom left, I got a three-day modeling gig with a New York photographer named Nancy Brown, who had come to Orlando to lead a weekend workshop for aspiring photographers. The models selected for the job weren't paid, but we did receive free photographs to use in our portfolios, and a chance to work with one of the leading commercial photographers in the States at the time. My elegant agency boss Cassandra and Nancy were cronies from their days at the Wilhelmina agency in New York. After their respective careers came to an end, Nancy stayed in New York and began building an extremely lucrative career shooting advertisements for major companies.

Out of all the models at the agency, I was one of the lucky three or four Nancy chose for the workshop. It was like winning the lottery. I didn't know what the payout was going to be, but I knew I would do everything in my power to use this opportunity to get out of Florida.

The shoot took place in Cypress Gardens, a lush, tropical tourist attraction near Disney World. I was on my best behavior. I didn't drink (much) the nights before the shoots and made sure to get to the location on time. Over the course of the shoot I made a new friend in Sharland, Nancy's assistant, a young woman from Connecticut who was just a few years older than me. We exchanged numbers and she told me that if I ever made it up to the "Big Apple" to call her.

On the third day, Nancy uttered a few sentences that completely changed my concept of what would be possible for my career in fashion. It was during the lunch break and we were standing near each other at the spread set out for the workshop.

"You know, Sil Lai, you're a very beautiful girl," she said. "You should come to New York. I think you can work there."

My heart started beating as if I had just run the fifty-yard dash. Gulping, I hoped she didn't feel the shift in my energy. I had come this far and didn't want to seem like what I was—a seventeen-year-old girl from Winter Park, Florida, who had just been given a shot to try out for the big leagues. Although my insides were twitching, I played it cool.

"Really, Nancy? You think so?"

She nodded her head affirmatively while simultaneously taking a bite of her sandwich.

"Wow, I would love to do that, but I don't know anyone. I wouldn't have anyplace to stay, or . . ."

Nancy cut me off.

"That's okay, kid. You can stay at my place for a few weeks until you get on your feet. I have an apartment in Gramercy Park, on Twenty-Second Street between Park Avenue and Broadway. I'm going out of town for a few weeks this summer and you can bunk there while I'm gone."

I couldn't believe what I was hearing. This woman had known me all of three days and was inviting me to stay at her apartment for free? In New York City? More importantly, she had validated my beauty as a successful New York City–based photographer. Someone thought that I had what it took to work in one of the leading fashion markets in the world.

"That's awesome. I mean, thank you! Thank you, Nancy. I can't believe it!"

Chuckling, she replied, "You just need to get yourself there and some spending money. But as far as a place to stay is concerned, I've got you covered."

I had gone to the shoot full of hope, and come back with something priceless: a vision. An escape hatch from a town whose boundaries, both culturally and professionally, had me in a stranglehold. At seventeen I was still too young to leave home, at least from a legal perspective. So I decided to wait it out a little while longer until I turned 18.

❧

A few months before my birthday, I encountered dazzling wealth up close for the first time. Exposure to it opened my mind to life's possibilities, and solidified my decision to flee from my family.

It was now the spring of 1988. I was invited by a New York City transplant to Winter Park named Chris to visit his father's home in Tuxedo Park, a hamlet about forty miles outside of Manhattan. Using money I had saved from my job at the deli, I bought a plane ticket and flew up to New York with Lars, one of my closest friends at the time. Lars was a closeted gay man who, along with several roommates, rented a home in downtown Winter Park. Chris had been crashing at Lars's home for the past few months, and had become a steady member of our party crew.

We flew up on a Friday to spend the weekend at his father's abode, or I should say estate, in this small village populated primarily by white, old-money bankers. Initially developed as a private hunting and fishing reserve by the tobacco heir Pierre Lorillard II in 1885, in time it became a town noted for its gentry. Emily Post wrote her classic book on etiquette from behind the walls that surround this two-thousand-acre enclave, and black-tie attire was created and first worn at the Tuxedo Park Country Club hidden behind its stony façade.

Chris picked Lars and me up at JFK airport in his dad's old Buick station wagon. I was unimpressed, especially since Chris had bragged that his father was a town big shot. Chris's parents were away that weekend, which is why we could even stay there. Had they known we were coming, his parents wouldn't have allowed any of Chris's friends past the front door, given their trust issues and his unbridled cocaine habit. At the age of twenty-two he had already been in and out of rehab a few times. Despite looking angelic in the stereotypical sense with his blond hair and blue eyes, he was his family's "black sheep."

To enter Tuxedo Park, one must go through a large, imposing stone gate manned by a security guard. The towering walls loomed over us as we entered. We drove past the town's private church, country club, and primary school as I sat awestruck in the backseat of the wood-paneled car. I was mesmerized by the dense forest and winding road that took us past mansions bigger than any I had seen in Winter Park.

When we finally pulled up to Chris's home, my jaw literally dropped.

Chris wasn't joking when he said his parents had a big house. It had been designed by a renowned architect, who in addition to creating elaborate private homes was known for public monuments such as the famous memorial to the USS *Maine* in New York City's Columbus Circle. The home was L-shaped and two stories high, with a gabled shingled roof that gently curved into eaves, giving the roof the thatched effect of an English country estate. Inside the home were real Chippendale doors and Tiffany stained-glass panels. The second-floor hallway was so long that you could run laps in it. I had never seen anything like it before, and could not believe I was staying there.

Chris assigned Lars and me to different bedrooms, and then we all went downstairs to the kitchen to plow through his parents' liquor supply.

On Saturday, we drove into New York City with his best friend from the "neighborhood," another young man named Chris. This Chris was a student at New York University and had an apartment near Astor Place where we were going to crash for the night. We drove into the city through the Lincoln Tunnel, which the two Chrises said contained air so toxic that if you rolled down your window you would suffocate. Lars and I, being the naïve suckers we were, believed them, and did our best to take small, shallow breaths in the car until we came out on the New York side of the tunnel.

As the city opened up in front of me, I was hit with a deep sense of belonging. Or perhaps it was longing. All I knew was that I *had* to live here. Peering up into the sky, I was overwhelmed with the sheer scale of everything. The buildings soared so high that it hurt my neck to crane back to peer at their peaks. Times Square was a luminescent, neon and light-bulb-filled adult arcade of strip joints and peep shows, interspersed with theaters and buildings covered with mammoth advertisements for the latest Broadway shows. The city's spirit was electric. Filled with a writhing energy that moved me to my core.

I was fascinated by the diversity of the city's inhabitants. Unlike the Orlando area, which was still in many ways segregated, everywhere I looked I saw people of all races and ethnicities. They seemed to move seamlessly by each other on the street, with no sense of hostility. Everyone was on their hustle, each intent on making his or her way in this land of opportunity. For the first time in my life I didn't feel the burden of my skin color. Within thirty seconds my mind was made up. Come hell or high water, I was moving to New York as soon as I turned eighteen that July.

After hours of drinking we made our way back to the apartment, and then the Chrises pulled out their stash of cocaine. I had never seen it before, but they assured me it was "good stuff," and offered me a line. Not wanting to appear cowardly, I took a rolled-up twenty-dollar bill and snorted the pinkish-hued crystalline substance up my nose. I did a couple of other lines that night, but really didn't get what the big fuss was about. The others were speaking rapidly and seemed enthralled. But I didn't feel anything other than wired and hyperalert, which was how I felt most of the time anyway. One of the main reasons I drank was so I didn't *have* to feel on edge all the time, and the coke was messing up my vibe. I stayed up all night grinding my teeth, while trying to bring myself back down with beer. Early in the morning, we all passed out. On Sunday, Lars and I flew back to Orlando. Back to Dad's home, with all its dysfunction, and the bland Central Florida lifestyle.

My body was there, but my heart was still in New York. I went through the motions for the next couple of months as I tried to hold the shreds of our family together. But I knew I was leaving. I wasn't going to miss Dad or Grandpa, although I did feel tenderness for Grandpa's many kindnesses to me. May Lai was by this time living in Cocoa Beach with her latest boyfriend and had dropped out of high school. She had recently turned sixteen, and there was no amount of convincing that I could do to keep her home. I loathed her lifestyle, but understood why she didn't want to live under Dad's roof.

It was my brother Dan who I worried about leaving. He was only fourteen and cowed under Dad's authority. His escape was into Christianity, which I believe saved his life. Mom, May Lai, and now I were done with this loveless, empty home. There were too many sad memories, too many disappointments, and too much anger for any of us to stay. But Dan was too young to leave and unable to stand up to Dad. Besides not having the benefit of age, he lacked the fiery temperament of his older sisters. If I could have taken him with me I would have, but that wasn't a possibility.

The only thing that gave me some comfort about leaving my brother was that one of the families down the street took him in emotionally, ensuring that Dan would have the support that Dad couldn't provide. This family was made up of devout Christians, which is how my brother ended up immersing himself heavily in Wednesday night Bible studies, youth retreats, and Sunday services. Through this family and his new church home, my brother had his own escape hatch from Dad's tyranny.

Once I left, the women would be gone and three generations

of Baber men would be left to fend for themselves. Grandpa, Dad, and Dan would have to do "women's work." There would no longer be a female to cook meals or do laundry, as I had been doing since Mom's departure. Someone else would have to clean the pool and mow the lawn, which I had taken over from Mom as well. One of them would have to be responsible for vacuuming the carpets and cleaning the kitchen and bathroom.

The funny thing is that Dad never asked me to do this. I assumed these responsibilities because I loved my siblings and felt sorry for Dad having to run a house by himself without a wife. None of my efforts were ever acknowledged. Just as he had with Mom, he took me for granted since he paid the bills. His ingratitude, along with the chance at a new life in a new city, was the final spark that pushed me out the door.

❧

After calling Nancy in New York and confirming that I could stay at her apartment, I put my exit strategy into motion. I borrowed money from Grandpa to buy a plane ticket to New York, along with $200 in extra cash. No one knew my ticket was one-way, and that I had no intention of coming back. Like Mom had done the year before, I packed as much of my clothes as possible into a large, light blue suitcase. I put important paperwork, like my GED certificate, birth certificate, and keepsakes I didn't want to leave behind into a small black Samsonite valise. That was all I was taking into my new life.

On the night of my eighteenth birthday I went out with my friends with the intent of celebrating my impending departure at Club Aahz, one of our favorite drinking haunts. The night was just getting started when one of the cops who moonlighted at the club saw me sipping a drink that had been handed to me by one of my friends who was of legal drinking age. Grabbing the cup out of my hand, he raised it to his nose and sniffed the contents.

"Come with me," he ordered.

I was led outside and read my Miranda rights. As the cop looked at my license, he noted my date of birth and sarcastically said, "Happy birthday!" I can't say I didn't have it coming, but it was totally lame that I was going to spend the first hours of my eighteenth year in a holding cell. I made my one call to a friend named Granville, who I knew could bail me out. He came down to the station, posted my bond, and I was released at around 3:00 a.m. Granville then drove me home and went on his way, while I stewed alone in my room. *What a fuckin' way to bring in your birthday,* I thought. If I needed one more sign that Orlando wasn't the town for me, this was it.

The following afternoon, my off-and-on-again boyfriend Jay, a skater boy from Satellite Beach, Florida, came by with his best friend, Israel, to drive me to the airport. It was July 14, 1988. Less than twenty-four hours after being locked up, I was on a plane to New York with no intention of ever coming back.

Model test shoot on Fire Island, NY, summer 1988.
Photo courtesy of Mishka.

CHAPTER NINE

With my ancient anger at everything, my newly-discovered sense of beauty, and the narcissism that often accompanies it, I landed in New York motivated to show other people that they had underestimated me. By now I had learned that my "exotic" appearance—the very thing that had condemned me to second-class citizenship in Central Florida—was now my greatest asset—and something I could use as a weapon.

It's a typical story, I know. A small-town social outcast makes her way to the Big City to prove to the world that she is *somebody*.

Still, it was my goal to show the world how truly special and unique I was—that I could escape my childhood and do what no one else in my family had been able to do: have a successful life.

As I was to come to learn, this wouldn't be as easy as I thought.

I actually moved to New York City during one of the hottest summers on record. We were in the middle of a scorching heat wave with high humidity and temperatures soaring close to 100 degrees. The weather was ironically almost identical to that of Winter Park, but it was aggravated by the walls of tall buildings holding the hot air hostage. The smell of urine in the streets, combined with the aromas from pizza and hot dog vendors, was nauseating.

True to her word, Nancy, the photographer I had met earlier that year, allowed me to stay in her apartment while she was away. You would think an eighteen-year-old girl from Central Florida would feel scared living in such a large city without a support network or financial safety net. Not me. I felt nothing but pure, unadulterated joy. In my naïveté, I was so exhilarated by my new-found freedom that I never considered the possibility that I could fail. As far as I was concerned, everything was up for grabs and I was intent on becoming the next "small-town girl made good." This was the first time in my life that I had complete autonomy and was committed to making my mark. In retrospect, I cringe at how I failed to see how much the odds were stacked against me.

During my first two weeks, I focused on acquiring the three most important things I needed to survive: permanent housing, a modeling agent, and a job. Also, I decided not to drink.

I was able to find a place to live when Nancy's assistant, Shar-land, suddenly found herself in need of a roommate. One of the three she lived with in a two-bedroom on the Upper West Side had abruptly moved out. The rent was $2,200 a month split four ways—the two who shared the larger bedroom paid $600 a month each, and those who shared the smaller bedroom paid $500 per person. I wasn't thrilled with the idea of living in such a small space with a complete stranger, but the rent was cheap by New York City standards and located in a luxury high-rise. At $500 a month, it was extremely expensive, considering that back in Win-ter Park I could rent a one-bedroom apartment a mile from my Dad's house for $300. But it was a place to call my own when my two-week sublet with Nancy ran out at the end of July.

Finding an agent turned out to be a much more difficult task. It never occurred to me that Nancy's assessment wouldn't be

shared by the modeling agencies in New York. On her recommendation, I went to open calls at every major agency in town—
Wilhelmina, Ford, Elite, Zoli, IMG, and Click—and was politely
turned down. At open calls you give your portfolio to the receptionist, who then walks your book back to the agents. If they have
an interest, they come out and speak to you. If not, the receptionist
simply hands your book back, and suggests that you try another
agency.

Out of all the agencies, only agents at two bothered to see me
in person—one at Elite and another at IMG. At Elite, the booker
told me my look wasn't right for New York, however, "You
might consider a smaller market like Chicago. They have a strong
catalog clientele that I think you're better suited for." (Catalog
meaning *not* high fashion.) Seeing the dejected expression on my
face, he added, "Feel free to come back when you have some new
photographs. I'm willing to give you another look."

My modeling career hinged on my ability to secure an agent
and IMG was my last option, after having been rejected by every
other major agency in the city. It was at this point that I began
to worry if I could pull off my big dream. I had left my friends
in Florida behind crowing about how I had been discovered by
a big-time photographer. If I didn't find an agent, I would have
failed before I started. It was this growing sense of desperation
that left me vulnerable to a man I'd hoped would be my salvation.
I had been in New York City all of two weeks before I experienced my first incident of sexual exploitation in the modeling
industry.

When I arrived at IMG, I handed my portfolio over to the
receptionist and waited for her to come back with the usual
"Thanks, but no thanks." Instead, I was greeted by the head of
the women's division who brought me into a boardroom with a
large conference table. He sat down but didn't offer me a seat, so

I stood awkwardly off to the side of the table as he quickly flipped through my portfolio.

"Uh-hum. Uh-hum," he muttered, before turning to me and saying, "You have some nice pictures. But in order to make a decision, I need to see your breasts. Do you mind showing me yours?"

I was so shocked by his request that I was struggling to process his ask. All I knew was that a top booker at one of the world's most prestigious modeling agencies had expressed a smidgen of interest in my look, and he was possibly my last chance.

Sensing my confusion, he rationalized his request.

"Models shoot naked all the time . . . You've seen the pictures in *ELLE* and *Harper's Bazaar*, right?" Nodding my head, I obediently unhooked my bra and lifted my shirt. With the antiseptic gaze of a gynecologist, he said, "Thank you. I don't think you're the right look for our agency, but you should try Click," before ushering me out the door.

I left the meeting feeling raw. Exposed. Stupid. Dirty. My mind was spinning as I desperately tried to reconcile what had just happened in that room. Was his request to see my breasts a legitimate part of the evaluation process? It didn't seem so. None of the other agents had asked to see what was under my shirt, but he did have a point that models were photographed nude all the time. But in my gut I knew I had just been had. In a matter of a few minutes I had been sexually coerced by a sleazy booker at one of the top agencies in the world. He preyed upon my ambition and inexperience, knowing how desperately girls like me were for the chance to become the next Cindy Crawford or Naomi Campbell. As I would come to learn, he was just one of many adult men in the industry who abused young girls and women.

Shame and embarrassment prevented me from telling anyone for years. Much later I would feel somewhat vindicated when this agent's supermodel wife divorced him and he was booted out of

IMG after multiple allegations of his predatory behavior became public.

Instead of signing with a top agency, I ended up being represented by a smaller, less prestigious one that primarily booked runway models. Avenue Models was housed above the famed nightclub Stringfellow's, owned by the nightlife impresario Peter String-fellow, whose eponymous London club was an international legend. After signing my contract with my booker, an Afro-haired, fair-skinned redhead named Stephen of either Jewish or black heritage, I was introduced to the agency owner, a seventy-something-year-old white man named Ed.

Ed was a gray-haired businessman with various interests who looked like and emanated the hurried air of then-New York City Mayor Ed Koch. When Stephen introduced me to him, Ed briefly looked up at me from his desk and grunted hello, before dipping his head back into his paperwork.

"Don't mind him. He's always like that," assured Stephen. He next ushered me into the office of the woman who actually ran the day-to-day operations of the agency, Pat Watson. Pat was a former model, a tall, elegant, cocoa-brown-skinned woman with legs that stretched for an eternity. Pat was distant, but courteous, and gave me a warm smile as she welcomed me to their small agency. Although she was only twenty-six years old, Pat was clearly a woman who knew what she wanted and how to get it. (Though Pat and I would drift apart as my life spun out of control, I never forgot her. The next time I saw her face was when she was speaking at the podium at Whitney Houston's funeral in 2012. Now Patricia Houston, she has married into the legendary icon's family.)

As I was leaving the agency, I told Stephen that I needed to find a new job but didn't know where to start. The week before I had found one as a hostess at a Japanese piano bar, but was fired after one night.

Stephen walked back into Ed's office.

"Hey, Ed. Sil Lai needs a job. Do you know if they're hiring at Stringfellow's?"

"Hold on a minute . . . let me find out."

While Ed made his calls, I went back to the office waiting area. After a couple of minutes Stephen came out and said, "I'm going to introduce you to Michael, the manager at Stringfellow's. They're looking for a cocktail waitress. Let's go."

Stringfellow's was the preferred haunt of celebrities from both the States and across the pond, an eclectic mix of wealthy bankers, drug dealers, paparazzi, international film stars, professional athletes, TV personalities, rock stars, models, and journalists. To get a job there was considered quite the coup, as far as nightclub employment was concerned.

We headed downstairs and rang the bell at the entrance to the club, a building with a sleek, black-and-pink granite façade. The main entrance doors were made of frosted glass embossed with butterflies. One of the Bangladeshi day workers let us in and we waited at the cashier's booth for Michael. When he finally showed up, I had to stop myself from giggling out loud, for like the club itself, Michael was a spectacle.

Michael was at least six foot three, and with his high-heeled boots towered at six foot six inches tall. His long, narrow face was painted with full makeup and dusted with translucent powder that glimmered on his skin. Even with his long blond ponytail teased in a slight bouffant, his style was more David Bowie à la Ziggy Stardust than RuPaul. His androgynous black suit with wide, padded shoulders tapered to a very narrow waist, and had drainpipe trousers. I loved his eclectic appearance, reminiscent of my days in the punk rock scene.

I was hired on the spot and instructed I had to quickly purchase my uniform at a Capezio dance store. Stringfellow's waitresses all wore pink sleeveless leotards, small tutus like circus bears that accented our waists and exposed our derrières, white or nude stockings, and nude heels. I was horrified at the uniform, but the waitresses made buckets of money, especially if you worked the Champagne Room. Just off of tips (and no "funny business"), the girls could clear three thousand a night.

On the evening of my first shift, I put on my uniform in the dressing room with the rest of the "tutus," as we were called. This group of women, aged twenty to thirty, ran circles around me in terms of sophistication. While I thought I was worldly by Orlando standards, here in New York the game was played on an entirely different level. And to be quite honest, my game had only one move: knowing how to party as much as possible while spending the least amount of money. These women were all angling for something larger. A recording career. A leading role in a Broadway show. A wealthy sugar daddy. I was just trying to pay my bills and have some fun, an outlook that earned me the derision of my peers, who criticized my lack of social and financial ambition.

It was at Stringfellow's that I served dinner to the first real celebrities I ever met, the singer Grace Jones and her then-boyfriend Dolph Lundgren, who was an international superstar due to his roles in the films *Rocky IV* and *Red Scorpion*. They wouldn't be the only celebs I would meet at the club.

Wilt Chamberlain, Robin "Lifestyles of the Rich and Famous" Leach, Brooke Shields, Samantha Fox, Eddie Murphy, Mike Tyson—the list was endless. Their money flowed plentifully, along with the wealthy bankers and drug dealers who wanted to mingle in the rarified air of what was then the epicenter of New York City nightlife. There were other clubs, of course, that were equally popular and even more famous, such as Peter Gatien's Tunnel, or the legendary Palladium. But when it came to star clientele, Stringfellow's cornered the market with its opulence and exclusivity.

For the first few months of work I tried to excel, but I simply didn't have the confidence to flirt with customers so they'd give me large tips. The other girls were making on average $400 to $500 a night, and the Champagne Room tutus were making thousands; I was only pulling in a measly $100 to $150. I just didn't have any "game." When a customer tried to engage in conversation with me, I'd nervously smile and then flee.

I did my job robotically. Take a drink order, place order, retrieve it from the bartender, then bring it back to the patron. One, two, three, four. As far as I was concerned, my job was to deliver drinks, not augment customers' egos. When the weather changed and the coatroom opened, I asked to work there, behind the scenes and away from the drunken customers and their demands. Coat check work was hard on the body, but it was lucrative and most importantly, I could wear my own clothes.

Most nights the club closed at 4:00 a.m., but on slower nights like Mondays we often shut down between 11:30 p.m. and 1:00 a.m. When Michael announced that I could leave, I would rush out the door and head straight home on the subway to my apartment on West 96th Street.

I had been asked on a few occasions to go clubbing after work with my coworkers but had always said no. It was now October and two months had passed since I'd had a drink. My life was operating smoothly, but I was lonely. Outside of my roommate Sharland, I didn't really have any other friends. But one night Ben, the head bartender, asked me if I wanted to go to the China

Club with some of the other tutus. Before I realized it, I heard my mouth saying the word, "Sure!" This small decision would completely change my life. This was the night that the city and I finally gelled, and I went from outside to insider.

Ben knew the bouncer at the door, so we bypassed the line rolling five deep. We walked down the steep stairs that led to a dark, unassuming basement. In sharp contrast to the grandeur of Stringfellow's, the China Club looked like a dive bar. But for some reason, it had become *the* go-to spot on Monday nights.

"What are you having?" Ben asked as we leaned on the bar. He sensed my hesitation, thinking it was because I didn't know what I wanted to drink. But he was wrong. What I was really pondering was, *Should I have a drink?*

Then he called out to the bartender, "Two Woo-Woos."

"What's a Woo-Woo?" I asked.

"It's vodka with a splash of peach schnapps and cranberry juice. Have enough of these and you'll be saying, 'wooo-wooooo!'" he laughed.

I took the plastic cup filled with pale cranberry-colored liquid, sipping it tentatively. As the alcohol began to flow through my veins, the invisible wall between me and my coworkers melted away. By drink number three I was bouncing on the dance floor with the crew to the sounds of Salt-N-Pepa's "Push It." Drink in hand, I flipped my curly hair back and forth and swayed to the rhythm. For the first time in months I was finally having *fun*. I felt like myself again, not a nervous, insecure creature grappling with insecurity and isolation.

In a matter of minutes, my Orlando party-girl persona was back.

As far as drinking patterns go, I was amazingly consistent. I drank way too much that night and ended up blacking out. Thankfully, I woke up in my own bed, unharmed, but dehydrated with a hangover from hell. Later that night when I showed up at work, I noticed a shift in my coworkers' attitudes toward me. Instead of indifference, Ben and his bar runner Poban greeted me with cheery hellos.

"Hey, Sil Lai! What took you so long to hang out with us? I had no idea you could be so much fun with, the way you always walked around like you had a stick up your ass. Glad you went out with us! You gotta do it again!"

The tutus who had been with us the night before surprisingly acknowledged my presence. After nearly two months of working side by side with them, I was finally accepted by my fellow workers. All because I had gone out drinking with them instead of going home.

The message was clear. If I was going to have any sort of human interactions outside of those with my roommates, I was going to have to drink. Sil Lai without any booze in her system was a bore. Sil Lai with some drinks was a member of the crew. Sobriety kept me out of trouble, but it also kept me isolated. After months of virtually no social life, I was ready to be a part of a group again. I knew that drinking created catastrophic unmanageability in my life, but at least I wouldn't be struggling alone in New York.

And so began the revolving door of parties, drinking, clubbing, hangovers, and brief sexual liaisons that I had tried to leave behind in Winter Park. The consequences for my choice to drink again came down swift and hard. Downing that first Woo-Woo at the China Club tipped over the first tile in the line of methodically placed dominoes that made up my life in New York. Each piece represented an area of my life that would fall.

One was sexual discretion. Another was thrift. Yet another, balance. And another, emotional stability. They all came crashing down with a rapid clattering the moment that I took that first drink. This decision made out of insecurity, denial about the extent of my alcoholism, and my need for acceptance, started a chain of events that would ensure my dream of modeling in New York would remain just that—a dream.

Now that I was drinking again, I felt freer to open up to my growing circle of racially diverse friends about my true identity. Actually, it wasn't so much an opening up to others as an embracing of their acceptance of my blackness.

Of course, I still received the usual question of "What are you?"—but instead of answering "Hawaiian," I would say, "I'm black and Chinese."

"Yeah, I can see the Chinese, now that you mention it" was as far as the conversations usually went. There was no questioning of the veracity of my claim, particularly in my newfound black community.

Over the years I've heard "Black people just know their own kind" repeated more times than I can count. The unquestioning, warm acceptance of my humanity was a balm to my soul. For the first time, I felt like I was truly home among people who looked like me, even if we didn't share the same cultural experiences.

In spite of my increasing comfort with the DNA that I had first unconsciously, then consciously, hidden my entire life, I was still very conflicted. Unlike before, it wasn't about who I was so much as trying to emotionally reconcile my past. It is natural when you're getting to know people that you swap stories of your childhood. Many people take great pride in their families; however, this wasn't something that I could do. When the holidays would come and go without any mention of my mine, invariably the question would come: Why I was estranged from my parents?

It was difficult and embarrassing to share, because none of my new friends had been present for the chaos and dysfunction. They only saw the result of the toxic environment in which I was raised. I would spend hours pouring out the intimate details of my family dynamics. Trying to gain the sympathy of my listener, to validate my feelings of betrayal. While some empathized, many would shrug at my experiences.

"At least you had a dad who took care of you," said one friend. "Hell, as far as I'm concerned, he's a saint. I can't say that I would've kept you under the same circumstances. My dad split before I was born. And you didn't have to eat government cheese, or live in the projects ducking bullets from drug dealers."

"Girl, you're lucky you still have your teeth in your mouth," opined another. "My mom would whip my ass with the extension cord when I came in late. And you're bitching about getting spanked with a belt. Puh-lease."

It was true that I had been spared many of the horrors that children experience at the hands of those who are supposed to love them. My parents never engaged in verbal abuse, or wanton physical violence. I didn't have a creepy uncle slipping into my bed at night. We had a modest, yet comfortable home, with running water and food in the pantry. A mom who fed us and tried to support us academically. While some things were definitely emotionally abusive, compared to others, my life could be seen as idyllic.

Exasperated, I would still try to convince the doubters that my childhood was *not* normal, and that my parents were not just well-meaning, but flawed folk. We would go back and forth, debating about who had it worse, until eventually we'd switch the subject.

Of course, I knew that my life hadn't been all bad. But why the hell did I *feel* so bad? If things were so "normal" for me, why did I wake up every day wishing I was dead? My parents' behavior didn't qualify them for a prison sentence for child abuse, but I was still exhibiting all of the symptoms of a person who had either (a) a serious psychological disorder; (b) experienced severe trauma; or, most likely (c) both. For while I did have the material trappings of a family, I grew up without feeling loved, and the hidden specter of my true origins tainting everything around me.

To many, that might not sound like abuse, but perhaps we all need to examine more closely what children really need to thrive and develop a healthy, normal sense of self. Few would dispute good parenting requires more than just providing discipline and material things.

My first boyfriend in New York was a sweet, attentive young man who worked in the menswear section at Barneys department store named Andrew. He adored me and treated me like a princess on his humble salary. He lived out in Queens with his mother, a small but domineering Colombian woman who, he had warned me in advance, "never likes any of my girlfriends." True to form, I didn't pass the test.

Like me, Andrew was of mixed descent, inheriting his Scottish surname from his father, a man who had disappeared from his life. He was tall and had the soft build of a man who used to be overweight. His olive-complected skin, full lips, and prominent nose, combined with a lush head of dark, wavy hair, gave him the combined features of a young Armand Assante and Robert De Niro. Andrew was the first "ethnic" man I had dated, for up until this point, all my lovers had been of European descent. Ours wasn't a grand love affair, but companionship. I had been in New York for a few months, and while he wasn't as glamorous as some of the models I had hooked up with when I first arrived, Andrew

offered something different. For the first time I was in a relationship with someone who actually treated me with compassion and
care. Although I wasn't in love with him, he said he was with me.

Our relationship didn't have any drama. Well, it didn't until
the night I brought him to Stringfellow's, where we partied with
my roommates. As he moved around the room, I couldn't help
but notice how out of place he was in the sea of wealthy men. All
of my fellow tutus were either seeking or had rich boyfriends.
They couldn't understand why a young woman with my looks
wouldn't date a man of means.

"Girl, why are you throwing your looks away on that broke
boy?" was a common admonition. "You can get someone that
makes fifty times more money than him!"

Although it shouldn't have mattered what they said, I was
beginning to think they were right. Yes, Andrew was sensible,
grounded, and treated me well, but he had none of the wealthy
trappings of the men I was meeting in droves. Slowly but surely, I
was being indoctrinated into this materialistic culture.

They're right, I thought to myself. *Why am I wasting my time
riding the subway with Andrew when I could be traveling around
town in a limousine?*

Not long after that night, I callously dumped him. I handled
his feelings just as carelessly as the men who had discarded me
in the past . . . dishonestly and without integrity. All because of a
man named Eddie Murphy.

❁

It was a Monday night and as usual, I had gone up to the China
Club with my coworkers. Standing off to the side of the dance
floor, I sipped my drink and chatted with my fellow tutu, a girl
named Keisha with whom I had become close. Keisha was a

black girl from New Jersey with a penchant for white boys and dreams of making it big on Broadway. She was sassy, confident, single-mindedly focused on her career, and could hold her liquor. Basically, my antithesis.

Sipping our drinks, we surveyed the room, looking for attractive men to dance with. The process was simple. We would spy a cute guy, and then slowly dance our way over to him so that eventually he'd be right next to us. Before he knew it, he'd be in the middle of a Keisha-and-Sil Lai dance sandwich, a white boy caught between two black girls. It was all done in the spirit of conquest and revelry, for as soon as the man would reciprocate our attention, we would dance away.

Out of the corner of my eye, I spied a football-player-sized man making his way over to us. The look on his face was stern and focused. He had the air of a man on a mission to achieve something. That, or make an arrest.

As he approached, he shouted over the music, "Hi. My name's Fruity. I work for Eddie Murphy. He'd like to meet you." His eyes were locked directly on me, not Keisha. And based upon his demeanor, it was clear that his "request" was more like a demand.

I looked over at Keisha and she nudged me. "Go on. I'll be fine."

I trailed behind his hulking frame as we wound our way through the writhing sea of bodies on the dance floor and over to the VIP section where Eddie and his entourage were gathered. The bouncer unhooked the black velvet rope that separated this exclusive area from the "regular" folk in the club. By the way, regular was all relative. For in the regular section were models, actresses, and well-known singers like Johnny "Just Got Paid" Kemp, Debbie Gibson, and Mike Hughes and Alex "Spanador" Moseley, of the wildly successful group Lisa Lisa & Cult Jam.

Eddie stared intently into my eyes while Fruity introduced us.

To say that I was nervous would be an understatement. Even with a couple of drinks in me, my diaphragm was twitching with excitement. It was a surreal moment. A year earlier I was watching him on television, or in a movie theater back home. Eddie Murphy was a bona fide superstar.

Leaning toward me, Eddie yelled over the music, "You're so pretty. You look like a damn China doll."

Trying to appear as unaffected as possible, I answered with a simple, "Thanks." He then flashed his multi-million-dollar gap-toothed smile, which put me a little more at ease. "Can I have your number?" he asked, and I nodded affirmatively.

"Fed, get me a pen and paper," Eddie called out to another member of his entourage. Shouting into his ear, I gave him my number, which he transcribed onto a white cocktail napkin.

"I'll be giving you a call" was his final response, signaling that our time together was over. Fruity then stepped aside to open the path for me to exit the VIP section.

Keisha was by then dancing with a blond-haired white man.

Grabbing her arm, I pulled her off the dance floor.

"Did you see what just happened? Oh my God! Eddie Murphy asked me for my phone number!"

"Did you give it to him?" she asked.

"Of course I did!" I said, pausing briefly before yelling over the music and adding, "I wonder if he's gonna call me!"

A little less than a week later I received a call from Eddie, and we chatted for a half hour about our backgrounds and interests. At the end of the conversation, he asked if I'd be interested in having dinner with him, to which I immediately said yes. A date was set, and I counted down the days until I would see him again.

I didn't tell Andrew about my new "friend." I rationalized that it didn't matter, because I was going to be breaking up with him anyway. He was kind, but I was bored, and wanted more excitement and a lifestyle that he couldn't provide.

Of course, deep down inside, it wasn't that simple. I was actually ill-equipped for any kind of intimate relationship. All my "relationships" up until that point had begun and ended so quickly that I was never at risk of any real emotional connection. Years of distancing myself from my parents made true intimacy impossible. I didn't realize that was playing a role in my decision at the time. Instead, I believed that my inevitable breakup with Andrew was due to his lack of money and sophistication.

The only person who knew about my impending date was Keisha, who supported it wholeheartedly. On the day of our dinner, my doorman called up to my apartment and said, "A gentleman is waiting for you in the lobby." I took one last look in the mirror. My outfit was sexy, but not too revealing. My wardrobe was limited, so I borrowed a coat from my roommate and threw it over my long-sleeved spandex shirt, black-and-gray-striped miniskirt, and black patent Aigner pumps.

I walked out through the revolving door and stepped toward a Jaguar waiting at the curb. As I approached, a tall, dark man named Ray Ray exited the driver's door and came around to open mine. I had never seen him before.

I was completely deflated when I realized that Eddie didn't think enough of me to pick me up himself. But Ray Ray was an easy talker, and by ten minutes into the drive to Englewood Cliffs, New Jersey, where Eddie lived, I felt comfortable.

We pulled up into the driveway of Eddie's estate, an enormous Georgian-inspired brick mansion affectionately referred to as "Bubble Hill." I followed him inside the large double doors that led into a massive marble-floored entry and then made a left toward the formal dining area.

As I entered the room, I was shocked by the number of people there for our "date." I counted at least fifteen bodies seated at the massive table. Surprisingly, Eddie was seated off to my right, not at the head of the table. Along with his entourage, there were a few other women there, and seemingly all of his immediate family. Haltingly, I entered the room and sat down next to him. To my relief, dinner was almost over by the time I arrived, so I didn't have to spend much time engaging with the others. The only exception was chatting with NBA star John Salley and a female friend of his named Ivelka, with whom I would eventually forge a friendship.

After dinner, Eddie took me on a tour of his home, which included a two-lane bowling alley, a billiards room, a spa, and a massive indoor swimming pool. Bubble Hill was 25,000 square feet of aromatic opulence. Aromatic because of the potpourri that was spread across every windowsill.

After the tour, we sat in his small library, away from the other guests in his home, and spoke some more. In contrast to his aggressive, highly excitable on-screen personality, privately Eddie was reserved, even remote. On occasion he would show his wicked sense of humor, saying things like, "Are your feet fucked up? C'mon. Tell the truth . . . when you're on the beach, do you dig your toes in the sand so nobody can see them?" But mostly he gently probed and asked me questions about my background.

I didn't know how to act. Yes, I was starstruck. But I was scared as well. Frightened that he would reject me because he could see through the curls and red lipstick what I really was: a scared, drunken party girl with no self-esteem, struggling to survive in a world that she was completely unprepared for, who had never been in a long-term relationship.

Eddie was also the first black man that I had ever gone out with. I wondered to myself, *Would I even be sitting here at all if this black man wasn't Eddie Murphy, superstar?* I knew the answer: absolutely not.

After an hour or so of talking, Eddie offered to drive me home. *Thank God.* I sighed with relief. I was eager to leave since I was afraid he would try to sleep with me that night. But he was a gentleman, and drove me to my door in another one of his vehicles, a Mercedes-Benz. Kissing me gently on the cheek, he said as I exited the car, "From now on, I'll be the one picking you up. No more Fruity or Ray Ray." Grinning, I waved goodbye and ran into my building, out of the bitter cold.

The next morning, I called my friend Lisa back home in Orlando and told her about my night.

"*No fucking way! The* Eddie Murphy, as in *Saturday Night Live?*"

"Yup!"

"Wait'll I tell everybody you're dating Eddie Murphy!"

"Whoa, slow down. I went on one date. Let's see what happens before you start that rumor."

Eddie and I scheduled another date at his home in New Jersey. True to his word, he picked me up himself—in a Rolls-Royce, no less, my first time in one of these mini-mansions on wheels. This time that we spent together was infinitely more interesting than the first. I had already eaten by the time he swung by, so we spent most of our time in his huge bedroom. It was almost entirely white, with a baby grand piano that had a vase of red, long-stemmed roses on it off to the side. Eddie sat down and expertly played Nat King Cole's "Mona Lisa," crooning and singing the lyrics with the flair of a seasoned performer. Afterward, he brought me into his huge walk-in closet that had fourteen-foot ceilings filled from top to bottom with clothes, then pushed another door on the back wall that opened into a secret room filled with Elvis Presley memorabilia.

And when I say filled, I mean from top to bottom. It was a shrine to Elvis, an homage to a performer that for some reason fascinated Eddie. The room, like so many other facets of Eddie's life, seemed to be a contradiction. Why would a black performer be obsessed with a white performer alleged to have copied everything from his hairstyle to his performances from black people? That question, I didn't ask him.

Finally, we lay down on his bed and roughhoused a bit, tickling and giggling. As the evening continued, I grew uncomfortable about the unspoken event that was to occur. I knew that night I would kiss him. But in spite of his wealth and talent, I wasn't really attracted to him. Here I was, nuzzled close to the biggest black male star in Hollywood at the time, yet I just didn't find him physically appealing. It had nothing to do with skin color. There were black men I did find attractive. He just wasn't one of them.

After a night of serenading and laughter, we were now on the precipice of some sort of intimacy. When Eddie leaned in to kiss me, I held my breath and pressed my mouth against his velvety-smooth lips. But I was totally sober, which meant uptight and unresponsive. I had chosen to not drink whenever I was around him because I didn't want him to think of me as a "loose" girl. And by not drinking, I also ensured that the self-conscious and insecure Sil Lai would be the only girl he met, qualities that don't make for passionate evenings.

After a few more pecks on the lips, he asked me if I wanted to go home, to which I replied yes. He drove me back to the city, still chatting, sharing with me the news that he had just bought Cher's house in Beverly Hills, and that I should come out to visit him.

"Do you want to come out and see me in LA?" he asked.

"Mmm-hhmm" was my tepid reply. I didn't want to go visit him in Los Angeles because that would mean staying the night, which would mean having to sleep with him. Which was something I simply did not want to do.

Eddie must have picked up on my ambivalence, because he cancelled our next date the same night we were supposed to get together. I guess the pecks on the lips and my general bland response just wasn't doing it for him. I was on my shift at Stringfellow's when Michael came rushing over to me and said, "Sil Lai, Eddie Murphy called for you and said that he can't make it tonight." Michael blurted out the message like it was breaking news, and everyone within earshot heard. Word quickly spread throughout the club that I was dating Eddie Murphy. Which in actuality was not the case, as that night was the last time I ever heard from him. But it didn't matter. To all of my coworkers I was now a bona fide "It Girl," elevated to a new level of coolness courtesy of my now defunct non-relationship with a superstar. It was the first time that I experienced the halo effect of being associated with someone famous, and it wouldn't be my last.

This was how things worked in the superficial world in which I lived. I learned that my proximity to a man of wealth and fame could change my social status. I had for all intents and purposes "arrived."

I broke up with Andrew soon thereafter, the first casualty in my search for the "glamorous life."

Cocktail waitressing at Stringfellow's nightclub, circa 1989.

CHAPTER TEN

$\mathcal{I}$ HAD BEEN IN NEW YORK FOR A GRAND TOTAL OF FIVE MONTHS and my life on the surface had entirely changed. Not just in terms of lifestyle, but also culture. For the past eighteen years I had been immersed in white society, and now I had crossed over to the other side. I was becoming a black woman by choice and full identification.

Some might say that the primary lubricant for my entrée into black society was superficially driven by my exposure to fabulous black celebrities. To some extent, this was true. Being surrounded by so much glamour and wealth *was* intoxicating. But as a young, attractive "exotic" I had plenty of opportunities to associate with wealthy white people as well. Yet, this isn't what excited me the most. The true driver of my avid pursuit of a black identity was living in an environment where I felt safe to do so.

What Eddie and other black celebrities, bankers, business executives, athletes, and models had shown me was that being black didn't have to confine you to living a small, oppressed existence. I was beginning to see that my black blood wasn't a curse. It was a testimony to the strength of the human spirit. The black glitterati showed me that despite society's pattern of keeping black people disenfranchised and lacking equal opportunities, many were still able to soar to the heights of fame and success. Proud of their achievements despite these extra challenges, I realized that being black was something worthy of pride. It may seem strange that a young woman who just a few years prior had washed the touch of a black man off of her skin would throw herself into an avid embracing and search for a black racial and cultural identity. The reality was that I had been aching to live openly and honestly based upon the truth. It really wasn't a difficult leap. I was ready to leave everything from my past, including my false racial identity behind.

My growing circle of black friends were a homogeneous group—with nearly all being in the entertainment industry, people who would be considered the "Beautiful Ones," as the old Prince song goes. Were they black and socially conscious? Largely, they were not. Like me, none had a real focus outside the avid pursuit of their chosen vocation. But they were passionate, direct, fun-loving, and accepting of me in a way that none of my prior friends had been. My friendships back home also had many good qualities, but very few there knew the truth about my racial background.

In my new milieu, I was no longer hiding my blackness in order to fit into someone else's construct of what was socially acceptable. But true acculturation into the black community was a much more complicated process. How does a person who knows nothing about blackness (save racial stereotypes), and who had had no deep interactions with black people growing up, actually learn "how" to be black? On a surface level I was able to assume mannerisms and colloquial speech by mimicking my friends. But I was troubled by my lack of lived experiences and historical knowledge. It didn't matter if we looked similar, or had shared interests. I still felt like a fraud.

Although I was accepted wholeheartedly into black society, my experience had still been white. My new friends had grown up in a world vastly different than the one in which I was raised. One that included black Greek-lettered organizations, historically black colleges and universities, family stories about their great-great grandparents' time sharecropping, or their experience in the black church.

I realized that I was woefully culturally undereducated. Concepts like racism as a larger social construct used as a form of oppression, not just as overt, obvious behaviors (like burning a cross on a lawn), were still foreign to me.

Despite my new feelings of kinship based upon the color of our skin, I still felt like an outsider in the black community. It seemed that no matter where I lived, or whom I was around, I would never belong.

❁

Although my job at Stringfellow's provided me with (barely) enough income to pay my bills, I wasn't actually paying them. Now that I was drinking again, I spent the money I made partying at other clubs. My cash flow was unpredictable, because it was largely contingent upon how busy the club was the night that you were working. Some nights I'd only earn $50, while on others I'd easily clear $300. My inconsistent income combined with my drinking had me locked in a tumultuous cycle regarding my housing.

Sharland ended up booting me from her apartment when I became irresponsible with my rent payments. My friend Keisha let me stay with her for a few weeks free of charge, but she soon grew tired of my constant drinking and taking up space on her living room couch.

Faced with potential homelessness, I reached out to Grandma Lou and asked if she would help me get my own apartment.

Always my champion, she loaned me $2,000, which helped me rent a studio apartment in a doorman building on 86th Street between Central Park West and Columbus. This rent-stabilized apartment was so tiny that when you opened the front door, you practically hit your nose against the back wall. It was a twelve-by-thirteen-foot room with an efficiency kitchen and an oversized salmon-pink and powder-blue tiled bathroom. I paid a paltry $486 per month, but with my drinking, food binges (my bulimia was still raging), and expensive cab rides home from work, I could barely cover the rent.

My life was in tatters, a reflection of the chaos and instability within me. By now, bulimia completely had me in its grip. Because I had gained weight, due in large part to my heavy drinking, I didn't feel comfortable eating. But food was another drug for me, and I would sometimes take money I couldn't afford and gorge myself on thousands of calories in a sitting, only to throw it up immediately afterward. Money literally flushed down the toilet. Instead of spending time with friends, I started to binge and purge repeatedly, on average five to seven times a day.

Eating disorders are one of the ultimate ways a person tries to create a sense of order. Consuming the rich, calorie-laden food that was denied to me as a child was in a strange way a form of self-nurturing. But the extra weight that was a consequence of my bingeing on food and alcohol was not something I was willing to bear, so I would purge. It was my way of trying to gain control.

Still, my weight ballooned by fifteen pounds and I was no longer thin enough for the fashion industry. My modeling career, the dream that propelled me to New York with $200 cash and a suitcase, had never taken off. Outside of a few test shoots and two showroom gigs, I had achieved nothing.

I had hoped that by moving to New York, I would leave the

damaged parts of myself behind. But I needed more than a geographic, racial, or cultural change—I needed serious psychological help. It would be years before I would have the resources, or
discipline, to begin a process of emotional healing.

Instead, I started moving down a religious path. I yearned to
connect to something greater, realizing that something was still
missing in my life. Although I had rejected the Baha'i faith at
thirteen, I still believed that there was something much larger at
work in the universe. I just hadn't found a religion that met my
spiritual and cultural needs.

The openness of the Baha'i faith *did* give me the foundation of
mental freedom to explore various forms of religious thought. For
a brief moment after reading *The Autobiography of Malcolm X*,
I flirted with the idea of joining the Nation of Islam. Yet, there
was something in their core beliefs and stories about the history
of mankind that struck me as unfathomable. After attending one
meeting, I abandoned the idea when I realized I wasn't willing to
give up my belief that women were equal to men, as well as my
right to wear bright red lipstick and tight black dresses.

Walking in Times Square, I would sometimes see muscular
black men wearing studded cuffs and sleeveless shirts, showing
off their often-tattooed arms, among other elaborate costuming.
I later learned that they were part of a religious group called the
Black Hebrew Israelites. Standing on milk crates, bullhorns in
hand, they would evangelize to passersby about the supremacy
of the black man and woman, and evil nature of the white man.
"Hello, sister!" they would call out to me. I liked that they called
me sister—their recognition of my blackness was affirming. Their
language was, of course, shocking. But they did make me think
about how I could combine religion with my growing sense of
black identity.

I took a more traditional route when I started attending the

Abyssinian Baptist Church in Harlem, where I would eventually be baptized by its head pastor, civil rights leader and Harlem living legend, the Reverend Calvin O. Butts III. But even Jesus wasn't able to get me off the path of self-destruction. The truth was I needed more than religion. I needed a full-fledged addiction intervention.

❧

The more time that I spent around my black friends, the more convinced I was that in order to authentically claim my cultural birthright, I had to teach myself about the history of black people. But clubs and parties were not the place to learn about such things, so I started where I always went when I wanted to learn: the library.

There began my self-education. Many of the initial books I read were written by black men. *Black Robes, White Justice. Invisible Man. Black Reconstruction in America. Roots. The Autobiography of Malcolm X. Black Boy.* Their well-crafted narratives taught me about the mechanics of blackness in America. In these carefully constructed tomes, I realized how whitewashed my entire world had been. How I had in fact been brainwashed to believe the reductionist and revisionist history of black people that all Americans are spoon-fed from the time we are infants. By reducing black history to a two-week area of focus in social studies classes, traditional education systems like the one I went through in Winter Park actually played a role in promoting white supremacy via omission. I became dedicated to unlearning this warped programming.

It was through the lyrical works by black female authors like Maya Angelou, Terry McMillan, Alice Walker, Ntozake Shange, and Gloria Naylor that I breathed in the emotional experience of being a black woman. Reading their words, I saw the similarities of our paths. It was curious. In spite of being raised white, the type of pain I suffered mirrored these stories by black women. Yes, there were differences in our experiences that could never be ignored; however, I now realized that my soul was forever intertwined with those of all other black women in our country, and throughout history. The compelling narratives of these brave, beautiful sisters, who managed to raise their voices above the throng in spite of being burdened by racism and sexism, filled me with awe. In these women I saw a path toward self-actualization that did not require one to lie, minimize, or deflect their race or gender.

Like many black women, I saw myself in Maya Angelou's poem "Still I Rise":

> *You may tread me in the very dirt*
> *But still, like dust, I'll rise.*

Her poem affirmed that I was still here, even though an entire community had tried to tear me down for my skin color. In spite of their best efforts, I was still standing, just not quite ready to rise.

As the white cultural conditioning slowly flowed out of me, I began to blend my increasing awareness and racial identification into my day-to-day life. My musical tastes, which had always mirrored those of my friends back home, transformed into a passion for classic soul, rhythm and blues, Afrobeat, jazz vocals, and the emerging dominant forms of popular music such as new jack swing. I still loved indie rock, but felt that to listen to it would be a betrayal of my blackness. Even when it came down to the television shows and films I supported, I made the conscious decision to watch only those shows that featured predominantly black casts.

Does one "become" black simply by reading a few books, changing your friends, and shifting your tastes in music and film? Of course not. However, although I had been raised with a white cultural identity, I had still suffered extreme racism because of the color of my skin. I had unknowingly carried the burden of my blackness since as early as I could remember. Now, I was learning context and understanding of what my identity truly meant in the world.

More than most, I actually knew from personal experience how extraordinarily biased white people could be. Conversations they would never have had in the company of someone they knew was black were conducted freely around me when I was "Hawaiian." For this reason and more, I knew unequivocally that my place was not with them, but with my black brothers and sisters, even if I had to construct my black identity, rather than being born into it. It was true that I was also half Chinese, but only racially. I was "too American," with values that ran counter to those in Chinese society, to ever really fit in. Plus, in the black community, my mixed heritage was a nonissue. But among the Chinese I met in New York, I saw in their wary eyes and distant behavior that I would never be accepted. Which, in all honesty, was completely fine by me. It was hard enough trying to immerse myself into one culture, let alone two radically different ones.

Some would argue that by ignoring my Chinese ancestry, I was denying half of my identity. But was it really denial when I had no relationship with my mother, or her family? My Chinese mother had abandoned me, and her racial group in the States rejected me, too. The only people who had ever accepted me were black, and I was not interested in trying to force acceptance from another group in America that actively rejected me after what I had experienced in Central Florida.

After years of enduring Dad's dominance, through my racial self-education I also emerged from his shadow as a strong, independent woman. We'd always fought, but now he finally listened.

During our phone conversations when I called from New York, he would sit in silence as I railed against the injustices done to black people—this after never having talked about race before. Perhaps it was due to his Baha'i beliefs on racial equality, or maybe it was a result of his guilt for lying to me for years, or a fear of talking about race that persisted. Perhaps because he was also a rebel who said whatever he wanted, he respected my escaping the family trap, living my own scrappy adventure, and throwing my anger at the world back in his face—something he had essentially done all his life.

Whatever the reason was, Dad didn't try to shut me down as I shoved my lessons about the "evil doings of white men" down his throat. May Lai and Dan never bothered to challenge me on race. (After their divorce, Mom and I had stopped speaking.) It didn't matter to me whether or not their minds were opened to the lessons in black history they now received on a regular basis. What was most important to me was speaking my truth, damn the consequences.

In some ways, I understood the apathy of my family and white society toward black people—having lived with this mindset myself. People are inherently self-serving in their interests, for the most part. It is the rare individual who would make an effort to respect and empathize with a group of people they were brought up to believe are violent, inferior, utilitarian creatures who refused to accept their second-place social role. None of the white people I knew were willing to acknowledge the fact that black people had created the very foundation of economic privilege that so many of them benefited from through slavery.

The more that I learned about this history and the resultant social reality, the angrier I became. Angry at my family for denying my racial heritage, because it didn't support my dad's convenient lie. Angry at the white people I knew who believed that blacks were inferior, even when many of them had never "achieved" anything other than being born with white skin.

But I was mostly angry at myself for becoming indoctrinated into a belief system that negated the legitimacy of my existence. I allowed my need to fit in to supersede my personal truth. Dr. Martin Luther King, Jr., said, "There comes a time when silence is betrayal." Out of cowardice I had betrayed myself and half of my bloodline by lying about being black.

While my pattern for rebellion against the status quo was well-established by this point, my election to "become" black wasn't just another act of defiance; it was a spiritual reckoning of revolutionary proportions. Instead of being self-destructive, as was my antisocial time as a "punk," it was soul affirming. My blackness also served a larger purpose, for I became one less person of color in the world who hated the color of their skin. In spite of nineteen years of counter-conditioning, I was emerging into my young adulthood defiantly and unapologetically a black woman.

❋

At this stage in my life, my boyfriends were without exception black. After my quick "relationship" with Eddie Murphy, I became involved with a handsome singer from New Jersey who was a part of the New Kids on the Block entourage. His name was Andre, and he was the first black man with whom I had a deeply sensual relationship. He was generous and creative, and introduced me to lovemaking as a true art form. In his arms, I felt comfortable in my skin, our spirits united by our shared experiences as people of color. Although we didn't last, he set the standard for the type of men I dated for many years.

My new lovers epitomized the opposite of the European beauty standards I had been taught were best. They were also as diverse in their social standing as they were in appearance. The beautiful Jamaican club doorman who took me shopping for a replacement outfit on our first date, because he didn't like what I was wearing. The music mogul who owned his own label and was equally renowned for being a world-class modelizer (a man who exclusively dated fashion models). The married, A-list Hollywood actor who would later go on to win an Academy Award. Beautiful male models of every shade of brown and physical build.

But for all the attention that I received from men, I was frustrated by my inability to establish anything more than short-term sexual dalliances. I was desperately seeking stability within this menagerie of lovers who saw me as nothing more than a plaything with which to momentarily distract themselves from their real lives and careers. All that I wanted was for one of them to show me some compassion and interest that extended beyond the release my body provided from the stress of pursuing their life's purpose.

I didn't know that I could have a man who truly delighted in my heart and spirit before I ever let him touch my body. So instead I traded on the currency of my beauty and sexuality in a vain attempt to secure affection, hoping it would lead to more. Failing miserably every time.

By 1989, Stringfellow's was in decline, its glitzy interior and tutu-clad cocktail waitresses a dated homage to mid-1980s extravagance. Nightlife in New York was becoming even more elite as high-profile artists began joining in the revelry that took place throughout the city. This emerging fusion society of rap stars and downtown art legends like Jeff Koons and Victor Matthews would never be caught in a garish environment like Stringfellow's. On the recommendation of a friend, I began working at another club that had become the hot spot of the moment, M.K., owned by nightclub impresarios Serge Becker and Eric Goode. There, music moguls, all kinds of professionals, society figures, and models intermixed in its simultaneously austere, extravagant, and elegant environment.

The money was excellent, and on a good night I would bring home $300 just for carrying drinks and popping champagne bottles. But as fortunate as I was to work at this elite club, I still hated serving. The only way I could confidently interact with a patron would be if I had been drinking, but when I drank I couldn't keep my drink orders straight. After a couple of months of anxiety-laden shifts, I requested that I be transferred to the coatroom, where once again I could hide from direct interaction.

In 1989 I met a woman who to this day remains one of my closest friends. Carol Ingram and I had met earlier that year and had quickly become inseparable. Despite the age difference between us (she was twenty years older), we revelled in each other's company. She became a maternal surrogate, and I, her daughter. As usual, I was on the verge of eviction due to nonpayment of rent. Carol, always the problem solver, found a friend who paid the back rent and moved in while I moved onto the couch of my friend Belinda, a coworker of mine at M.K., who had agreed to let me stay rent-free with her and her roommates while I got my life together. After living in the apartment my grandmother had secured for nine short months, I was couch surfing.

Belinda was a stunning, chocolate-skinned woman ten years older than me. She was signed to Elite Model Management, and had grown up on the tough streets of Baltimore. Belinda was the first person to check me on my use of the "n-word"; unlike before when I used it as a pejorative, I had taken to saying "nigga" as a show of solidarity. Many of the people I knew used it, and I ignorantly went along with them. One night I was recalling a story about a man that worked at M.K., saying, "Belinda, can you believe that nigga thinks he can get away with this shit?" Shooting me a withering look, she spent the next ten minutes lecturing me on the history of the word and how it would not be said "in her house." Shamed, I stopped using the term immediately. This wouldn't be our only run-in, and after a few weeks I moved in with Carol's friend Glenda. I had also moved on from my job at M.K., next working as a server at the world-famous Rainbow Room, thanks to my new roommate.

I had lost my previous job due to my tendency to call in sick for my shifts because of my constant hangovers. I knew my drinking wasn't normal. But it was the only thing that kept my pain, so long buried, away from the surface of my consciousness. Each morning after a particularly rough night, I would wake up and vow never to drink again. And then within hours I would be back at it. At one point I even attended a recovery meeting to see if they could help me quit, but I walked out halfway through because I couldn't identify with the attendees. They were all middle-aged white men, sorrowful creatures who shared how they had lost everything in their lives due to drinking and were now fighting to get things back "one day at a time." At nineteen, I believed I was too young to be a "real" alcoholic. Besides, I wasn't willing to give up drinking until after I was married and had the requisite champagne toast with my husband.

It was now November of 1989 and I had been living in New York City for a little over sixteen months. During this time, I had lived in six apartments and held at least the same number of jobs.

Like many heterosexual young women without self-esteem, family support, discernible job skills, or financial stability, I wanted nothing more than to find a man who would help secure my life. Unfortunately, over the past year and a half I had only succeeded in becoming a jump off (A.K.A., occasional consort) of various celebrities.

In fact, years later, I would look back on this time and realize that I did not like the woman I had become. After I dumped Andrew to "date" Eddie Murphy, I was courted by throngs of celebrity men enchanted by my appearance. Many of these men's best assets were their looks, power, or wealth. Instead of focusing on their characters as intently as I did their big names and big dollars, I chose to overlook behaviors in them that I would never have accepted in a "regular" guy. This was of course shallow, but the Universe punished me for my superficiality. In exchange for choosing the external over the internal, I received shoddy treatment from these highly-coveted men.

It came to a point where if a man couldn't afford to buy an expensive bottle of champagne during our date, or take me out to the most expensive restaurants in town, I lost interest. I wanted extraordinary power, or beauty, or fame in my lovers. I thought these things would heal me, making me powerful and whole. Seeking a panacea externally only led me to avoid building myself up from inside out, making me vulnerable to being used by the very people I thought would save me.

Yet, as low as my self-esteem was, and as horrible as this cycle became, I would only play this game to a certain degree. I often shied away from the most famous men who chased me—and there were many—at the final moment of conquest, sensing that I would just become one more pretty young thing, used and discarded. I wanted more.

But, although I was considered beautiful, I was not stable enough for anyone to take me seriously. I was about to give up on my dream of finding my own Prince Charming, when someone I thought was the perfect man entered into my life and irrevocably changed it forever.

Keith Diamond in the recording studio while producing
Mick Jagger's *Primitive Cool* album, circa 1987.

CHAPTER ELEVEN

Keith Diamond was a Grammy Award–winning music producer that I had met a year earlier at the China Club through his friend, the one-hit-wonder Johnny Kemp. Although we had exchanged numbers, I wasn't interested because, honestly, I thought I could do better.

At the time, I was being pursued by men who were more successful, more attractive, or both. It wasn't until almost a year later that I decided to give him a call, mainly out of boredom. We spoke for a few minutes before he suggested that we meet for dinner, to which I gladly agreed. I was just coming off the heels of being dumped by a male model who didn't approve of my happy-go-lucky ways and needed the company.

Keith was a charming dinner companion. He exuded confidence, but more important had all the trappings I was seeking at that time. Keith was ferried all over Manhattan by a car service, owned multiple houses, and could pick up the tab for group dinners after being welcomed eagerly at the most exclusive restaurants in town.

Over the next several weeks, I became more and more enchanted by his worldliness and gentle demeanor. By Sil Lai standards, I took things slow, and didn't sleep with him until after we had dated for a couple of months.

Our relationship was consummated in a suite at Le Parker Méridien hotel that Keith was occupying while his new apartment was being renovated. We'd been kissing on the couch when he removed the hat he always wore. In fact, I had never seen him without it. I chalked it up to a style statement similar to the way the rapper LL Cool J always kept his head covered. But I was momentarily shaken when I saw what was underneath.

Keith, it turned out, was completely bald, save a fluffy fringe circling the dome of his head. It immediately became clear that I had no idea how old he really was. Keith's face was round and full, a result of his portly stature, plus his Trinidadian roots with a Chinese grandmother on one side. With a hat covering his bare head, he looked quite young.

On one of our first dates I had asked him his age; however, he evaded the question.

"How old do you think I am?" Keith asked.

"Thirty?"

"Well, if that's what you think, that's what I am." He laughed. Later I would discover that Keith was actually thirty-nine, nearly two decades older than me.

Now, some say that "age ain't nothing but a number," but looking back I wince at the power imbalance our age difference represented. Keith rationalized it by saying, as so many men do: "You're so mature for your age."

I didn't realize then that this was a common line used by older men to pick up younger women. Tell a young woman she's smart, or mature, to boost her ego and it is almost guaranteed to remove any reservations about the age disparity. After all, what young, naïve girl wouldn't be flattered that someone close to your parents' age considered you their equal?

Had I known his true age when we met, I probably wouldn't ever have gone out with Keith. But by the time I saw his bald head, it didn't matter. By now I was hopelessly in love. As we lay in bed together following our first tryst, he whispered in my ear the words I had been longing to hear for my whole life from a man who represented everything my father wasn't:

"I love you, Sil Lai."

"I love you, too" was my grateful reply.

Keith was mature, successful, intelligent—all the qualities I had been searching for in a man. And he apparently loved me, in spite of myself. Nuzzled in his arms, I felt safe for the first time. After years of instability, I finally had my knight in shining armor who would save me from the big, dangerous world that swallowed up young women who lacked protective male familial figures. He turned out to be one of the biggest miscalculations of my life.

Although we had only been officially a couple for a few weeks, I thought our relationship was rock solid based upon our mutual declarations of love. Without any prodding, I called the men I had been either dating or talking to over the past few months (including the A-list Hollywood actor) and told them I was off the market. I even called my grandma and told her that I had finally found true love.

I would come to learn that love is a subjective term. After months of daily phone calls, three days after we consummated our relationship Keith suddenly didn't call at all. Now, in 1989, there were no cell phones, only pagers and pay phones. The only way you could track a person down was to actually go out and find them. So I took a cab that I couldn't afford to the China Club in the hopes of finding Keith, but he was nowhere to be found. Instead, I ended up striking up a conversation with a man named Nile Rodgers.

Nile was an incredibly successful music producer with a string of monster hit records with artists like Madonna, the B-52s,

David Bowie, and Duran Duran. After an hour or so of talking
by screaming over the club's music, he asked if I wanted to grab
breakfast at a quieter spot around the corner. We ended up chatting into the early hours of the morning at a 24-hour diner, largely
in part because his company distracted me from thinking about
what Keith might have been up to that night.

I wasn't interested in Nile in "that way," but I thought he
was a funny, interesting, and cool dude who would make a good
friend. At the end of our breakfast, we exchanged phone numbers
and promised to keep in touch. His driver took me back to Glenda's apartment, where I collapsed into a fitful sleep. I may have
made a new friend, but my mission to locate my boyfriend had
failed.

The next morning, I called Keith, hoping for an explanation
for his disappearance. He sidestepped my inquiry by putting the
focus on me.

"So how was your night?" he asked. The tone of his voice was
falsely cheerful.

"Oh, it was cool. I went to the China Club . . ." He cut me off
midsentence.

"I *know*, Sil Lai. I know you were there, and I know you left
with Nile."

"We just had breakfast around the corner . . . nothing happened!" I protested.

"I have people *everywhere*, Sil Lai. Just because I'm not there
doesn't mean I don't know what you're up to! I can't believe you
would do this. Of all the people in the world, you had to leave
with *Nile*? NILE?"

I wondered why he was so upset. His words so accusatory. It
wasn't as if I had done something wrong. In fact, he was the one
who had vanished, and still hadn't answered for it.

"Keith. I don't know why you're so upset . . ."

"Of course you don't. How could you? Why should I expect you to understand?" he said contemptuously. "Let me spell it out for you. I'm a black Grammy Award–winning music producer. So is Nile. Do you know how rare that is? Do you? And my *girl-friend* is having breakfast with my main competition."

As he continued his tirade, I was amazed at his hubris. I mean, Keith had won a Grammy for his song with Billy Ocean, "Suddenly," in 1984 and had gone on to work with big names like Mick Jagger, Sheena Easton, and Michael Bolton since then. But Nile really wasn't his competition. To be quite frank, Nile was on a totally different level. Keith's most recent albums, although with big names, barely made the charts.

"I think we should take a break . . ." he began.

I felt my stomach drop. Panicked, I pleaded for a second chance.

"Keith. I love you. I don't know Nile. I don't have to know him. I promise I'll never speak to him again, okay? Baby, I would never cheat on you. I had no idea you would be so upset. I promise I'll take care of this. I'm going to call him right now and let him know. Please don't do this."

He issued a terse, "Fine. But don't let me find out that you're spending time with any men again, or else it's over between us. Do you understand?"

"Yes, Keith. I understand. I'll take care of this right away," I said, hands trembling as I hung up the phone.

My pulse was racing. In the space of a little over a month Keith had become my entire world, and somehow I had thrown our entire relationship in jeopardy, because of an innocent break-fast with a man I barely knew.

I fumbled around in my purse and found the cocktail napkin with Nile's number. My hands were still shaking as I punched the numbers into the phone.

After a few rings, he answered.

"Hello?"

"Hi. Nile?" I inquired.

"Yeah, this is Nile."

"This is Sil Lai. The girl you met last night at the China Club."

"Oh, heeeeyyyy! How's it goin' . . ."

I cut him off.

"Um, my boyfriend isn't happy that I had breakfast with you last night, so I'm not going to be in touch with you again. Please don't call me, either. I'm sorry. I don't want to do this, but if I don't I'm going to lose him, and I can't have that happen."

"Uhhhh . . . it was just breakfast, Sil Lai."

"I know, I know. But he's mad because he's a music producer, too, and felt disrespected."

"Your boyfriend's a producer? What's his name?" Nile asked.

"Keith Diamond."

"Keith Diamond is your boyfriend?" Chuckling lightly, he said, "Okay. Whatever you want. Take care of yourself," and hung up the phone.

As I placed the receiver back into the cradle, my face burned with embarrassment. I couldn't believe what I had just done. I had allowed myself to be intimidated by my boyfriend into making a humiliating call to a man I barely knew simply to placate his ego. Somehow, in spite of all of my efforts, I had fallen in love with a man as controlling and overbearing as my dad. Despite vowing to never let this happen, I had become Mom.

❀

Just as quickly as we came together, our "love" began to unravel. The change in Keith seemed to happen overnight. He had always been slightly paternalistic, but I had chalked that up to our age gap. But his behavior shifted from paternal to increasingly demanding and critical. We had only been dating a short while when he shut down my social life.

"You need to stay out of nightclubs, Sil Lai. And off the lips of everyone, too," he insisted. Which was puzzling, since we had met at a club, a place he still liked to frequent—just without me.

I was next instructed to find a new job, since "Keith Diamond's girlfriend can't be a cocktail waitress." So I quit my job at the Rainbow Room, telling my boss that "my boyfriend thinks I should get an office job," and registered with a temp agency. This was a serious pay cut, but one I was willing to take because in Keith's mind an office receptionist making $8 an hour was more respectable than a server earning two or three times that amount.

Without his asking, I stopped drinking entirely. This, out of all my actions, was a testament to my commitment to our relationship. The longest I had gone without drinking was nine days when I was seventeen years old. Still, it was a sacrifice I made willingly because he was a teetotaler and I didn't want to give him any additional ammunition to use against me.

Yet in spite of all of my efforts to solidify our relationship, he continued to slip away. His affection toward me cooled with each passing day, while I did backflips trying to regain his favor. It didn't matter what I did. I could feel his boredom begin to permeate our interactions, then his judgment and wariness. Just weeks before, he couldn't wait to spend time with me. Now, I could barely get him to respond to my calls. I had made the terrible mistake of making him the center of my world, and now his erratic behavior was throwing me off my axis. This is what happens in relationships when a person doesn't have a strong sense of self. We give away our power in the hopes that this will gain our beloved's favor, not realizing how incredibly unhealthy a dynamic this creates.

I didn't want to lose Keith. He was the first "real" man to ever "love" me—but suddenly he didn't want me. His behavior touched on my deep, primal fear of abandonment. The more I tried to please him, the more he pulled away. Just as when I was a little girl, I wracked my brain trying figure out what was so wrong with me that he was avoiding my company. Why was I so inherently unlovable? What was I doing that caused the people I loved the most to leave me?

During this rocky time, Keith chose to spend New Year's Eve in Atlantic City—without me, announcing, "I'm going to watch Sheena perform with my friend Dane and his girlfriend." Sheena, as in Easton. A woman he had told me was his former lover. I was crestfallen, but tried not to show it. "I'll try and call you later to wish you Happy New Year," he said.

"Okay" was my quiet response. I was bereft after we hung up. My roommate Glenda tried to console me, or more pointedly, tried to talk some sense into me.

"Sil Lai, don't you see what he's doing? He doesn't love you. If he did, he'd be with you tonight instead of letting you sit here with me."

Her words just upset me further. While I didn't want to admit it, deep down I knew that what she was saying was true. Still, I held out hope that his behavior was just a phase that would soon pass. It didn't occur to me that it was probably best that our relationship ended. But he had said those magic words, "I love you," and I was holding onto the promise behind them with every fiber of my being.

"Come out with me tonight," she offered. "Rudolf has opened up a new club in the old Wetlands building and they're doing a New Year's celebration. Don't sit here by the phone, girl. He ain't thinking about you, and you need to stop thinking about him."

The last thing in the world I wanted to do was go out. I would have much rather preferred to stay under the covers on the couch, feeling sorry for myself while waiting for his call. But the more I thought about Keith ditching me to celebrate New Year's Eve at a performance by a former lover, the more incensed I became. So in the end Glenda prevailed, and we headed out into the cold to the latest hotspot of the legendary nightclub king, Rudolf, of Studio 54, Danceteria, and Mars fame.

The night was a flop. Poor Glenda would have been better off going out without me. I was completely distracted, worried that Keith would try to call and I wouldn't be there to answer. That would then be just one more reason for him to leave me. I went through the motions of providing her company, but after a couple of hours we returned home. Of course, Keith didn't call that night. Or the night after that. When we finally did speak, it was three days later. There was no formal breakup announcement, but I knew it was over between us.

At the same time that Keith dumped me, Glenda kicked me out. She was always very generous with her belongings, and let me borrow her accessories when I went out. When I lost one of her pieces of costume jewelry, I tried to replace it with a less expensive version (simply because it was all I could afford). The jewelry was the excuse. It wasn't the real reason why she was kicking me out. The truth was that for two months I had slept on her couch, drained her home bar, and couldn't maintain a job. That, combined with my tendency to avoid dealing with my problems by flinging myself headlong into another whirlwind romance, led her to the conclusion that I wasn't going to change. She was right. It would take many, many years for that to happen. So I don't blame her now for the final showdown that occurred.

Angry at my attempt to replace her jewelry with a knockoff, Glenda told me that I had to leave her apartment immediately, and that I would only be able to get my things once I replaced her necklace with an exact replica. I was being put out with only the clothes on my back. While I felt bad for losing the jewelry, I also knew that her holding my belongings hostage wasn't right either. Instead of leaving as she requested, I made a dash to the bedroom to grab my things. Alex, a houseguest who had started staying with her the week before, lunged at me. He and Glenda grabbed me, and pushed me out the door. Alex was what was then called a "drag queen," who loved to walk back and forth in the style of a runway model while wearing his size-13 heels and a silk robe. He was so good at it that he eventually started teaching it at modeling agencies in Europe. Alex was tall and thin as a rail, with a rather plain face and large, expressive eyes that would bulge out of their sockets when he was trying to make a point. But as wiry as he was, he possessed decent strength, and between him and Glenda clawing and tugging, they were able to successfully get me out of the apartment.

Rushing downstairs into the frigid January cold, I went to a pay phone and called 911. Within forty-five minutes a police officer had arrived at the apartment to help me retrieve my belongings.

"But she owes me money for my necklace!" Glenda insisted, as Alex stood by, staring me down.

The officer responded, "Ma'am, you can't keep her personal belongings as collateral for any outstanding money. She is allowed to take her things and if you want the necklace replaced, you can take that up in small claims court."

Glenda seethed as she watched me rush about the apartment, gathering my belongings into my two suitcases. Within the span of fifteen minutes, I was gone and headed downtown to stay on the couch of our mutual friend Carol. That was the last time that I would see Glenda or Alex for over a decade. The next time I saw Alex, he had resurfaced as Miss J. Alexander, a judge and runway coach on *America's Next Top Model*. Alex attaining professional heights by teaching young aspiring models how to sashay down the runway on television was proof that *anything* could be commoditized in our culture.

It was the first week of January in 1990. I was jobless, sleeping on the couch of another friend, and had just lost the love of my life. I didn't think things could get worse, but of course, they did.

❖

For the past week I had been waking up feeling nauseated in spite of not drinking. Plus, my period was late. Frightened, I called my friend Eva, a law student at NYU, and asked her to keep me company while I went to Planned Parenthood for a pregnancy test. Within an hour it was confirmed: I was carrying the child of a man who had unceremoniously dumped me without any conversation or explanation.

Bidding Eva goodbye, I returned back to Carol's apartment and shared the news with her and her husband, Emmanuel.

"I don't know what to do!" I exclaimed. "He isn't talking to me."

Emmanuel chimed in, "Sil Lai, you need to tell him immediately. He has to know."

The last thing in the world I wanted to do was to call Keith. It had been over ten days since we had spoken and I had no idea how to approach a conversation with a man who had zero interest in speaking to me.

The next day, I called his apartment and he picked up the phone.

"Keith?" I asked. "I need to talk to you."

"I'm getting ready to go someplace. I can't talk right now" was his terse response. But this conversation couldn't wait.

"I'm not trying to waste your time," I started, cautiously. "I know you have to leave . . . but I need to speak to you."

"Sil Lai, it's gonna have to wait for another time. I've got to go. People are waiting for me."

I knew that if I didn't speak to him then it would become increasingly difficult, as he would start screening his calls. So I just blurted it out.

"I'm pregnant."

He laughed.

"So, what do you expect me to say, let's get married?"

"Of course not! I'm not asking if we should get married or not. I'm asking you what we are going to do about this."

"What do you mean 'we'? I don't even know if that baby is mine."

"But Keith! I love you! You're the only man that I've been with during this time. How could you think that about me? You said that you loved me . . . Why are you acting like this?"

"Sil Lai. I have to go." *Click.* Dial tone.

Keith's reaction wasn't at all what I expected. I anticipated shock. Anger. Disappointment. Confusion. Not laughter and dismissal.

Emmanuel was sitting on the couch next to me. He had heard everything. Collapsing into his arms, I buried my head on his chest and wailed as the tears flooded my face and his shirt.

"He doesn't love me! He doesn't care! I'm alone. ALOOOON-NNE!" I wailed. The cruelty of his response hit me in the solar plexus. "All I ever wanted was for someone to love me. That's all. Someone. He told me he loved me! Why would he say it if it wasn't true?"

"He's an asshole, Sil Lai. You are loved. Carol and I love you. Your friends love you . . ." But as he spoke, his words droned into unintelligible sentences, overshadowed by the sheer enormity of the terror enveloping me.

And that is when my concept of love shattered. At nineteen years old, I learned the hard way that to some people, words are meaningless. Simple utterances that spring forth from the throat in the pursuit of a goal, be that a business deal, or to ease the opening of a woman's legs, or a man's wallet. In my first experience with "love," I had learned that seemingly adult men will lie to young girls just to sleep with them. They were willing to say whatever they were feeling in the moment without caring about how their words could destroy another's spirit.

This loss highlighted how my move to New York City had proven to be an epic failure. I was a high school dropout with a GED and a ninth-grade education, an alcoholic wannabe–fashion model who had come to the city that never sleeps, and fallen into its hypnotic embrace. Like a mariner in Greek mythology, I had thrown myself into a churning sea of false hopes and iffy dreams, lured by the city's siren song into believing I would easily reinvent myself, a woman freed from her past. A woman who could soar above her flaws and failures to eventually become *somebody*. Instead, I was another casualty in this city of a million wiped-out wishes. There were so many people searching to find relevance or, at the very least, deliverance from the place whence they came. I would come to understand that more people were destroyed by the city than saved.

Strangely, my life was mirroring Daisy's in so many ways— this in spite of her not being in my life for nearly fifteen years. Somehow, through DNA or some unseen spiritual thread that connected me to her, I had managed to replicate an almost identical life pattern. Like her, I had a drinking problem. Like her, I didn't finish high school. Like her, I suffered from incredible mood swings, and a reactive temper. Like her, I had fled my father's home to fulfill a fantasy of what I believed life could be like free from the bondage of my past. And like her, I had become

pregnant by a man around the same time that I had stopped dating another one—the married, A-list actor.

While I was 99 percent sure that the life forming in my womb
was Keith's, there was the thinnest sliver of a chance that the actor
could be the father due to the closeness in timing of my last liason
with the actor and my first with Keith. However, unlike when
Daisy became pregnant with me, there was no man waiting in
the wings to claim me as his wife. Outside of that, our lives were
almost perfect mirrors. Broken ones, in fact. Within the frame,
in each remaining shard of glass, I saw how my distorted vision
of womanhood had been imprinted in me by my birthright as
Daisy's daughter, spanning time and distance to grip me in a similar pattern of destructiveness.

For me, love, pain, and longing were inextricably linked
from the beginning of my short life. The love I had as child for
my mother and father, as well as my love for Keith, were both
streaked with abuse. My parents provided the mold of what love
looked like, and Keith picked up where they left off. Of course,
I didn't see him or our relationship in this way at the time. But I
would come to see that, while Keith never laid a hand on me, he
did emotionally, verbally, and psychologically violate me.

Coincidentally, a few days after I told him I was pregnant, I
attended a Knicks basketball game with my girlfriend Ivelka and
a friend of hers who I later learned had previously dated Keith.
Through Ivelka, her friend passed along a warning to me: "Tell
your friend to watch out for Keith. He likes to hit women." I
didn't believe her at the time, thinking instead that she was just
a jealous ex with an axe to grind. When I look back at how he
used and spit out teenaged-me as a middle-aged man, I can (along
with his controlling behaviors) now see that he had the character
traits of a man capable of physically harming a woman he dated
over time.

I soon realized that staying at Carol's in my current state wasn't an option. She and her husband shared a small L-shaped studio and there wasn't room for a third body, let alone a baby. Without a job or home prospect in sight, I packed my things, bought a one-way ticket, and headed to the only place where I knew I could stay—my sister May Lai's house.

Eight months pregnant, saying goodbye to my host "Mom"
Kay Clarke, Santa Barbara, CA, August 1990.

CHAPTER TWELVE

$\mathcal{E}$VEN THOUGH SHE WAS HERSELF INCREDIBLY UNSTABLE, I'D MADE the decision to call May Lai for help as I had no other options. As I pulled up to my sister's cottage, I marveled at how quickly my freewheeling life in New York City had come to an end. Despite the best of intentions, I'd frittered away my dreams through a series of bad choices. I had spent only eighteen months living on my own before everything came to a screeching halt.

May Lai didn't hesitate to open her home to me, which wasn't a big surprise. She was prone to taking in strays of all kinds, be they pets or people. One infamous story about her generosity involved the time she was living in Orlando with a boyfriend who managed an apartment complex. Finding a homeless person in the neighborhood, she took pity on his plight, and created a makeshift sleeping area for him in the building's laundry facility. Much to her chagrin, her boyfriend evicted his new "tenant" when some of the other residents took exception to navigating around him while washing their clothes.

By seventeen May Lai had made it to California, and was living in Santa Barbara of all places. Somehow she managed to find yet another boyfriend to take care of her, and was living a relatively quiet life in this small, artsy town.

Their small bungalow-style house with its red clay roof was

within walking distance of the Presidio, the historic area of the town, which was good since I didn't have a car to get around. I did not have my own bedroom, per se, as her boyfriend had paying tenants who occupied all the other rooms. Instead, I slept on a small cot in a multipurpose back room that also housed their washer and dryer. Still, I was thankful. I had a place to stay and looked forward to spending time with my younger sister, whom I had not seen much of since I left Florida.

The culture in Santa Barbara was a shock to my recently-acculturated New York City sensibilities. People wore colors, for God's sake, and walked around in flip-flops. The town was a hodgepodge of wealthy, silver-haired residents mixed with artists who seemed to be leftover from a Grateful Dead tour. City blocks were interspersed with cafés, elegant art galleries, and head shops where you could buy tie-dyed shirts, Jimi Hendrix posters, and ornate bong pipes.

Unfortunately, my reunion with May Lai and our shared living arrangement was short-lived. Two weeks after my arrival, she met a man from Los Angeles visiting Santa Barbara for the weekend. He invited her to attend a party with him later that night in LA, and she ran off with him, returning briefly only to grab her belongings a few weeks later. May Lai's boyfriend Eric was a recovering alcoholic who had been trying to manage my sister's heavy drinking. She had shared with me how tired she was of his controlling behavior, so she used this latest man to break free.

Eric had only agreed to let me stay with them because I was her sister. Humiliated and angry over losing her to another man, he gave me two weeks to find a new place. I had come to Santa Barbara with the hope of finding some sort of comfort and stability, yet was again facing homelessness.

The precariousness of my situation, especially considering my pregnancy, was not lost upon me. While many women in my situation, faced with the same bleak circumstances, may have had an easy decision on their hands, I wrestled with whether to continue my pregnancy. Having grown up in a nonreligious household, I didn't carry any guilt or fear about the "sacredness of unborn life." In fact, I had always assumed that if I ever were to become pregnant, I would simply have an abortion. I honestly could not understand why the pro-life movement was so violently opposed to a woman's right to choose. To me, abortions were an easy fix to an issue that could derail a woman's life forever. I considered them to be a minor outpatient medical procedure. It was only when actually faced with the choice that I discovered the complexity involved with making such a decision.

One of Eric's roommates, a woman named Sophia, took interest in my situation and offered to help me figure out my next steps. Petite and possessing an abundant head of curly brown hair, she was the sympathetic ear that I so desperately needed. After listening to my story, she advised me to terminate my pregnancy—advice which I found to be unnerving, because she also told me she was unable to have children due to having a botched abortion back in her homeland of Italy. Still filled with reservations, I reluctantly agreed to let her take me to the local Planned Parenthood to look into the procedure.

As we pulled into the short driveway in front of the clinic in Sophia's small red pickup, I was surprised to find a small throng of protesters holding up various-sized makeshift signs. Some of them were quite graphic: photos of embryos and fetuses on vividly colored poster boards highlighted with large, black marker writing.

As Sophia slowed down to enter the parking lot, a roundish woman in bright floral prints leaned toward my window. She extended two colorful pamphlets toward me.

"Get away from her!" Sophia called out to the stranger, admonishing me, "Sil Lai, don't take that . . ."

Perturbed at her bossiness, I countered with, "Why not? I've always wanted to see what these pro-lifers are about."

I reached out the car window and took the brochures.

"God bless you," the protestor said, smiling as she walked away.

What I saw inside the pamphlet gave me extreme pause. Interspersed with prose about the sacredness of life were statistics about the developmental milestones of fetuses.

"Did you know that an eleven-week-old fetus has fingernails and a heartbeat?" I asked Sophia.

"Sil Lai, that stuff is designed to get you to doubt . . ."

"To doubt my decision? They haven't done that . . . I haven't been sure of what to do since I found out I was pregnant."

Sophia pleaded, "Don't let this change your decision . . ."

"Sophia, *this* isn't my decision . . . this is *your* decision. I can't do this. I love Keith too much to do this . . . I just can't!"

"I was just trying to help you . . ."

"Well, thanks for your help, but I've made up my mind. I am keeping this baby."

When I called my friends back in New York and told them that I was moving forward with my pregnancy, they were disappointed. But the person most disappointed was Keith, who hung up on me when I shared the update. If I had any doubt about his position before this call, I was now crystal clear. I was completely on my own.

❖

The clock was ticking fast, and I knew Eric wasn't going to give me a reprieve. I needed a plan. Quick. Asking my parents for help wasn't an option. In all honesty, it actually never occurred to me to go to them given how vocal they'd been about their desire that I move out of their house while I was still living at home. Besides,

Mom had remarried, Dad was busy creating a new life with his latest girlfriend, and the last thing either wanted was for their wayward child to return—pregnant, no less. After mulling it over for a day, I set out to find a government agency that would help me.

After making a call to the local social services office, I was dismayed to learn that the State of California would only provide financial assistance to pay for an abortion or benefits to help support your child after you had given birth. Undeterred, I began flipping through the yellow pages for pregnancy counseling, seeking another option.

The majority of the ads were for abortion services. Out of all the listings, only two offered counseling to women who wanted to carry their child to term. Both were Christian-based agencies, but I would not let that deter me from seeking their help. If conservative right-to-lifers were the only people I could go to, then so be it. Beggars can't be choosers.

I selected one of the two and thought to myself, *Here goes nothing*. A friendly female voice answered my call. I gave her a brief overview of my circumstances, and said I was looking for help. She told me she had an appointment available that afternoon, and invited me to meet with her to discuss my options.

The counseling center was housed in an attractive Craftsman-style home on the edge of the historic district of Santa Barbara. Pressing the doorbell, I waited a few moments before hearing footsteps approach the door. When it opened, I found myself looking at a very thin-faced, petite white woman. She introduced herself and extended her hand.

"Thank you so much for coming by. I'm Sally, the woman you spoke with on the phone earlier."

She ushered me into the cozy office, where a periwinkle-blue sofa featuring an array of floral pillows beckoned. Sally motioned for me to sit down.

"So tell me why you are here today," she said.

Over the next twenty minutes, I recounted the situation I was currently facing. She didn't say much, only interrupting me from time to time to nod her head and say, "Uh-huh." Her presence was strangely calming, her demeanor beneficent. It was such a relief to speak to someone with experience in dealing with my situation, someone who could potentially help me. By the time I got to the part about the crisis surrounding my current living situation, I noticed how intently she was watching me. It was as if she was sizing me up.

"And my ex-boyfriend won't do anything to help me, and he can!" I exclaimed. "He told me he loved me, but now he won't even talk to me!"

Sally then began to tell me about the various services they offered, which included religious and pregnancy counseling.

"Well, do you know of anyone that can help me find a place to live?" I interjected, hoping she would refer me to another Christian agency. "I don't want to go back to New York and be around the same people as before, but I don't have anywhere else to go."

Sally paused for a moment and then took a deep breath. "I know we just met, but you seem to be a really nice girl. Right now I have another teen mom named May who is staying with me and my daughter; however, there is another bedroom available."

My eyes widened as she continued, "I would like to speak to May about you coming to live with us. It shouldn't be a problem, but I want to run it by her just the same."

Tears welled up in my eyes. This woman was willing to do for me what my child's father and my own parents wouldn't, or couldn't. I stood up and shook her hand, thanking her profusely before making the mile walk back to Eric's house to wait. The next morning, she phoned and said that May was fine with me moving in. Within a week, I was ensconced in my own bedroom in a beautiful home in the Montecito area of Santa Barbara.

I spent my days lounging around her house, sharing the responsibilities of light household chores, and writing letters to Keith that I never sent. Sundays were spent in Sally's house of worship, a small Presbyterian church not far from where she lived that was housed in a Mission-style building. I had never been very religious; however, I immersed myself in reading the Bible and Christian life. The church's fundamentalist teachings gave me much-needed strength and hope to cope with my out-of-control situation. I was so committed to the lifestyle that at one point, I even went away on an all-women's weekend church retreat.

This was a very peaceful time, save the increasingly frequent arguments between May and me. Our arguments continued to escalate until Sally told me that I would have to find another place to stay only a month after I had moved in. In another stroke of luck, one of the members of Sally's church was also a supporter of the pro-life movement, a woman named Kay whom I had met at the women's retreat. I called and told her that Sally was asking me to leave. She offered to help, but made it clear that she would have to talk it over with her family. After discussing it with her husband and daughter, they opened their home to me. They, too, lived in Montecito, in a rambling house trapped in 1960s décor that lay at the foot of the Santa Ynez Mountains. Despite its spaciousness, their home only had two bedrooms, so they converted their dining room into my makeshift bedroom.

I spent the remainder of my pregnancy attending secretarial school, learning basic office skills that would enable me to leave waitressing behind, praying, and reading the Bible. My school expenses were covered by grants and student loans, and my nominal living expenses were paid for by social services.

My time in Santa Barbara provided me with a stable living situation and a break from the instability of my drinking, as I had ceased all alcohol consumption upon learning of my pregnancy. Instead of chasing parties and men, I focused on learning how to type and developing a relationship with the Lord.

As beautiful and peaceful as my surroundings were, I felt completely out of place. It was too quiet and reminiscent of the hometown I had done everything in my power to escape. New York City had given me a year and a half completely immersed in black community and culture. Now I was suddenly living in a town that had a black population of less than two percent. This lack of racial diversity pained me terribly. Separated from New York and its dazzling cultural melting pot, I was hell-bent on continuing to dive into my blackness.

I kept up my reading on black history with books from the local library. The more information I took in, the more compelled I felt to share what I was learning with anyone who would give me an ear—irrespective of whether they were interested. Subtlety has never been my strong suit. True to my nature, in this case I soon boorishly anointed myself as Montecito's de facto guest lecturer on all things related to black culture.

I was foolish. In retrospect, my audacity in shoving the "sins of the white race" in the faces of a white family I was dependent on is embarrassing. But my intentions were not born from a need to punish these people, but from a desire to remain connected to the black identity I had just recently embraced. There was nothing about them that screamed racism, or white guilt. They were truly kind, sincere Christians who happened to be white and took a chance on a strange girl in order to give her and her child a shot at life. Sadly, I was all too willing to alienate my benefactors— simply because I prioritized my needs over theirs.

Intellectually, I recognized their difference from the whites I had grown up with; but another sad level to this story is that my experiences of being taunted for my skin color in Winter Park still haunted me, tainting my interactions with my hosts, regardless of their compassionate characters. I couldn't stop discussing racial inequality and trying to "cure" them of their white privilege. With the subtlety of a sledgehammer, I'd pass off my newfound knowledge with the assuredness of a tenured Africana studies professor, even though my knowledge of black history was superficial at best.

Plus, while my living situation was the most supportive and stable of my brief life, Santa Barbara was not the environment in which I wanted to raise my child. The town was too white and close in culture to my hometown. The class divisions were marked, and I hated dealing with the constant suspicion that they were only helping me because I was "acceptably black," due to my light skin and "exotic" appearance. Always sensitive to power imbalances, I noticed how I was treated differently than the other blacks in the community. None of them (that I was aware of) had wealthy white patrons willing to help them carry, give birth to, and raise their illegitimate children. The awareness that I was an "acceptable Negro" compared to the few others that lived in the area was troubling. There was no way I could remain in a city that was so similar in many ways to Winter Park, Florida.

Additionally, I secretly harbored hope that Keith would take me back once our child was born and he recognized his mistake in dumping me. Our contact during my time in California was sporadic. He called once a month and we would speak for an hour or so. Between these calls, I lived in suspended animation, waiting for the times when Kay, my host mom, would tell me that Keith was on the phone.

Still a child myself, I naïvely believed that Keith's rejection of me was temporary. That once he saw me again and held his child in his arms, we would pick up from where we left off, and I would ultimately have the happy, financially stable home I had always dreamed of as a child.

For these reasons, I ignored the pleas of my surrogate family to stay with them after the birth of my son, and despite not having a job, hopped on a plane back to New York when I was eight months pregnant to sleep on the couch of my friend Ivelka's sisters' apartment. I wanted my child to be born in a city I loved. Besides, the writing was on the wall about my time in Santa Barbara with my foster family. Our relationship was increasingly strained due to my clashes with their fourteen-year-old daughter, Kim, who had branded me a "bitch." Apparently, my constant waxing about my glamorous life back in New York, combined with my nonstop proselytizing about white supremacy, was not appreciated.

Daisy and me, summer of 1997.

CHAPTER THIRTEEN

My son, Christian, was born two weeks late following inducement and twenty-nine hours of labor. Holding his tiny body in my arms, for the first time in my life I finally had someone I could call my own. A person into whom I could pour all of the love that I wished had been given to me. Peering into his cherubic face, I marveled in awe at his perfection. Of course, every mother says this, but he truly was the most beautiful creature I had ever seen.

My bond to this tiny human being was instantaneous. I knew our circumstances were less than ideal, but I was committed to doing everything within my power to ensure he had a better life than mine. This baby boy was going to know what it was like to be accepted and loved for all that he was and all that he could be. Not just because he was my son, but because he was living proof that I had not succumbed to the brainwashing of my youth.

My son was black. He was beautiful. He was mine.

The only dark moment that clouded this initial meeting between mother and child was the whiff of doubt I felt when the nurse handed him to me for the first time. Christian's skin was very light and his hair was not curly like I had expected. He had a small flattened tuft of fine, thin strands on the crown of his head and his skin had a slightly yellow cast to it. (I would later learn this was due to a mild case of jaundice.) Keith was brown-skinned and I was half-black. How was it possible that our son had such fair skin?

Several friends, including Carol, had come to visit us in the hospital.

"Carol, look at him," I said, motioning her over to me. "Why is he so light? He looks like me, but shouldn't his skin be darker?"

"Babies often grow into their skin color, Sil Lai. Plus, you never know which side of the family a child will take after. Your genes are strong, girl. It's like you spit him out!"

Secretly, I was disappointed. I had hoped my son's skin color would be deeper. At least that way he wouldn't have to live with the constant questioning of his racial identity. I wanted the African blood from Keith and my ancestors to release him from the curse of my racial ambiguity. Yet despite Carol's prediction, Christian's skin color never deepened to more than café au lait brown. He would never be confused for white, but he never became dark enough to assuage my fears about what his life would be like as a light-skinned male, which sounds crazy considering that statistically darker-skinned blacks are treated more harshly by society. At this stage in time, I was unaware of light-skin privilege. I guess it was because despite being lighter myself, I still experienced horrific racism.

Any reunion fantasies about Keith came crashing down when he visited his newborn son in the hospital. Seeing his child, holding him, and even naming him didn't change his attitude toward me or Christian. Keith continued living as if we had never known each other, let alone created a new life with me.

After a month off, I went back to work, leaving my newborn son in the care of a Colombian babysitter who lived down the hall. I struggled to support us on a meager receptionist's salary of $26,000 a year while Keith refused to contribute anything more than $150 for one well-baby doctor's visit. Total. It didn't bother him that his child's existence had been made possible in part through California's public assistance program, and now with the help of the good State of New York's WIC program.

After eight months, I realized the only way Keith was going to pay child support was if I took him to court. It was now that I was able to see how far he was willing to go to fight for something he believed in, which in this case was *not* being declared my son Christian's biological father. What should have taken six months to settle spread out into a court battle that took nearly four years to resolve due to a small flaw in the paternity test. This tiny glitch opened up a legal loophole surrounding the competency of the only lab licensed by the state at that time to do paternity tests—Roche Laboratories. When his eagle-eyed attorney noticed the inconsistency, it threw my entire case into legal limbo, and opened the door for the fight. Keith even hired Barry Scheck, the renowned DNA law expert, to refute the test results that clearly showed he was my son's father. In the end, I accepted the settlement he offered that was a fraction of what he would have had to pay if the lab had not made the error, because I was too exhausted to continue the fight.

Although I was torn, my lawyer assured me that this was the best course of action.

"I know it's hard to see this now, Sil Lai, but this is better for you and your son," he said. "Think about it. A man like this will only make your life miserable. Let him go and move on." As heartbroken as I was over Keith's continued refusal to be a part of his child's life, I took the settlement. My son's paternity had been proven through multiple tests; however, it was never established in court. As part of our agreement, Keith could continue to deny paternity, while I could continue to assert it. It didn't matter. After the case was settled, we would never speak to each other again.

Nearly five years after I had given birth to her brother, my daughter Amanda was born in 1995. Her father and I came together quickly in a relationship that, like the one I had with Keith, started with much promise, but quickly devolved into a five-year cycle of verbal, emotional, psychological, and physical abuse.

Nelson was an outgoing and personable model whom I'd met when on assignment in Dallas during the summer of 1992. After my failed attempt in New York, I was finally able to give my career another shot when I was signed to a respected agency in Miami Beach that had an outpost in Dallas. In the early '90s, South Beach was a strong fashion market due to its weather and the beautiful locations that were highly desirable to the city's largely European clientele. While never wildly successful, I managed to build an inconsistent career comprised mainly of catalog work for clients like J.C. Penney and Sears and runway shows in Milan, Italy. By contrast, Nelson had done reasonably well for himself (prior to us meeting) by regularly doing catalog work and even appearing in some campaigns, the most notable being a Guess jeans ad featuring the supermodel Anna Nicole Smith.

Nelson was physically beautiful, with the requisite chiseled facial features and build of a lightweight boxer. The only obvious quirk he had was a cartoonishly high-pitched voice that was better suited for the show *Looney Tunes* than a human being. He was of Dominican and black American descent, and when learning of his background my friends would tease me, saying that I needed to "leave those Caribbean and West Indian men alone." Little did I know how prescient their joking was, and how much suffering I could have avoided if I had taken their advice.

What drew us together was strong sexual chemistry, shared career goals, and our similar childhoods filled with abuse. Most men dragged their feet making a commitment to a relationship; however, he was willing to claim me as his girlfriend after one date.

Having no exposure to healthy relationships and "normal" dating behaviors, I didn't know that one of the warning signs of a potential abuser is their desire to solidify their bond with a partner as quickly as possible. Anyone who has ever bought a used car knows this fact: if the salesperson is rushing you through the process, it's generally because there is something wrong with the car. In my opinion, the same principle applies to people and relationships of all kinds.

Eventually my son and I would move in with Nelson in an efficiency apartment on Washington Avenue in South Beach. We didn't know each other well, but he was the first man since Keith who called me his girlfriend and accepted my son as his own. Having a steady boyfriend was of utmost importance to me for two reasons. The first was that it provided my son with a father figure and someone to help share the various responsibilities of parenthood. Those first two years of my son's life were hard for many reasons, financial reasons being just one of them.

Secondly, and probably of equal importance, was that through this relationship I was no longer a single black mother. I loathed the idea of being another statistic, a stereotype of black failure—a single black woman without a man in her (or her child's) life. So I accepted the first man who would have us, without stopping to consider why he so quickly "claimed" us both.

Nelson had been raised by his mother in a violent home filled with poverty and neglect. His background didn't turn me off; if anything, it softened my heart. Nelson's personal history of abuse made me want to wrap my own broken wings around him to prove that someone could love him unconditionally in spite of his past (which was of course a projection of what I wanted for myself).

Our whirlwind courtship had us both on such a high that we were envied by the network of friends who observed us together during the starry-eyed beginning of our courtship. I loved him fully and completely, confident that in return for my loyalty he would love me with the same intensity and tenderness. Yet no matter how mightily I endeavored to prove my devotion to him, I couldn't earn his trust. He was emotionally wary from the damage from his childhood, and had a latent hatred of women masked by his outgoing personality.

I made the mistake that so many broken people make, which is to focus on fixing someone else instead of themselves. The reward I received for trying to "fix" him? Nearly five years of abuse.

The constant rancor in our relationship caused wounds that led us into a pattern of regular breakups, during which time we might see other people. After a few weeks or months went by, invariably we would reunite and begin our dysfunctional dance all over again. Our longest time apart took place during the summer of 1994, when we had a huge blowout while both working overseas. Nelson was stationed in South Africa and I was working in Italy. His expectations of daily check-ins and endless accusations of infidelity were wearing me out.

In Italy, I was living in a *pensione* ("boardinghouse" in Italian) filled with models from around the globe. The last thing I wanted to deal with was his insecurity, so I cut things off with him and took up with Ismaele, a wealthy Italian businessman whom I'd met through one of my flatmates. With him, I was finally living the glamorous model life I had dreamed of for the past five years. Ismaele was the handsome, firstborn son of a business magnate, and our relationship immersed me in the sort of over the top, luxurious lifestyle usually only seen in the pages of *Town & Country* magazine. Our days were spent shopping, dining at the finest restaurants with his friends, yacht hopping, and traveling up and down the Amalfi coastline in his Cigarette Café Racer boat. Our home was a beautiful converted stable house on the land of his family's estate located an hour's drive from Milan. We had a maid, a chef, and his father's main house across the road had a swimming pool with a view that overlooked the rolling Italian hills, as well as its own chapel for worship.

When Nelson realized I had quickly replaced him, he made sure that our breakup was messy and public. In his bid to ruin my reputation, he faxed messages about his concern for my son's well being and my heavy drinking to my agencies in Milan, Dallas, and South Beach—documents that became the talk of the bookers. I was mortified. He did all he could to get me blacklisted from my agencies, and succeeded with at least one—his own agent in South Africa, who had recently taken me on for representation. Our breakup unfortunately coincided with editorial bookings I had confirmed with the South African editions of *ELLE* and *Glamour*, which would have provided me with magazine tear sheets that could have pushed my career to the next level. Knowing how vital these bookings were to me professionally, Nelson gave the South African agency an ultimatum, stating that if they kept me on their roster that he would leave. Given he was their most popular model at the time, the choice was easy. I never made it to Johannesburg.

During the time we were both overseas, my son Christian had been staying with Nelson's family in Florida. With the recent turn of events, it was no longer acceptable for him to stay with my ex-boyfriend's family, so I made a trip back to the States to take custody of him and move my belongings out of the home Nelson and I shared into storage. Carol had agreed to take Christian in so that I could continue to pursue my professional dream in Italy. Grateful for her support, I brought him with me to New York to settle him into preschool and into his temporary home before heading back to Italy.

It was during this brief time frame in New York that a music mogul raped me.

My son and I were both staying at Carol's, when I went out drinking with my so-called friend. At the end of the night, I went back to his home to pass out on his bed in a drunken stupor.

Barely coherent, I could not fend him off when he climbed on me and, in spite of my protestations, forced himself on me.

When I woke up the next day and remembered what had happened the night before, I snapped. Grabbing a handful of prescription pills, I polished them off with a bottle of white wine. I was out of my mind with grief and went so far as to call him, my family, and Carol to tell them what I had done. Fortunately, due to these calls my friends—and my rapist's assistant—brought me to the hospital, where I would remain for the next five days because of my suicide attempt.

I never pressed charges against him, and to this day have never publicly named him. Given my history of emotional instability (as evident by my suicide attempt) and our prior sexual relationship, I wasn't the perfect victim. The power imbalance between us was another reason why I never came forward. At the time he was worth $30 million versus my $30. I had already seen what happened to women who pressed charges against rapists of power and influence. Complete and total character assassination of the victim, who would end up in financial and emotional ruins because of the trial (if it even made it to court). I may have only been a drunken twenty-four-year-old model, but I knew better than to try and seek justice for a crime that no one would believe ever happened.

Like many rape victims, I blamed myself for stupidly allowing myself to get drunk, and be alone with this man in his bedroom. It was a male friend who helped me realize that I wasn't responsible for what had happened.

"Sil Lai, you didn't make him do this. Do you understand? He did this because he's an asshole," my friend Julio said, continuing, "If you had gotten drunk and come over to my apartment, I wouldn't have had sex with you. He took advantage of the situation and is the only one to blame for why you're in this hospital . . . not you."

To this day I am grateful for these words, spoken to me in the visiting center of St. Vincent's psychiatric ward. Even though I accepted what he said at face value, I still remain conflicted about what happened to me. Not because I don't understand that I was a victim of sexual assault. It's more because I know I will never receive justice, and my anger at the knowledge that, if I were to come forward today, I would have to come armed with over fifty other women sharing a similar story—and would most likely still be branded a liar by society.

After my five-day hospital stay, I was released to Ismaele after he assured the doctors that I would receive follow-up psychiatric care. I flew back to Italy to rest while Carol cared for Christian; quite frankly, I was in no shape to be parenting. He didn't send me to a psychologist like he had promised. Instead, Ismaele decided to treat me himself by confiscating my passport, cutting off my alcohol supply, and throwing away my antidepressants (he said I didn't need them). After six weeks of his "treatment," I planned my escape from his stifling behavior. I pleaded with him to give me back my passport and let me visit my son in New York.

"I'll be back. I just need to see my son," I promised.

Once I got to New York, I broke things off with him over the phone and returned to Nelson, immediately becoming pregnant. With my son in tow, we moved into his sister Barbara's apartment on Valentine Avenue in the Bronx sharing a bedroom with his niece and nephew. Christian slept in his "cousin" Andrew's bed, while Nelson and I slept on an old twin bed placed directly on the linoleum floor. The mattress had a spring popping out of one side, so we wrapped it with a military blanket to ensure that the protruding metal didn't slice our arms. The mattress was too small for two adults to sleep on, so Nelson placed a pillow on the floor next to the bed where he rested his extended arm.

My reversal of fortune was total and complete. Two months

earlier I was sunning myself on the deck of King Hussein of Jordan's mega yacht. Now I was sleeping on the floor of a tenement building with peeling paint on the walls and a urine-stained elevator. Oh, how the briefly mighty had fallen.

❦

After a short honeymoon period, Nelson and I began our regular arguments over money, my pregnancy, and his resentment over my leaving him that summer. Many couples lash out at each other when upset, but he was absolutely lethal with his verbal attacks. When angered, Nelson would put such a tongue lashing on me that I wished he would just hit me instead. To him, no subject was off limits as a weapon.

During one of our arguments he yelled, "You know why you got raped, Sil Lai? Because you always need to have a dick between your legs!" I curled into a ball on the bed and cried, saying over and over again, "Why? Why would you say that? How could you say something so mean to me?" Once he calmed down he would profusely apologize and I'd forgive him. This attack-and-apologize pattern would continue between us unabated for the duration of our toxic relationship.

As is often the case, his abuse didn't stop at the verbal level. He also used choking, hair pulling, punching, and shoving to try to silence me. Yet despite years of trying, he couldn't break my spirit. My will, whether directed in a positive or negative direction, has always been ironlike. This isn't to say that I wasn't harmed by the abuse. It's simply to point out that because of my upbringing, I was conditioned to stand my ground, no matter what the ramifications.

Like my dad, there was a schism between Nelson's personal religious beliefs and his actual behavior. He was a fundamentalist Christian who devoutly prayed every morning and night, and before each meal. Yet he "lived in sin" with me and our child that was born out of wedlock, a direct contradiction to the core principles of his faith. He espoused Christ's teachings on forgiveness and charity, but couldn't demonstrate this in our relationship. Instead, he rationalized his behavior when I confronted him on his hypocrisy by saying, "Only God can judge me. I know my sins have been forgiven by Jesus's death on the cross."

Much like Daisy and Dad had done decades earlier, we were locked together by trauma, parenthood, and the struggle to survive on a meager income. Except in this case, it wasn't the man who was the provider: it was me. We had only stayed with his sister Barbara for a couple of months before I used one of my settlement payments from Keith to move us into our own two-bedroom apartment just down the street from her. Our new home was clean and in a well-maintained prewar building just off of Grand Concourse in the Bronx. We were supported by my $15-an-hour full-time, long-term temp assignment at J.P. Morgan, which combined with my quarterly annuity payments, allowed me to take care of my family.

Nelson didn't want to face up to his financial responsibilities and avoided getting a "real" job for years. He was too busy playing Sega video games while waiting for casting calls for modeling assignments—work that dwindled away until I was the only source of support for what was now our family of four once our daughter, Amanda, was born. It wasn't until I threatened to cut off his weekly $50 allowance that he actually sought employment as a mailroom clerk. His small paycheck helped ease the financial burden off my shoulders, for which I was grateful.

Out of thirty days a month, we spent close to twenty-seven of them arguing. It was a horrible time, which in the past I would have tried to cope with by drinking. But I knew what would happen if I picked up again, so I started attending local recovery support groups. Within these church basement meetings, I gained tools that helped me maintain the sobriety that began during my pregnancy with Amanda. In these rooms, I could talk about Nelson's behavior and learn coping mechanisms that didn't include a drink. These meetings were my only safe haven from the abuse in our home. Any other attempts on my part to socialize were incredibly threatening to Nelson, eliciting accusations of my intent to cheat on him. Over the course of our nearly five years together, I probably went out by myself a handful of times. No outing was worth the inquisition and verbal accusations that would happen when I came home. He'd check my purse for evidence of my supposed cheating, smelling my body to make sure that I hadn't been messing around. Instead of allowing myself to be subjected to the humiliation that followed an outing with a girlfriend, I spent all of my time at home with him and the kids.

Our relationship had cost me everything. By now I was completely isolated, save a handful of friends. No one understood what kept me committed to this deeply harmful union of broken souls. Least of all, me.

People usually deny the truth when they are too afraid to face it, and fear is what is at the root of many destructive relationships. Fear of being alone, fear of further abuse if we leave, fear of financial insecurity, fear that no other man would want a woman who was "damaged goods." Fear of being a statistic—another "single black mother with two kids by two different men," and the social ramifications of that diminished social standing.

In the world we live in, singleness, especially for black women, is viewed as not only a sign of social failure, but as an indicator of our inherent defectiveness as well. Almost every girl, irrespective of race, grows up in a society that is wedded to the superiority of male-dominated households. To be a single black woman, and a mother to boot, was proof that you were just not good enough to get and keep a man. Rather than face the world alone as a single mother, I chose to stay in a violent, unstable relationship for years, because the alternative of being alone would have been the ultimate proof of my unlovability. For me back then, being a single mother would have also confirmed society's negative stereotypes of black women as irresponsible, and further stigmatized my children. The burden of feeling responsible to push back against this larger narrative about black women (and the ramifications of my choice to leave my batterer) was as oppressive as the actual abuse I suffered.

Neither of my children had been wanted by either of their fathers. In fact, Nelson only stuck around due in large part to religious guilt. Still, I thought I had a man invested enough in *me* to fight for our relationship (even if that meant beating me during the process). Keith had never fought for our love, and although I now know how completely erroneous the following statement is, I believed Nelson's behavior was somehow indicative of his commitment to me and our family.

Over the course of our union, I was sent to the emergency room a handful of times. I was slammed into walls, dragged around the apartment by my hair while pregnant, choked, pummeled, and verbally assaulted on nearly a daily basis for not knowing "when to shut my mouth." However, it wasn't his physical abuse of *me* that led me to walk away from our relationship. The final straw was the day he laid a hand on my son.

One day in a gesture befitting a child, Christian had made the mistake of taking the tag off the ear of a stuffed animal that Nelson had bought me for Valentine's Day. Grabbing his tiny arm, his long brown fingers entwined around Christian's small bicep so tightly I feared it would snap as he bellowed into my boy's face, "Didn't I tell you not to take the tag off this dog?"

My heart was racing as I eyed the scene unfolding with panic.

How could I protect my sweet boy? The distance between my son and I was probably ten feet. Nelson's tall, dark form loomed menacingly over my firstborn, and I instinctually ran to protect my child. But suddenly, with a swift scoop, Nelson picked up my son and threw him across the room as if he were casually tossing a Nerf football. Fortunately, he threw him in the direction of Christian's bed, where he landed with a small bounce on its cushiony surface.

I snapped. Nelson had broken my one cardinal rule. I'd been willing to work with him while he sought court-mandated counseling and individual therapy to deal with his abusive behavior, but touching my children killed any willingness I had to stand by his side.

"GET OUT!" I screamed at the top of my lungs. "GET THE FUCK OUT OF MY HOUSE! How DARE YOU touch my baby! GET OUT OF HERE!"

Nelson left that day and never moved back home.

Fear had kept me attached to Nelson for years. This final straw in our relationship forced me once and for all to decide whether I wanted to live or die. And for the sake of my two children, I chose to live.

I used every resource available to get the help needed to begin healing, starting first by seeing an individual therapist once a week who specialized in working with women in abusive relationships. In addition to attending individual therapy, I joined a support group for battered women. They were a great comfort and helped break me out of the deep sense of shame and alienation I felt about being abused. It was in those sessions that I finally realized that what I had witnessed as a child, and the environment that I had been raised in, was actually an abusive one. As my mind replayed Dad's relationship first with Daisy, and then with Mom, and the relationships I had with all of my partners, it finally clicked that my childhood was where I had learned to accept mental, emotional, and physical violence as the norm. This was why, in spite of my promise to never be subjugated by any man after leaving Dad's home, the blueprint for my adult relationships had been set. My actions, as self-destructive as they appeared to those around me, originated beyond the space of my conscious reasoning.

In time, with counseling and a permanent order of protection, I was able to break ties with Nelson, and my children and I were able to live free from the threat of abuse hanging over our heads. By now it was 1997, and I had been working as the executive as-sistant to the senior vice president of sales at a corporate news dis-tribution service called PR Newswire for the past year. The work, while unchallenging, provided me with a small but stable income and great family health benefits that I could use in conjunction with the settlement I had received three years before from Keith.

For the first time ever, I had steady employment, consistent income, housing, a social life, two healthy, well-adjusted children and most importantly—I was free from abuse.

❀

The rage I had long directed at Dad and Mom created a push-pull dynamic between us where I would go for long stretches of time without communicating with either of them. However, by the time the physical abuse had begun in my relationship with Nelson, I had reestablished a relationship with Dad. Our fresh start was the result of a "Come to Jesus" conversation that I ini-tiated in the hope that I could break down the walls between us, while letting him know how much his behavior had hurt me as a child.

Although I didn't know what the outcome would be, I had

come to a point where I had decided that I was either going to permanently cut him out of my life, or we were going to rebuild our relationship. Everything would hinge on how receptive he was to hearing my criticisms, especially of his lack of compassion and woefully inept parenting skills.

Surprisingly, instead of rejecting what I had to say, he listened without argument. At one point, I believe he may have uttered something along the lines of, "I didn't know that you felt that way," which was all I needed from him—acknowledgment of my feelings. With that one conversation behind us, we slowly began the task of repairing over fifteen years of painful estrangement. It was around this time that I began communicating with Mom again as well. Our reconnection was more gradual and didn't have any big "a-ha" moments, but as a young mother myself I had developed compassion for her, especially in the wake of my time spent with Nelson.

While my relationship with my dad was now relatively "normal," in my gut I felt that only half of the puzzle was complete. On the surface, my life had all the trappings of an adult woman: My own apartment. Employment. Healthcare. Sobriety. A 401(k) plan. A used 1992 Honda Civic I used to tool around the city with my kids.

Despite these markers of adulthood, I was in many ways, at least emotionally, very much the same neglected and abandoned little girl who desperately longed for her mommy. Mom had taken over her responsibilities when I was a girl, my friend Carol had become a surrogate during my twenties, but Daisy was still my mother as far as I was concerned. Decades had elapsed, but there was a remaining void only she could fill. At twenty-seven, I was convinced that, in order to truly reconstruct my life, I would need to find her. It had been decades since we had last set eyes on each other, yet I felt that she contained the key to unlocking why I had spent so many years consciously and unconsciously destroying myself.

There were so many questions left in the wake of her absence. As a mother myself, they burned brighter in my mind with every passing year. What kind of woman could leave three children behind? Did she ever think of us? Did she have new children who had replaced us in her heart? Why had we never heard from her again? Was she dead?

Neither May Lai nor Daniel ever spoke about her unless I brought her up. Still, I was curious about whether they were interested in seeing her again; I knew a reunion wouldn't impact just me, but them as well. Daniel was indifferent to the idea, and May Lai was only mildly interested. Their attitudes, while disappointing, didn't come as too much of a surprise. My sister was three years old and my brother just shy of his first birthday when Daisy disappeared. They had spent the majority of their lives being raised by our stepmom, who was the woman they considered their mother. For me, it was different. I needed to see her again. Unlike them, I could still remember her. Not just the emotional memory, but visual ones as well, like her long, thin fingers with crimson painted nails, cigarette dangling from the tips.

I tried to bridge the gap between us by trying to connect with the Chinese side of my heritage. Without access to Daisy or her family, I asked a former Chinese coworker to teach me how to celebrate Chinese New Year. I did everything instructed, from cleaning every inch of my home from the ceiling down (to eliminate any leftover energy from the past year). I cooked a traditional meal of fish with black bean sauce and made fried rice in a wok I had purchased in Chinatown. Aware of my limitations, I didn't bother to try making pot-sticker dumplings, but instead served premade ones along with stir-fried bok choy. My children received money in lucky red envelopes, and I made sure we all wore red to celebrate the new Lunar Year. We even went outside to light sparklers in lieu of the usual fireworks. It took a week of preparation, and was over in a matter of hours. While I was proud of my attempt to connect to my Chinese culture, I knew that was probably going to be the one and only time I celebrated Chinese New Year in a traditional sense. It was simply too much work for me as a single working mother.

But going through the motions of Chinese New Year and making sure my children visited Chinatown to see the other side of their mother's racial heritage wasn't enough. I had no emotional connection to the people who milled around me in this busy section of New York City. Just like in Winter Park, Chinatown made me feel invisible. An outsider.

My identity as a black woman was rock solid, but the woman who had birthed me was not black, which created a conundrum of sorts. There was no emotional need driving me to acculturate into Chinese society. They were as foreign to me as any other ethnic group outside of the black community. Besides, it was hard enough reconciling just *two* cultures and identities: the white one in which I was raised, and the black one that I had embraced. The thought of now "becoming" Chinese as well made my head spin.

But the strong possibility that mainstream Chinese society would never accept me on top of these challenges didn't stop me from needing to find Daisy.

I thought that finding a person who has been missing for twenty-two years would be difficult. After all, there are decades separating you from the person you knew, decades erasing the person's tracks. Decades destroying old memories.

Fortunately, I found my biological mother within two months of beginning my search. It didn't cost me much. Only ten dollars, plus tax, on a book aptly entitled *How to Locate Anyone Anywhere Without Leaving Home* by Ted L. Gunderson and Roger

McGovern. In their concise tome, the authors share that if you arc searching for a lost family member and have information from their driver's license or license plate, that particular state's Department of Motor Vehicles will forward a letter to the latest address on file. Of course, finding a missing loved one will work only if the person in question has an up-to-date license or vehicle registration on file at the time you send the letter.

In the decades since their divorce, Daisy's name was no longer verboten in our family. Yet, I was still surprised when, after I told Dad that I wanted to find her, he was actually supportive. Not in a "That's a wonderful idea, Sil Lai" kind of way, but more like "Well, let's see if you're able to pull this one off, kid."

So I got to work.

"Dad, I bought this book and they're saying we can track a person through the DMV if you have any information on that person's license or car. Do you remember if you kept any paperwork from when you were together?" I asked. "What kind of car did Daisy have?"

"Give me a few minutes. I'm gonna check. Call me back in a half hour," he answered.

Time moved at a tortoise's pace while I counted down the minutes. There was plenty of busywork for me at the office, but I couldn't focus. At thirty minutes on the dot, I picked up the phone and called him back.

"I've got something for you," Dad said. "In our divorce papers she was given her car in the settlement. The license plate number is in the document. Do you have a pen handy?" He then recited the license plate number to the vehicle Daisy owned in 1975. This one small, seemingly inconsequential bit of information from a divorce decree over two decades old was all I needed. Typing rapidly, I wrote a brief letter that would be read by the random clerk who would receive my note at the State of California's Department of Motor Vehicles, plus a letter to Daisy that I sealed in a postage-paid envelope. Placing both inside a larger manila envelope, I said a brief prayer before dropping it into the mailbox.

Approximately three weeks later, I was seated at my desk at work when an unfamiliar number came up on the caller ID. Nonplussed, I figured it was one of our clients and answered the phone with a brisk, "Good afternoon. PR Newswire. This is Sil Lai speaking."

"See You Lai."

It had been twenty-two years, but I knew that voice. I froze as I realized I was having a once-in-a-lifetime moment, the nonsports equivalent of landing a three-point shot from way downtown during the final seconds in the fourth quarter of the NBA playoffs. Seated in my cubicle, surrounded by my coworkers who were busying themselves with their daily tasks, my entire life was changing. Everything around me faded from my consciousness. I was completely fixated on the voice on the other end of the phone.

"Yes? This is she," I replied, to which I heard her response. Light sobbing.

"See You Lai. This is your mother. Daisy."

I wanted to run a victory lap around the office, to stand up and shout, "Eureka!" Of course, that was out of the question. I was in the office and my phone wasn't cordless. Instead, I kept my voice low while my spirit soared and eagerly chatted with her for approximately a half hour, until my boss summoned me to his office with a wave of his hand.

"Sorry, Daisy. I have to go . . . My boss needs me."

"Of course. You're at work. Maybe we can speak later today?"

"Absolutely! I will call you tonight once I get home from work."

The rest of my day, I was halfway in my body, floating on a high that was unparalleled. I couldn't believe my good fortune, yet I wasn't entirely surprised. Somehow, information always had a way of reaching me. For instance, I had discovered earlier that year that my son's father, Keith, had died of a massive heart attack when I did an internet search of his name. Instead of turning up anything on his current work or family, I had stumbled across his obituary in the *New York Times*. Dated January 27, 1997, the headline in the Arts section simply said, "Keith Diamond, 46; Produced Pop Songs." A strange coincidence? Perhaps. But I've always had many unexpected discoveries, an almost sixth-sense ability to stumble across the truth, no matter how unpleasant.

So here it was again that I had managed to find out information about someone from my past in the most random of ways. At the time, there were no paid locator sites like Intelius or People Search available to help you find someone (at least to my knowledge). I couldn't afford a private detective. And I didn't have any contacts within the government to break the rules and comb through a database as a favor. Yet somehow, for the cost of a paperback book and a postage stamp, I was able to achieve the impossible: locating my long-lost biological mother.

We spoke that evening for hours, and then every night following it, cramming as much discussion as possible into calls that were simply inadequate to bridge the time that had elapsed since we had last seen each other. Although it had been over a quarter century since she had left Hong Kong, she still spoke with a slight Cantonese accent. After spending a week on the phone, we planned a family reunion together that would include May Lai and Daniel. Ten days later, all four of us, along with her husband of nearly twenty years, Bob, met face-to-face in New York.

Daisy had chosen the Grand Hyatt hotel restaurant connected to Grand Central Station as the location for our first "family" dinner. As far as restaurants went, this was on the expensive side, which led me to wonder if she and her husband were wealthy. Looking at her navy Ralph Lauren jacket with its gold-embroidered logo on the breast, I hoped she was. Not for my sake, but for hers. For Daisy to find a loving husband and financial stability after her time with my father would have been poetic. (It turned out they weren't rich, but comfortable.)

Glancing around the circular table, I saw my mother sitting next to her husband, a tall, average-looking white man with kind, blue eyes and sandy brown hair, then my sister's exotic face, and finally, my brother, who at twenty-three had matured into a younger version of Dad, with just the slightest hint of Chinese features. Unless he told you his middle name (Cheung), Dan appeared to be just a better-than-average-looking white boy.

In the center of the table was an impressive tier of seafood from the raw bar that stood three levels high. But instead of focusing on the food, I sat transfixed by my mother's face. Its planes were simultaneously rounded and angular, with almond-shaped eyes that had just the slightest overhang of skin above her eyelids. Her skin was no longer alabaster smooth. Instead, faint lines crisscrossed under her eyes and lined her forehead. Her cheeks, while still prominent, had the faintest flush of rosacea (which I learned was a side effect of her thyroid medication). Still, she was the most beautiful woman in the world to me.

While May Lai, Dan, and Bob chatted breezily, I watched her every move with an almost hypnotic focus. In the middle of this rather generic restaurant, something incredibly unique was happening inside of me. It was as if for the first time in my life I had entered into the fold of humanity after spending a lifetime foraging outside of emotional civilization. In Daisy's face, I finally saw what so many people take for granted every day: history. A connection to the past. Someone outside of my siblings with whom I shared bloodlines and common ancestors. A living repository of my matrilineal lineage.

In the middle of our dinner, I excused myself to go to the

ladies' room. Daisy accompanied me. Walking side by side, I noticed her upright posture, an almost regal way of carrying herself that belied the additional fifty pounds she now carried on her frame. Like me, Daisy moved with a cool but slightly nervous energy. What was extraordinary was how similar our behaviors were as well. For example, after we had used the toilets and washed our hands, Daisy reached for the door. My eyes opened wide and I bellowed with laughter as I watched her extend her arm as far as it could go, so that her hands almost touched the top of the door frame. Using her fingertips, she pulled the door open from the top, not using the door handle.

"I can't believe you do that too!" I exclaimed. "I do the *exact* same thing! The door handle is where all the germs are!" What were the odds that two people who hadn't spent time together in over two decades would have the exact same odd way of evading bacteria in public restrooms? Nature in this case had clearly overtaken nurture. She smiled and nodded her head, and we laughed while heading back to the table, where we concluded our dinner.

The rest of her trip with us was spent sightseeing and trying to compress twenty-two years of life experiences into a week-long visit. May Lai had chosen to stay with friends in Manhattan, while Dan stayed with me and the kids at our apartment in the Bronx. Daisy and Bob had elected to stay at a simple hotel in Westchester, not far from the Bronx, and would visit us every day, either at my apartment, or at a location downtown.

Finally, I thought, *I am complete*. Although I was an adult, I hadn't realized how much I needed to have her back in my life. That unbeknownst to me there was a little four-and-a-half-year-old girl who still cried out for the touch of the woman who had given her the gift of life. It didn't matter that she had abandoned us all those years ago. I had my Daisy back.

Another serendipitous part of our meeting was that, when

my letter arrived, Daisy and Bob had returned from Japan only a few months before. In fact, Daisy had just renewed her California driver's license the previous month. Had I sent the letter two months prior, they would never have been able to forward it to her new address, because she had been living out of the country for almost eight years. Our finding each other was not just a strange group of coincidences coupled with a well-timed letter; it was divinely ordained. Kismet. An intended reunion of souls.

Of course, a plethora of unanswered questions were put on the table, mainly by me. It wasn't May Lai or Daniel's style to probe too deeply into much of anything. Besides, I was speaking enough for the three of us. Daisy candidly answered my questions and explained the circumstances around her disappearance all those years ago. I peppered her with a barrage of inquiries into my parents' marriage and divorce, her life growing up in Hong Kong, and what her life had been like in the time since. I was shocked to learn that she lived in her car for two weeks after leaving Dad and was only able to rent a room when she received her first paycheck from the job she had gotten at the commissary at the local marine base. It was there that she would meet the man who would become her second husband not long after leaving Dad—her current one, Bob.

Contrary to the story Dad had told us over the years, she claimed that she didn't abandon us. That, in fact, he had taken us away from her. Daisy didn't attend the custody hearing because she never received the notice in the mail and didn't have the money for an attorney. After they split, she had tried to visit us, but he refused, saying that the time wasn't right. The second Christmas after their divorce she called asking to spend time with her children. Dad said he would let her know. In anticipation, she had bought all of us presents and awaited the call from Dad saying it was okay for her to see us. The call never came. She was heartbrokcn. By the time she mustered up the courage to stop by our house near Moon Park, we had moved to the house near Disneyland and the new tenants didn't give her our new address. Less than two years later we would move across the country to Florida, while she and Bob would be relocated to Okinawa, where he was stationed for years. Granted, to me the obvious solution would have been to hire a private investigator, but that was an expense that she and her husband, then an active marine, couldn't afford.

"I kept those presents for almost a decade, hidden in the back of a closet. I didn't give up hope I would see you all again," she recounted bitterly. "Eventually I threw the presents out, but I never stopped hoping to see you all again. I still kept these," she said, handing over the passports that May Lai and I had used when we took our trip with Daisy to Hong Kong some twenty-three years earlier. This small gesture confirmed what I had always hoped: that she hadn't forgotten about us, or thrown us away. In spite of thousands of miles and almost two dozen years, she had held onto a piece of us, even if it was just government-issued passports with small black-and-white photographs inside.

It was then that I realized that Dad had been lying to us all of those years. That Daisy didn't abandon us because she didn't love us. She had been kept away because she had done the unforgiveable by leaving him. When I told Dad that I had found Daisy he was shocked, but he also seemed genuinely happy for me. Little did he know that I was learning more about his character than he would have liked. Like his willingness to lie in order to protect the agendas he had that were beyond his convenient lie about my race and paternity. The more Daisy shared, the more I came to realize that Dad had in fact committed an act of parental alienation.

At this stage, I was finding it increasingly difficult to separate the past from the present. Dad and I had enacted our peace treaty based upon incomplete information. Yes, I had forgiven him for being emotionally abusive most of my early life. But this new information was not a part of our "settlement." I found myself becoming disenchanted with him again and started pondering how I was going to come to terms with this latest piece of intel on what truly happened all those years ago. Yet, in spite of my reawakened anger at him for the things he had done to Daisy during their marriage and afterward, I kept what I had learned about him out of our conversations. The time would come for reckoning, but it wasn't now. I still needed information from him, and knew if confronted directly about what Daisy had shared, he was liable to shut down. Instead, I began using my weekly phone calls with Dad as vetting sessions for what Daisy shared.

It was Daisy's nature to be reserved, and this wasn't just limited to me and my siblings. She cautiously engaged with my children as well. I watched her interaction with them closely, seeking any evidence of racism on her part toward my black children. But she treated them as any person in her situation would—kindly, not too friendly, but not too distant either. The best word to describe her interactions with them is *respectful*.

By now, my entire cultural existence was rooted in black America, but if that made her uncomfortable, she never showed it. I paid close attention to the content of our conversations, furtively hoping that neither she nor Bob would say something racially insensitive, or outright racist, that could rupture the bond that was beginning to develop between us. But despite my clear identification with black culture and the absence of Chinese culture in our home, they never said anything about race that was even remotely offensive, even when the inevitable subject of the identity of my biological father came up.

"What was he like?" I asked as we sat around my simple dining room table.

"He was a gentleman. An Air America pilot. That is why

you are so smart. Not like George," she said dismissively of Dad. "He was married, with a wife back in the U.S. He would visit me when he came to town. He bought me my first bottle of real perfume. Chanel Number 5."

"Dad said that he was black. Do you know where he was from? His family background?"

I saw her jaw tighten ever so slightly.

"Not black black, like Africa. More like Brazilian. He wasn't dark. He looked like George's friend Mike Marcial. Have you ever seen a picture of him?"

Shaking my head no, she continued.

"Ask George to show you his photo. He looked more like him."

While her lack of clarity around my biological father's race was slightly troublesome, I figured it would be easy enough to determine once I found him. So I asked the next logical question.

"Do you remember his name?"

"No" was her short, terse answer.

"Really? Like, is there anything at all that you can tell me about him? A first name perhaps?"

Mouth tensing, Daisy answered again, "No."

Up until this point in our conversations she had been an open book. But I was for some reason coming up against a wall. How could she not remember the name of the man who impregnated her? A man that she carried on an affair with for over a year? Someone who left such an indelible impression on her life that decades later she could recall the name of the bottle of perfume he bought her twenty-eight years prior?

"So there is nothing at all that you can tell me about him other than he was of Brazilian or South American heritage and that he was a pilot?"

"That's all I remember, See You Lai."

Subject closed.

It was then that I saw how quickly she could shut down when placed in a situation she didn't like, or didn't want to face. I should have seen this behavior as a red flag, but I just assumed she had her reasons for not wanting to discuss the subject any further.

To this day, I'm not clear if Dad learned I wasn't his biological child before or after I was born. According to Daisy, she told him while she was pregnant that there was a possibility I wasn't his child. This would be an unbelievable statement coming out of most people's mouths, but Daisy was a very literal and direct woman. She proudly shared that she didn't tell Bob that she loved him during their first ten years together. When I asked her why she waited so long to say these words to her husband, she said matter-of-factly, "I didn't want to say something that wasn't true. I had to know for sure that I truly loved him."

When I recounted to Dad her story about the race of my biological father, he chuckled. "Sil Lai, I saw that man and he was black. No, he wasn't dark . . . he was very light, but he was definitely a black man," he said. "I don't know why she's saying that he's Brazilian. And he was darker than Mike Marcial."

"Well, where was Mike from?"

"I think Mike was from somewhere in South America. Either Brazil or Colombia. I can't remember."

Daisy's refusal to acknowledge my biological father's race was the only time that I picked up any potential racism on her part. Granted, my dad didn't have the best track record with being honest, but at the same time, I trusted his judgment before hers. He had nothing to lose, either way. Brazilian or black made no difference to him. Plus, he grew up in a country that was a literal melting pot of people from around the globe, whereas Daisy grew up sheltered in a very racially homogeneous environment—sans foreign-born visitors. So while their stories never completely jibed, I knew how the indigenous people of Brazil had their bloodlines mixed with the Portuguese who colonized their country and the African slaves brought over to work the plantations. Daisy, in her explanation, was missing the obvious fact that *if* my father was in fact Brazilian, he was more than likely of African ancestry. And my appearance was proof positive that he had black blood in his family. My skin was too dark and my hair too curly to be explained any other way.

Instead of getting into a debate about the colonization of Brazilian people with her, I left the subject alone, as it was obviously something that she wasn't prepared to discuss. If she was unwilling to reveal his name, there was no way she was going to go any further into a discussion about my biological father's race.

At the end of their week in New York, Daisy and Bob returned to their home in Torrance, California, and we continued to speak on a weekly basis. My brother and sister both returned to their respective homes in Florida, and from what I understood, had limited contact with Daisy. May Lai had relocated from Los Angeles and Paris, having lived in pampered wealth in both cities for the past few years with a French pop singer named Félix Gray. Despite the expensive jewelry, clothing, and jet-set lifestyle (he had once chartered a private jet to fly from Paris to Ibiza for the night just to attend a birthday party), she had left him and his wealth behind.

During a visit to South Beach she managed to reconnect with a petty drug dealer named Israel whom we had both met when I still lived at home in the 1980s. At the time I was dating his best friend Jay, and this duo of skater boys would drive in from Satellite Beach, nearly fifty miles away, to visit. (The same Jay who dropped me off at the airport in 1988 when I moved to New York.) May Lai and Israel never dated when we were teens, but they hooked up following a final breakup with Félix. Similarly to when I left Italy for the Bronx, May Lai went from living in a mansion in Beverly Hills and an elegant apartment overlooking the Eiffel Tower to slumming at her new boyfriend's mother's house on the Florida Panhandle. For Dan, and now for me, things were much tamer. He went back home to his job as a UPS worker in Orlando and I returned to my day-to-day life of office work and child rearing, invigorated with a sense of pride and knowing that at long last, I had found the woman who had brought me into this world.

As our calls continued, I completely opened myself up to this woman who was, in all reality, a complete stranger. In my naïveté, I didn't consider that there may have been other explanations for her prolonged absence from our lives. A childhood fantasy was being fulfilled. Like a child, I blindly accepted everything about her at face value.

As time went by, I noticed a strange dynamic developing between my mother and my other siblings. She pushed my brother and me away while pulling my sister in closer. When I first noticed that she was distancing herself from Dan, I questioned her about it. Her response was a bland rationalization.

"Your brother is so hard to talk to," she said, continuing, "He never really has anything to say. He is just like his father."

"Yeah, Dan is an island unto himself," I agreed. "But he is nothing like Dad. He just needs time to get to know you before he opens up."

Although I felt that she was scapegoating my brother for the anger she still held toward our father, I hoped that she would eventually work past her feelings. Secretly, I suspected that the real motivation behind Daisy's distancing behavior with my brother was that she realized she had been replaced in his heart by the woman who raised us—Julie. While Dan was interested in Daisy, he didn't embrace her the way that I did, nor did he put much effort into staying in touch with her after our face-to-face visit. What Daisy didn't realize was that Dan was pretty disconnected from every-one. But instead of trying to understand him, she rejected him.

Not long after she made her statement about my brother, I noticed that her calls to me were slowing down as well. When I asked May Lai if she had been speaking with Daisy, she said, "Yeah, pretty much every day." I was envious. At first I thought it was my feelings of sibling rivalry being kicked up. That I was just jealous of my mother and sister's growing bond. Having spent the past several years sober, I had learned many techniques through my involvement in a recovery group, such as reminding myself that "feelings aren't facts," and to "take it one day at a time." In-stead of panicking at what I felt was some distancing on Daisy's part, I decided not to jump to conclusions and gave her the benefit of the doubt. After all, I had gone through the time and effort to bring us all back together and was heavily invested in my rela-tionship with her, and she knew it. In me, Daisy didn't just find a daughter. She had gained a bona fide fan.

One evening while Daisy and I were on the phone, the subject of Dad came up. While I don't recall exactly what was said, I do remember telling her that although I hated *the way* in which he had raised me, I did respect him for at least putting a roof over my head and food in my stomach while I was growing up.

Her response to my statement was a curious silence. Noticing the shift in her energy, I tried to smooth things over. The last thing in the world I wanted to do was hurt her feelings. I knew she hated George, and I wasn't his biggest fan either. But I had to give him credit for doing what my children's biological fathers were unwilling to do, which was to care for their physical needs. Had

I paid more attention, I would have realized that silence does not equate agreement. Particularly for a highly emotionally-guarded Chinese woman like Daisy.

Instead of responding to my statement, she turned our conversation to the topic of long-lost family members who reunite only to end up estranged again. Specifically, she referenced reunion episodes on television talk shows.

"You know, See You Lai, those talk shows never share the reunion stories that don't have happy endings." Continuing, she said, "Bob and I have been doing research and most family reunions don't work out. Especially when a long time has gone by."

"No, actually I didn't know that, Ma." "Ma" was the name that I had begun to call her instead of Daisy. "Mom" was Julie's name, and "Mother" was too formal. "Ma" was also short for the Cantonese word for mother, *Ma Ma*.

While I thought her choice of topic was odd, I assumed that she was bringing up the subject because she was anxious about one of *us* rejecting *her*. It never occurred to me that she would walk away from us again, although in retrospect, had I any objectivity at all, I would have seen it coming.

❀

Given my work schedule and the difference in time zones between us, Daisy and I often spoke at night once my kids were asleep. So when I received a call from her one night at 2:00 a.m., I wasn't too surprised to hear her voice.

"See You Lai, I have to tell you something," she began, in slightly slurred speech.

"Is everything okay?" I answered with a start. Something about the sound of her voice immediately triggered an anxious feeling.

"I don't think we should talk to each other anymore."

I sat up in my bed and shook myself awake.

"I'm sorry. Can you say that again? I was sleeping and I'm not sure if I heard . . ."

"I said we shouldn't talk anymore."

Her words wiped away any lingering drowsiness from my mind, rendering me hyperalert and light-headed at the same time. I had to resist the urge to pinch myself to see if I was really awake. Unfortunately, this nightmare was real. My heart was pounding so hard that I could hear it in my ears.

My two-year-old daughter, Amanda, was lying next to me asleep. Not wanting to wake her with our conversation, I quickly got out of bed and walked down the hall to the bathroom, shutting the door firmly behind me.

Dad and his entire family had told me stories about Daisy's problems with alcohol back when I was a child, but in the time since we had reconnected I had never seen her drunk. Given that she was always sober in our prior conversations, I figured any tendency to over-imbibe was in the past. Clearly that wasn't the case if she was drunk dialing me in the middle of the night.

"What are you trying to say? Did I do something to offend you? If it was something I said, let's talk about it," I responded as calmly as you can when you've just been told by your mother that she doesn't want to have a relationship with you. Ever.

Praying she wouldn't catch the slight panic in my voice, I continued, "I am sure we can work this out. It would be a shame to walk away from each other without giving our relationship . . ."

She abruptly cut me off.

"You are controlling and bossy! You remind me of my sister Judy in Hong Kong. I can't stand her! You are both alike: so materialistic and concerned about what you have."

I was dumbstruck as she continued, "I wouldn't choose you to be my friend! You just happen to be my daughter, but we don't have to be in each other's lives."

The words slipped out of her mouth with such an icy precision that it almost seemed rehearsed. As I replayed instances of her growing disconnection from me over the past month, I realized that she had probably been practicing this speech for weeks.

By now large tears were streaming silently down my face. Remembering that she was drunk, I considered that she might not really mean what she was saying. Like a criminal defense attorney, I spent the next hour questioning her decision from many different angles, hoping to see a sliver of possibility that this was not truly a kill shot but a warning.

In spite of my most persuasive efforts, she never once wavered. Her mind was made up. Nothing I said was going to stop her from severing ties to me and her grandchildren. Somehow, through no specific action, just the nature of my personality, I had managed to make my mother hate me. To despise who and what I was so much that she felt compelled to cut me out of her life.

The realization that this was going to be the last time I spoke with my biological mother again was excruciating. It was as if she had taken a hunter's knife, shoved it into my abdomen, and ripped me open from navel to sternum with no anesthesia. She had just eviscerated her daughter. Again. But this time was worse, for I knew unequivocally that unlike before, she was consciously *choosing* to reject me. I felt the same familiar longing and panic descending over me. My mother didn't love me. In fact, she couldn't stand me.

I whispered into the receiver, "I'm sorry you feel this way, but I want you to know the door is always open for you to come back, if you change your mind."

After a moment of uncomfortable silence she finally responded, "Uh, okay. Bye," and then the phone went dead.

It had taken twenty-two long years for me to find my mother and bring her back into my life and only four brief months for us to break apart again. Never in my wildest dreams did it occur to me that Daisy would just walk away.

Clawing at the cold tile walls in the bathroom, I slid off the edge of the tub where I had been sitting and curled myself up into a tight little ball on the bathroom rug. A lifetime of rejection began to slowly spill out of my mouth in low, pitiable sobs that wracked me to my core. Frightened of waking my children, I grabbed a towel off the towel rack and shoved my face inside it to muffle the sounds of my crying.

With each passing minute, I felt the connection between us sever. There was a vortex of energy pulled out of my body and life as the magnitude of my loss descended upon me. After almost an hour of crying on the bathroom floor, I finally dragged myself back into my bed, wrapping my arms around my daughter, who lay there quietly sucking her fingers in her slumber. Breathing in the scent of her hair, I collapsed into a fitful sleep. While I may not have had my mother anymore, I still had my children. They were still my blood. My family.

In the days and weeks that passed after that conversation, I still held onto the hope that Daisy would change her mind. That she would wake up one day and realize she had made a huge mistake and desperately wanted me back in her life. But the call never came. And slowly, I began to put the pieces of my heart back together while struggling to come to terms with the savagery and lack of empathy from the woman I had put on a pedestal. The woman I had dreamt about for years who had unexpectedly rushed into my life like a tsunami and pulled back out again with the same amount of lethal force. Unbeknownst to us both, this would not be the last time we would speak.

May Lai Baber

April 16, 1972–February 24, 1998

CHAPTER FOURTEEN

Like me, for years my sister May Lai had lived with a seri-
ous drinking problem. She was also a runaway and a high-
school dropout, but she never tried to get her GED. Thanks to
her extraordinary beauty, she was able to survive in the world
because men were willing to foot the bills as part of the price of
being in a relationship with her. She wasn't a gold digger, but a
survivor, a girl who began at the age of fourteen to live with various men who idealized her. The men she chose weren't necessarily well off. For the most part, they were average, and in some
cases, below average.

Except for a brief period when she was twenty, she never
worked at a "real job." Eventually she would become a successful
fashion model, whose image graced many campaigns. But modeling was just something she did for fun. She never took her career
seriously. With the proper direction and drive she could have
been, according to her agents, "the next Kate Moss." But May Lai,
like I had been for a time, was firmly rooted in a lifestyle based on
the pleasure principle.

I have always needed a physical place to plant myself, but
not my sister. May Lai preferred living out of her suitcase, drift-
ing from city to city, from man to man, in a quasi-Bohemian
existence. She wasn't materialistic in the least but she was an ex-

ceptionally vain woman, as most beautiful women are. Her god was named Freedom and her most cherished possessions were her wardrobe, makeup, skin-care products, and her collection of music and poetry.

For years she had been living her nomadic lifestyle without any serious issues other than her drinking that I knew of, but things changed quickly when she reunited with Israel.

Israel, it turned out, was a junkie and a small-time drug dealer. Soon my sister would find herself "chasing the dragon" as an intravenous drug user.

We were standing in the old administrative passport office near New York's City Hall when she dropped this bomb on me.

"I think I am going to try heroin," she said as banally as one would say, "I think I want tacos for dinner tonight."

She was always losing her identification and had lost yet another passport. I'd taken a half-day off work to vouch for her by signing an affidavit of her identity as she reapplied.

At this point I had been sober for a little over two years. I had heard enough horror stories in my recovery group about how hard "smack" was to kick to know that no good was going to come of her "experiment" with heroin.

"What in the hell are you talking about, May Lai?" I scolded. "Are you kidding me? Tell me why you are doing this."

"I don't know . . ."

"Are you outta your fucking mind?" I hissed. Seeing the stunned look on her face, I continued my attack. "You know you are going to get hooked, right? That's the only thing that happens, May Lai. We already have addiction running through our family. Tell me, in your infinite wisdom, how you're going to end up the one person who can defy the odds and *not* end up an addict!"

I kept up my tirade, berating her for her stupidity. May Lai was never a very confrontational person. If someone had come at me that way, there would have been a shouting match in the middle of that office. Not my sister. She tended to hold everything in until she exploded, which was rare. I could see she was getting more and more agitated, but I wouldn't let up. Her life was on the line and I was trying my hardest to smash it into her skull that she must not do this. Of course my blitzkrieg approach failed. Instead of changing her mind she finally stormed off in a huff, leaving me standing alone.

Years later I would wonder whether a different approach that day would have kept her from experimenting with the drug. What would have happened if I had tried a loving and compassionate response? Would that have stopped her? For the life of me, I didn't understand why she told me what she was planning to do. She knew me just as well as I knew her and had to have foreseen my response. Maybe she did it for shock value. Or as a cry for help. Or maybe it was her way of letting me know that she was giving up on life and taking a slow trip to the grave.

I had hoped my tough-love approach would deter her from trying it, but it didn't. I would come to learn, during her first call from jail after being arrested for possession, that my sister had become a full-fledged heroin addict within a few short months. I tried to help her get clean by taking her to a recovery meeting, but after attending one she said she wouldn't go back. She simply wasn't ready. Staying true to her nonconfrontational style, she would just smile sweetly and nod while ignoring my desperate pleas for her to get help.

To say that it's a nightmare to watch someone slowly kill herself through drugs and alcohol is an understatement. It was true that I had put my family through a similar hell when I was drinking. The chaos and destruction caused by both addictions is the same, but between the two, drugs typically will kill you quicker. Maybe that's why I viewed her heroin use as worse than my drinking. While I had gotten used to the irresponsible behavior that came along with May Lai's drinking, I couldn't accept her hardcore drug use.

It was incredible to see that the little sister I had played Barbies with, the one I had taught how to put on makeup and scrapped with over coloring books, was now a junkie. Lord knows, my family was incredibly dysfunctional, but heroin addiction was something that happened to other people's families, families that you saw on made-for-TV movies, or in documentaries on the impact it had in the parts of our country that had been ravaged by poverty and racism. Yet despite my "othering" of a very universal issue in our society, my precious little sister was a junkie who needed a fix more than she wanted to live, and there was nothing that I or anyone else could do about it.

By the time she had been arrested, May Lai was no longer modeling and was living off handouts from her friends and her ex-boyfriend Félix, the French pop singer. This was a far cry from her days as a top-tier party girl coveted by the Hollywood elite. May Lai's career brought her into contact with those in the highest echelons of rock and roll—even appearing in different music videos, the most famous being Guns N' Rose's "Don't Cry." Like me, she had found that being perceived as a great beauty was an equal burden and gift. May Lai had her own horror stories of sexual abuse at the hands of powerful men. How much these traumas played in the development of her own drug addiction, I will never know.

Now in New York, in an attempt to jump-start her career again (and because Israel's mother had kicked her out of the house), my sister had moved into the apartment of my former boyfriend Jay.

Jay's apartment was disastrously located near the epicenter of the city's heroin trade, Tompkins Square Park. My home in the Bronx was miles away by train, but May Lai and I stayed in contact and tried to see each other as much as possible. Between my busy work schedule, raising my kids, and her constant partying, however, we didn't actually spend much time together. I lived each day in a sort of emotional limbo with my sister and her addiction. They weren't connected in my mind. May Lai was my sister. Her drug addiction was an interloper that could be cast out of her life, if only she made the decision to eliminate this destructive guest, or so I hoped. Of course, as a recovering alcoholic I knew that you cannot separate the addiction from the person. When addicts in recovery do this they often find themselves using again, which is why those of us in recovery acknowledge each day that our addiction runs through our system just as readily as blood does in our veins. The day we try to mentally separate the two is the day we are at risk of finding ourselves back in the throes of a full-blown relapse.

I knew that May Lai's odds of surviving heroin addiction were slim, but I believed that she would be one of the fortunate ones that would get clean. And through our phone calls, I learned that Daisy had been trying to help her by offering her a place to stay while she "kicked" and was working with her husband, Bob, to get May Lai treatment. It hurt to know that Daisy, again, was choosing May Lai over me, but my feelings were irrelevant. My sister was in trouble, and getting her help was the most important thing on my mind. My feelings were a distant second to saving May Lai's life.

❦

I have always found it amazing that the most defining moments in our lives can often happen within minutes, or even seconds. One ill-considered decision can have an impact that resonates forever.

It seems like it was only yesterday, when I was in the middle of reading the Dr. Seuss book *Green Eggs and Ham* to my children as their bedtime story, that my telephone began to ring.

"'Would you? Could you? In a car? Eat them! Eat them!' . . ." *Brriiing!* "'Here they . . .'" *Briiing!*

The ringing was grating, but I decided to ignore it so I could finish reading them their story. I had just tucked my kids into their beds when the ringing started again. Closing their door behind me, I rushed over to the phone in the living room and answered it, slightly out of breath, with an annoyed "Hello?"

On the other end of the line I heard a young woman's voice sobbing.

"Sil Lai? It's Yvette. May . . . May Lai . . ." she stammered.

I already knew what she was going to say. It was a call I had been waiting for with anxious foreboding over the past year.

"What happened!?" I barked.

May Lai's friend then began rambling about the jumbled events from the night before. How they had started out their night at a party at The Coffee Shop for the band The Black Crowes and ended up partying over at their friend Kip's apartment afterward. According to Yvette, May Lai had left the group at 5:00 a.m. to go home and pack for her flight that morning at 11:00. She had to get to a court appearance the following day in Florida for a heroin possession charge.

Yvette tearfully blurted out that Jay had found her dead in his bed that night when he came home from work. "I am sooooo sorry, Sil Lai," she wailed.

"So Jay just got home right now from last night? He just went straight to work without stopping home first?" I said suspiciously.

Although I had stayed out for days at a time when I was an active alcoholic, I didn't work the day after a good party. The idea that Jay would roll straight from Kip's apartment to his job at a real estate office without changing clothes seemed far-fetched.

"Where's Jay?" I demanded.

"He's at home with the police."

"I'll call you back."

By now, my entire body was shivering uncontrollably, adrenaline surging. How I was able to punch the numbers into the phone with the way my hands were shaking is beyond my comprehension, but I somehow managed to dial Jay's number while walking into my bedroom. He answered as I closed my door.

"Sil Lai . . ."

"Jay, what the fuck is going on?" I demanded. "What happened? Tell me what happened to my sister, dammit!"

"Um, Sil Lai. Hold on a minute."

Another man's voice then came on the line.

"Hello. Who am I speaking to?"

"My name is Sil Lai. May Lai is my sister! Someone just called my house and said she was dead and I want to talk to Jay! Where is he? Why am I speaking to you? Who *are* you?"

"Ma'am, I'm a detective with the New York City Police Department. Your sister . . ."

I didn't need to hear him utter the words that would excruciatingly confirm Yvette's. Dropping the phone on my lap, I shrieked at the top of my lungs. A long, piercing wail that rose from the bottom of my stomach and scraped off the back of my throat, reverberating off the walls of my small bedroom. I picked the phone up again and held it to my ear in time to hear him say, "Ma'am, I need you to calm down."

Hand clawed around the receiver I'd dropped down by my side, I doubled over the edge of my bed, shrieking again and again.

"NO! NO! NO!" I wailed, each word punctuated by a shriek, then followed with brief, shallow breaths. Putting the phone back to my ear, I sat doubled over, head between my knees, on the edge of the bed. Hyperventilating and weeping as I listened to the officer tell me how May Lai's body had been discovered that evening, dead from an apparent heroin overdose based upon the drug paraphernalia on the nightstand.

Sobbing, I asked him to put Jay back on the phone.

"Jay, I don't understand. What happened?" Not waiting for his response, I pressed, "So you just got home at 8:00 p.m.? You didn't even stop in at all during the day?" I said warily.

"No, I got in from work not long ago and found her in my bed. I swear."

The sordid story sounded so clean and convenient for Jay and Yvette. How incredibly coincidental it was that he had found her thirteen hours after she left them following an all-night party. Thirteen hours was more than enough time for them to distance themselves from her and any illicit drug use they had all engaged in that morning. Something inside me didn't buy their tale. I knew Jay had a history with drugs. I had also heard stories about addicts panicking when someone in a group overdoses, leaving their friend to die in order to avoid a possession charge. Although there wasn't any evidence other than my gut feeling, it wasn't beyond the realm of possibility that he had been with May Lai when she overdosed, and had bailed to save his own ass.

"No, I was out showing apartments all day. My roommate was here, though. He was working from home and saw her lying in the bed around 10:00 a.m. He thought she was sleeping, so he just closed the door and left her alone."

At this point I couldn't hold it in any longer. I blew up.

"So you're telling me that fucking idiot didn't think there was anything strange about May Lai sleeping straight through the afternoon?"

Due to his inattentiveness or utter cluelessness, their roommate had unwittingly sat by idly and done nothing while the final breaths of air escaped from May Lai's lungs. He had chatted on his phone, eaten lunch, peed, and watched television all while my very alive sister was transforming into a corpse.

Paralyzed with rage, I hung up the phone. As I struggled to wrap my head around what had happened, another thought popped into my mind.

My parents! Lord! I gotta call them and let them know that May Lai is dead.

I spent the rest of my night calling my entire family to let them know May Lai had overdosed. That included the woman who had explicitly told me not to call her, Daisy. When Bob answered the phone, I told him that I knew she didn't want to speak to me, but it was an emergency about May Lai. That, I knew, would get her on the phone. Of all the calls I had to make that night, this was the hardest. I couldn't imagine what it was like to be in her shoes—to have lost and found her children, rejected all but one, and have her die within seven months.

I fell into a fitful sleep around 4:00 a.m., but not before calling in to my job and leaving a message on the main company voice-mail that I wouldn't be coming in to work due to a family emergency.

The following day I began to take care of May Lai's funeral arrangements—alone. Everyone in my family lived far from New York and I was relieved when no one stepped forward to help. It made it easier for me to handle what had to be done, without any interference or group consensus. Once I figured out the date of the wake and the funeral, I called Daisy back to let her know so she could begin making her travel arrangements. I was shocked when she said that she wasn't sure if she was going to go.

"Why wouldn't you come?" I asked.

"I don't want to see George. I don't want to be in the same room with him."

At this point I'd had enough of her nonsense. It was one thing for her to make a decision not to speak to me. It was something else altogether to not attend her own daughter's funeral.

"Daisy. This isn't about you. This isn't about what happened between you and Dad two decades ago. This is your opportunity to say goodbye to your daughter. This is about *May Lai*. I can promise you this: if you don't come to this funeral because you're still mad at Dad for what he did to you, you will live to regret it! You're bigger than that. You're stronger than that. And you know this is what May Lai deserves."

"Fine. I'll come, but I don't want him near me."

"I promise that won't happen. You and Bob will be kept clear away from him."

I then called Dad and told him what Daisy had said.

"I don't understand why she's still mad at me. After all, she left, not me. And it's been over twenty years."

Apparently, in his mind at least, there was a statute of limitations on how long a parent is entitled to hold a grudge when the other parent takes her children away. *Christ*. The denial with this one was too much.

"Dad, just promise me that when you see her you won't say anything, okay? Just stay away from her. She doesn't want to see you . . ."

"Fine. I won't speak to her. But I still don't understand . . ."

Cutting him off, I said, "I have to get back to making the arrangements. I'll see you on Thursday."

Somehow, I managed to make it through the week on autopilot. I walked through the funeral home in a daze while selecting the steel casket that would hold my sister's body. Sifted through her suitcases for the clothes I thought she would want everyone to see her in the last time the light of day shone on her face. Feet shuffling through the dirt, I plodded through the cemetery, coat wrapped tightly around my body as protection from the cold air. Selecting the final resting place where she would be buried, curiously only fifty yards from where my son's father, Keith, was interred.

How I was able to go through this painstakingly intricate and unfamiliar experience is beyond the scope of my understanding. Yet despite feeling like someone had shot a syringe of battery acid straight into my aorta, I managed to hold it together up until the day of May Lai's wake. By then everyone was in town: my brother Dan, stepsister Julia, Dad, Mom, Daisy, and Bob. In a short amount of time the word of my sister's death had spread throughout her social circle, and at least fifty people showed up to pay their respects at Redden's Funeral Home on East 14th Street in Manhattan.

True to his word, Dad stayed on one side of the funeral parlor, entertaining himself by being overly friendly and, dare I say, flirtatious with May Lai's twenty-something-year-old female friends. Watching him out of the corner of my eye, I was disgusted. He hadn't even offered to pay a penny toward his daughter's funeral, instead opting to call everyone he knew and beg for money. When I asked him if he had money in his IRA to use, he said that money couldn't be touched. Fortunately, May Lai's former fiancé, Félix, had flown in from France and kicked in $6,000 toward the funeral costs, which at least covered the wake. The remaining balance for the burial plot was my responsibility since I was the one who'd signed the paperwork. Apparently, my having to shoulder the burden of paying for the funeral while being a single mother raising two children on a salary of $33,000 and small, quarterly annuity payments in New York City didn't matter to Dad.

Julie, Julia, and Dan stayed close together and behaved in a manner that was more expected of a grieving family, greeting those who came in. Politely speaking in hushed tones with the mourners. Daisy and Bob sat off to the side, watching everyone interact with each other, avoiding me, and speaking only to my brother Daniel or any of May Lai's friends who came over once learning that Daisy was May Lai's biological mother.

All day I had been operating on caffeine and adrenaline, scurrying around to ensure that everything was in place. After an hour or so of milling about in the parlor area, it was time for the viewing, which was being held in a room upstairs. I climbed the stairs and as each foot landed on another carpeted step, I was acutely aware of my lack of emotion. I was nervous, but not any more so than I was ordinarily.

Maybe this isn't going to be as bad as I thought.

Looking back at my friend Carol, who was coming up behind me on the staircase, I said, "This is so strange, but I don't feel anything."

She simply responded, "It's okay, Sil Lai, everything is going to be okay."

I wondered what in the world she was talking about. *Everything is okay.* Well, it was until my foot hit the landing at the top of the stairs. Turning my head so that I had a straight view of the casket, I saw May Lai, lying still and quiet in the coffin I had chosen for her. And that is when whatever had been binding me together suddenly ripped apart. My knees buckled and I burst into a torrent of tears so violent that I fell to one knee, hand planted on the carpet to brace my fall. My then boyfriend, Terry (a man I had begun dating after Daisy's rejection), and my brother lifted me up and partially carried me to her side. I nearly collapsed twice as we approached, but somehow made it to the casket. Finally, I was able to stand, teetering slightly in my three-inch heels, tears flowing in a torrent down my face.

She looked so peaceful. So still. With the exception of the unnatural stiffness of her body and the flatness of the skin covering her eyelids, you would think she was asleep. But this was not some deep sleep. If I didn't have a room full of spectators, I probably would have screamed at the top of my lungs and clawed at the curtains and flowers in the room.

So many people survive heroin. Why couldn't my sister? It wasn't fair. It wasn't fucking fair at all. How did the sun dare to shine on a day that plunged my soul into darkness? Nothing had the right to shine on the day my sister was lying dead in a steel coffin in that funeral home with its tacky floral drapes. How could people be walking around outside, going about their lives as if everything was normal, when my life as I had known it had ended?

I wanted to take my life and breathe it into her, to shake her and force her to open her eyes.

Wake up, baby! Wake up!

In the biblical chapter Exodus, the God of Israel had given people an opportunity to protect their firstborn child from death by marking their doors with the blood of a lamb. May Lai wasn't the firstborn—I was. I was the one who should have died, not her. Why could I get sober when she couldn't?

This was something I couldn't fix or control. It was another finite period at the end of a sentence. The loss of one-third of the people in my immediate family (outside of my children) I personally knew and loved who shared my bloodline. Of the one person in the world with whom I had shared most of my life's experiences. My best friend and biggest rival. My sister would never grow old or have children. She would remain twenty-five. Forever.

The next day we held the funeral at a Catholic church on the Upper West Side. Only a handful of people showed up. Inside the cathedral, the beautifully lit, ornate Gothic marble interior echoed with the light sobs emitting from the forms sitting in the hard wooden pews. After the priest made his remarks, there was an opportunity for people to come up and share their stories about my sister. No one moved from their seats. I don't know if they were too grief-stricken, or just shy. After a few moments, only one person, Charles, an owner of The Coffee Shop restaurant in Union Square and one of May Lai's ex-boyfriends, got up to speak briefly.

Peering around at my dad, Mom, Daisy, and May Lai's friends, I waited to see if anyone else was going to speak. The priest rocked back and forth slowly on his heels as he patiently waited. After an awkward few minutes of silence, I realized that no one else was going to say anything. And while I was terrified of speaking, there was no way I was going to fail to eulogize my only sister. I made my way up to the podium and said a few unprepared words, then rushed back to my seat. I hated every second of it, but my conscience was clear. I couldn't leave May Lai unacknowledged.

At the conclusion of the service, six men carried my sister's casket to the waiting hearse, and our funeral procession made its winding way up to Woodlawn Cemetery in the Bronx. My boyfriend had hired two limousines to transport us to her final resting place. Dad, Mom and Julia, and a few of May Lai's friends were in one limousine, while my brother Daniel and I rode over in the car with Daisy and Bob, my boyfriend Terry, Charles, and Félix.

It was a somber ride, largely silent, broken up intermittently with polite conversation. I sat with the bright sunlight shining through the windows onto my face, eyes hidden behind my dark glasses. Staring absently at the scenery, I watched the cars fly by, musing over how many times had I driven past a funeral procession myself and never thought twice about the people in the cars. Now, I was one of those people, looking from the inside out.

In an effort to make small talk, I thanked Félix again for paying for part of May Lai's funeral.

"We couldn't have done this without you, Félix. Thank you so much for making the trip from France to say goodbye."

Before Félix could reply, Daisy shot out, "At least *someone* cared about May Lai."

These, not the drunken phone call from a few months earlier, would be the last words Daisy uttered to me. I couldn't believe the gall of this woman to speak with such disrespect to everyone, including me, in that car. She had shown up in our lives again only because I had found her and brought her back. There were twenty-two years of time between us during which she could have done her part to "care" about May Lai. But in her grief, she chose to indict us all for failing to protect May Lai from herself.

Fortuitously, our drive ended a few minutes after Daisy's outburst when we pulled up to the gravesite. Our small group of mourners made its way from the cars to the burial plot. The coffin was closed and on a hydraulic lift that would lower May Lai into the ground.

Weeping, I asked one of the graveyard workers if they would open the casket for just a moment.

"Please . . . I just want the sun to shine on her face before you lower her into the ground," I pleaded.

"Ma'am. You don't want that. The coffin is sealed, but trust me, you don't want to see her in the sunlight. I can't do it."

Not wanting to make a scene, I let the subject go, forced to accept that yesterday was the last time I would ever see her face outside of a photograph.

Once the burial was over, Daisy climbed into the other limousine and rode back to the funeral home where we were all dropped off. She and Bob exited the vehicle and walked away without saying goodbye to anyone. As I watched her form recede from view, all I could think to myself was *Thank God the kids weren't here for this.*

Now, both of the women in my life that I most closely shared blood with were truly gone. I had no way of knowing that in the years to come I would, through a fortuitous cycle of events, embark upon a search that would reunite me with the other women with whom I shared a genetic link.

Four generations of Lui women together again after thirty-two years estrangement. Kowloon, Hong Kong, 2005. (L to R) Me, Aunt Judy, Grandma Mei Ying, Great Aunt Hong Ying, Aunt Esther, seated Great Grandma Sau Ying.

CHAPTER FIFTEEN

⁂

$\mathcal{A}$s our plane began its descent into Hong Kong's airspace, I felt a rush of adrenaline surge through my body. Enough energy to shake off the lethargy of a sixteen-hour flight in Cathay Pacific's coach class. Fortunately, the flight wasn't full and I had an entire center row to myself that enabled me to spread out for the duration of the trip. That, coupled with the Ambien I had taken, allowed me to sleep through half of a flight that for many (except those in first and business class) must have been an extremely uncomfortable experience.

Our flight was scheduled to land at 9:00 p.m., which made the approach to Hong Kong International Airport an opportunity to see the city lit up like a glittering disco ball. Stretching my neck to have a better view, I saw that our plane was virtually skimming the surface of the bay, wings outstretched like a crane sailing low over the water. Landing at this airport is like the approach at LaGuardia in New York—minus seeing the miles and miles of low buildings in Brooklyn and Queens. I couldn't believe that I was on the last leg of my journey to finally meet Daisy's family. My Chinese family.

The years of complete alienation from her had left me culturally incompetent regarding my Asian heritage. To prepare for this trip, I did my best to learn more about the local customs by purchasing a traveler's guide and rewatching *The Joy Luck Club*, one of my favorite films, based on the best-selling book of the same name. As we descended, I envisioned a teary reunion with Daisy's family where we would grab onto each other as the sisters did in the final scene of that movie. Yet despite this melodramatic fantasy, I also knew how standoffish I could be with strangers, and didn't bet on any tearful hugs from people I was meeting for the first time.

It was now 2005, and in the time since I had last spoken to Daisy, I had gone from being a single mother, to a wife, to a single mother again. Reeling in pain from my sister's death, I'd hastily married a man that I had met several years before when I was modeling in Milan, only thirteen months after burying May Lai. David was a sweet, white Canadian man two years my junior who became a willing and adoring surrogate father to my children. At the time I was struggling with a serious depression that followed on the heels of my sister's death and financial difficulties. David was not put off by my having two children by two different men who were not a part of their lives. He was vastly different from any man I had dated prior, the result of an incredibly solid base of values instilled in him during a loving childhood.

Even though I had stopped dating white men years before, I had made the decision to break my rule after my disastrous five-year relationship with Amanda's father. Since I was eighteen years old I had been in a series of unfortunate relationships with black men. I needed a break from the complications of dating, and David entered my life at the perfect time. He was so incredibly *normal,* so present and open to me, that at the time I assigned these traits to his white upbringing, not his parents' healthy chil- drearing practices. A blind spot for sure. It never occurred to me that the reason for my consistently poor selection pattern in men could be originating from within me. That it had nothing to do with race, but with how I was conditioned poorly by *my* family. That Dad, a white man, had primed me through years of psychological terrorism and neglect to seek out men who, irrespective of race, treated me the same way he had—or worse.

My marriage to David was functional, yet had its difficulties, the main being that, as the saying goes, opposites attract, but they also repel. The contrast of our temperaments and backgrounds was charming in the beginning, but over time exposed the radical difference in values we shared. That, combined with our youth and constant financial problems, placed tremendous pressure on our very new union. David was a model who had switched to sales to support our family, while I pursued a new career in event planning. Despite two incomes, there was never enough money to go around.

Eventually our marriage would end, slain by my own hand. And for what reason did I leave the kindest and most respectful man I had ever known? His race. David, in spite of being attentive, honest, faithful, and patient, was white and not as ambitious as the men I had been accustomed to dating. Also, while he wasn't racist, he was woefully ignorant about what it meant to be black in America. David was tall, handsome, charming, blond, blue-eyed, and completely impervious to his privilege. In time I grew to resent the need to constantly educate him on what it meant in this country to not look like him, and how it was patronizing to greet black men with fist bumps and "What's up, brother?" when he never used this same language with his white friends.

Out of my desire to make the marriage work, for a few years I did my best to ignore his racial ignorance and focused instead on the positive aspects of his character. I was so grateful to have him in my life that I never questioned how the issue of race could become a problem, at least for me—at first. Yet, walking down the street, I felt the eyes of the men and women who watched us curiously. A feeling that was reminiscent of my childhood, when the Baber clan walked through the mall and had to endure the curious stares of passersby. It never occurred to me that I would end up feeling shame when David and I were around my black friends. Over time, I would resent what I feared he represented to the people in my social milieu—that I had sold out on my brothers. Equally disturbing was my concern that by having a white man raise my black children, even if he was a good man, they would end up with the same crisis of identity that I had worked for years to undo in me. After a few years I could no longer ignore my inner conflict around our incongruent identities.

When I told David that I wanted out after four years of marriage, he was devastated. I did my best to explain why—citing our constant financial problems and his lack of ambition as the primary reasons. However, we both knew that these weren't solid reasons to divorce. It wasn't as if he was loafing around the house playing video games like his predecessor. David was hardworking, and given enough time, these issues would most likely have worked themselves out. He intuitively felt the ripple of something else underneath the surface of my resolute decision, so I told him the truth about how I felt about our interracial marriage. His whiteness was not something that he could defend any more than I could defend my pro-blackness. For another woman of color, one who didn't have a complicated history with race and identity, David would have been heaven sent. In many ways he was to me, but I could not get over the sense that I had somehow succumbed to a "white savior complex."

In the end, I felt comfortable with my choice to end the marriage for my personal reasons, but I couldn't (and never did) reconcile the impact that my decision would have on my kids, depriving them of the only stable and healthy father figure they ever had in their young lives. Our divorce was granted in 2004 and I went back to the cycle of unhappy relationships with men I could identify with, emotionally and culturally.

A year after my divorce was finalized, I began to focus my attention again on Daisy, perhaps in part because in David's absence, I was for the first time in six years feeling the loneliness that came from not having an extended family to call my own. May Lai's death and Daisy's absence surged to the forefront of my consciousness after being buried for the past several years in the routine of family life. Seven years had passed since I had spoken to or heard from Daisy. Although she had re-wounded me in a way I didn't think possible, the perpetual child in me still held on to a fantasy that we would be reunited yet again. That one day the phone would ring and I would hear her familiar voice on the other end. As the years went by, my hope waned but didn't disappear; it just shrank away into a tiny space in my broken heart.

My desire for a reconciliation was like a mild heart arrhythmia. You know that it's there. Occasionally it's uncomfortable, and you know how it limits your body's ability to fully function at an optimal level. But for the most part you ignore it, and deal with the intermittent reminders of its presence only when symptoms flare up. That's when you remember it exists, at which point you do something to try and treat it.

On those rare moments when I had a "flare-up," my typical "treatment" was to search for Daisy's name on the internet. I usually came up with nothing, other than some general information from paid search providers listing her name, with five different variations of her profile, listing her in three different states. Even though paying for a search result was inexpensive, I was leery of spending money on information that would end up sending me on a wild goose chase. Plus, what would I say to her if I found her? She had made it crystal clear that she didn't want to have anything to do with me. What was I going to do? Call and say, "Hi Daisy! It's Sil Lai—you know, the daughter you basically told to get lost back in 1997? Just reaching out to see if you've changed your mind about not wanting to talk to me." Reaching out was a crapshoot. Unwilling to risk another rejection, I left the paid services alone. But it didn't stop me from wondering about her—if she was even still alive.

In February of 2005, I typed in her name and used a technique that I had learned over the years as internet search protocols became public knowledge. My browser was open to a Google search tab and I typed in the words *Yau Lai Lui*. I narrowed the search to the keywords in her name by putting quotation marks around her first and surname, and including a plus symbol between the three words, so it looked like this: "Yau+Lai+Lui."

As I scrolled down the first page of responses, my eyes paused on a result that was on an international missing persons website:

Yau Lai Lui (Baber)
Mother of Siu Lai, Mei Lai, and Daniel
Anyone with information please send to Esther Lui.

The post was followed by an address in Chippenham, England.

My heart started pounding with a force so intense that I feared it would jump through my rib cage. As I felt my pulse throbbing, a high-pitched, tinny sound began ringing in my ears.

It was somewhat of a relief to know that I wasn't the only person in the family that Daisy had rejected, nor the only person thinking about her. Then I remembered a story Daisy had told me in 1997 about how she became estranged from her family. From what I recall, she felt that they hadn't shown her husband, Bob, proper respect on his birthday, which was in contrast to the way they treated her sister Judy's husband, Philip. If Daisy was one thing, she was consistent. Piss her off and you'll be tried, sentenced, and executed for any one of a million possible infractions to her unspoken code of acceptable behavior.

To learn that my mother's sister was looking for her and that her address was listed on the internet was nothing short of a miracle. For decades I had wondered about my extended family, and in this moment I was one step away from potentially reconnecting with them for the first time in thirty-one years.

It was late afternoon and counting the hours, I realized it was now 10:00 at night in the United Kingdom. Despite the time difference, I had to find some way to act. Right then. To mail a letter to England based upon the information at my fingertips meant I might have to wait a week or more to connect with Esther. I needed to speak to her *now*. Grabbing my wallet and keys, I ran around the corner from my apartment in Park Slope, Brooklyn, where I had settled the year before, to buy a calling card. My thought was that I would call directory assistance in England, give them my aunt's information, and get a phone number.

Plunking down my ten dollar bill on the counter, I asked the owner of the deli which card had the best rates per minute to call the U.K. "This one here is very good," he said in a thick Pakistani accent.

"I'll take it." Grabbing it off the counter, I ran the half block back to my brownstone apartment and leapt up the stairs two at a time to our second-floor unit. My son, Christian, now fourteen years old, was in his room playing video games, and Amanda, age nine, was already asleep, as it was a school night. Which was a good thing, because I didn't have to worry about being interrupted by either of them. I was too hyped up to pay attention to anything but the matter at hand: contact with my aunt.

Rushing to my room, I sat down at my desk and scratched off the code on the back of the card. Hands shaking, I searched online for the correct number to directory assistance in England and made the call. Once I got an operator on the line, I was disappointed to learn that Esther's phone number was unlisted.

Damn.

Spinning around in my chair, I tilted my head back and closed my eyes.

Think, Sil Lai. Think. How can you get around this?

And then it clicked. While I couldn't find Esther's number through a search, or directory assistance, her address was right there in front of me. With some luck, I just might be able to get her contact information through one of her neighbors listed on the internet.

Typing in her address, I scanned the results and saw a listing for a graphic designer located at what had to be a few doors away. Her house number was 83; this business listing was 95, and had a phone number. Given that by now it was almost 11:00 p.m. their time, I decided to wait and call the next day.

First thing in the morning after the kids had left for school, I called the number I had found online. A congenial-sounding man with a British accent answered the phone.

"Hi. My name is Sil Lai Abrams. I know this is going to sound weird, but I'm looking for my long-lost aunt and you happen to be down the street from her."

There was a brief pause, and then he asked me to continue, with a little skepticism in his voice. Over the next five minutes, I rushed through my story of having lost touch with my mother and finding the listing on the missing persons website. "Would you be willing to take my phone number and give it to my aunt? I know this is asking a lot of a stranger, but I'm desperately trying to get in touch with her."

Chuckling, he said, "No worries at all. I'm happy to oblige. It's not a big ask. I'll take care of it later today when I go out to run some errands."

"Thank you so very much. I'm very, very grateful for your help. Bless you!" I exclaimed. I was grateful, but also very impatient. What I really wanted to say was "C'mon, mate! I've waited thirty-one years. Let's get to it now! Chop chop!" or some variation of what I imagined a British person would say.

Now it was just the waiting game to see if (1) he would actually do what he said, and (2) if Esther was even still alive, and living at that address. The posting at this point was three years old.

The next day my cell phone rang. The number coming up on the screen said *Unavailable*. Praying it wasn't an ex who was blocking his number, I answered the phone quickly with a breathy, "Hello?"

"See You Lai? This is your mother's sister, Esther. I got your note yesterday. I'm sorry I didn't call earlier, but I had to work." Her voice had a slightly wheezy quality to it, like she had some sort of lung problem. Despite her measured tone, she let me know she was extremely happy to hear from me.

Collapsing onto my bed, I exhaled deeply with relief. My mother's abandonment of me not once, but twice, could not keep me away from my kin. Esther and I spoke for two hours that night, and then again the following night. I caught her up to general speed about what had happened in my life over the past three decades since we had seen each other last. She shared stories about her life in England and her children, my cousins Phil and Dave. It was the first time in my life that I had cousins. Not the "fake" cousins I inherited through Julie as a child, with whom I never connected or spent much time, unless forced through family gatherings. This was different. These were my real cousins. My blood. Regardless of my skin color, we were kin.

In what was another huge stroke of luck, she shared that she was heading to Hong Kong to visit her family—*our* family—in a week's time. At this point she asked me if I, along with my siblings, would like to go as well. She had already called the family in Hong Kong and they had said they would like me to come. My accommodations were taken care of—I would stay at the home of her sister, my aunt Judy, Daisy's nemesis, irony of all ironies. I would just need to get a plane ticket.

"Umm . . . I spoke to my brother and he said that he can't make the trip. He can't take the time off of work." I didn't share that after the debacle with our mother, Dan had little-to-no interest in getting to know the rest of Daisy's family. Quite frankly, I couldn't blame him.

"As for May Lai going, that isn't possible. She died in 1998."

Esther paused for a moment and then offered her condolences. She then asked for additional information about May Lai's death, which I painfully recounted. It had been seven years since she had passed away, yet the wounds were still fresh.

"Well, when you come you must not tell Grandma about this. It will be too much for her to handle."

"So what do I do when she asks me about my brother and sister? Do I just lie to her?"

"Just tell her they couldn't make it. Grandma is sick. Stomach cancer. We don't want her to get upset."

What I didn't realize at the time was that her request for me to lie was a part of the Chinese concept of *mianzi*, or "saving face." "Saving face" is the Chinese concept of personal honor. It is not particular to China; there are many societies in which the gravest infraction you can incur is to lose honor in society. It doesn't matter if you caused it intentionally or not. For example, in some cultures, a woman will be murdered by her family because she brought shame to her family name by being a victim of rape.

In the United States, we are taught that the truth is the ultimate good. Our personal sense of honor, public or private, is based upon our telling the objective truth no matter what the consequences. Those with high personal integrity are those we respect the most. In China, ethics aren't based on basic principles of right or wrong, good or bad. The strong emphasis on relationships, and the potential that specific information has to affect them, is what determines whether the truth is told in a given circumstance. What we call "situational ethics," which is frowned upon as cowardly in the West, is acceptable in Chinese culture. To the Chinese, it is okay to tell a lie if it serves to protect a family's honor. My sister's death from a drug overdose was not honorable. Not only would it cause my grandmother pain (which was a good enough reason in Esther's mind to lie), but the unspoken fact was that it would cause my family to "lose face," something to be avoided at all costs. Our collective family honor came before my individual need to be transparent about my sister and how her loss had impacted me. Any sort of family scandal, which my sister's drug overdose would qualify as (and coincidentally, pretty much all of my own life's history), needed to be covered up.

Of course, I didn't realize this at the time, because despite my Chinese bloodline I was an American through and through. What she was suggesting struck me not only as blatantly dishonest, but also cruel. Who were we to take away my grandmother's right to the truth?

I was deeply troubled by the prospect of starting my relationship with my grandmother with a lie sitting between us, but this was Esther's call, so I begrudgingly agreed to let her believe that May Lai was still alive. I personally felt that Esther was being unintentionally dismissive of my sister's life. But at the same time, she was offering me an opportunity to meet my blood relatives. So despite my disagreement, I sucked it up.

As I packed and prepared for this trip, I reflected on the fact that I was three and a half years old the last time I had seen Daisy's family. Now, three decades later, I was an adult woman with children older than I was the last time we'd laid eyes on each other. I knew that this trip was a miracle. There are so many people in this world who go to their graves never knowing their blood relatives. As a woman who wasn't a true "adoptee" in the traditional sense, I had always felt conflicted when asked about my family of origin. There was always a disclaimer uttered at the onset of any conversation, for I didn't have an answer.

Now, due to a complete stroke of luck and timing, I had the opportunity to gain more closure on the fragmented parts of my life history. During this visit, I hoped to learn how Daisy had been able to walk away *again* from her children. And perhaps in learning more about her, I would understand more about why my life had taken its twists and turns. Why at thirty-four years of age I'd had only one decent relationship with a man. Why I kept choosing men who were incapable of loving me, or making a commitment to our relationship. Equally important, I was eager to see how I fit into the larger picture of a cohesive and organized family structure, unlike the one in which I was raised.

Our plane touched down with a gentle bounce, and soon our group of weary passengers were exiting and entering the main terminal. The terminal was mammoth, and I would come to learn later that it was (at the time) the largest airport terminal in the world, with an area the equivalent of 140 acres. Inside this gargantuan space I somehow had to locate Daisy's sister Esther and my cousin Janet. We had exchanged photographs over email, but I had failed to print them out.

"Damn it. Why the hell did I wear these?" I cursed myself for opting to wear high-heeled boots instead of more practical sneakers as I struggled, dragging my luggage across the smooth, polished concrete while teetering on the balls of my feet. The truth was I didn't want to meet my relatives dressed like a typical American tourist. You know: blue jeans, Reebok sneakers, Abercrombie sweatshirt, with hair pulled in a topknot tied with a neon scrunchie. Not that I would dare wear any combination of this sort of clothing anyway. But I could have at least worn some stylish kitten heels.

As I exited the glass area that separated the arriving passengers from those in the main terminal, I continuously scanned the faces of the people lined up to greet their family members, business associates, and lovers. It is horrific to admit, but the stereotypical words I've often heard said about Asian *and* black people "all looking alike" popped into my mind. Of course, it's not true. But for a harried American entering a terminal filled with people of Asian descent, I was overwhelmed by the uniformity of the features of the faces I saw in front of me.

Exasperated, I continued my tenuous clattering across the floor, and then I saw the arms flailing in front of me. Beaming smiles and eyes met mine. *Yes. This must be them.* Hurrying my steps, I rushed over to my relatives and was greeted warmly.

"Hello, See You Lai. I'm your cousin Janet. Lisa's daughter." Nodding, I smiled, and a short, bespectacled woman stepped forward and gave me a hug. "I'm your Auntie Esther."

"Let us help you with your bags," said Janet as she grabbed one of my luggage pieces. We made small talk about the flight as we navigated through the terminal and into the parking area, where we boarded a cab.

Hong Kong is comprised of three main regions: Hong Kong, Kowloon Bay, and New Territories. The actual airport is located on the island of Chek Lap Kok, about sixteen miles from our destination, my aunt Judy's home in Kowloon. Traversing the highway that brought us into Kowloon proper, my eyes gawked at the diorama of sights unfolding before me. Kowloon, which is located on the mainland adjacent to the island of Hong Kong, was swarming with people and a giant display of flashing lights. Many of the buildings we passed were low, but there was neon everywhere. And I mean everywhere. At 9:00 p.m., the city was a buzzing hive of activity. It was like New York City's Times Square on steroids.

"We're almost there!" exclaimed Esther. "Just five more minutes. Sorry take so long. Traffic is bad here," she said in her heavily accented English.

Our taxi made a left-hand turn onto a quiet street that wound up a sloping hill. As it made its way through the development, Esther said, "We're in Kadoorie Estates. This is the most expensive area in Kowloon. You know Judy and Philip have money."

"I didn't know that," I replied. Later I would learn that not only was Judy wealthy, but she and her husband, Philip, were bona fide Hong Kong socialites, complete with a membership in the ultra-exclusive Hong Kong Club, which up until 1970 didn't even accept Chinese members.

Kadoorie Estates is an exclusive residential community located near West Kowloon. The homes are a mixture of detached and semi-detached buildings, all designed in an elegant blend of Mediterranean and modern architecture. In a city known for cramped housing, Kadoorie is an oasis of beautifully designed buildings sheltered from the bustle of the surrounding city. The best way to describe it would be if someone were to create a high-end, low-rise housing development in the middle of New York's Central Park. Each house had a private garden, some with pools. This sanctuary was blanketed with eucalyptus and cinnamon trees that lent an aromatic fragrance to the heavy, humid night air. Horsetail plants, which look like thinner versions of bamboo, rose up to the sky around the homes, and plentiful flowering flame tree branches stretched like a fiery canopy over the winding streets. Interestingly, none of these homes were for sale. Their owners, the Kadoorie family (an Iraqi-Jewish family that settled in Hong Kong in the 1880s) were not willing to let go of this precious sanctum in the city. All of its tenants lived there for years, paying exorbitant rents. I found this curious, since one of the principles of wealth building that I knew was that home ownership was a primary way to increase your net worth. This place must be special for wealthy individuals to be throwing away money on rent for decades.

After what seemed an eternity, our taxi pulled up in front of a semi-detached three-story home. Grabbing my luggage, we made our way to the front door. As it opened, I was greeted by a tall, attractive, middle-aged woman whose gaze met mine.

"Hi, See You Lai! I'm your Aunt Judy. Come inside. Welcome to my home."

As the three of us entered the small vestibule on the entry level, I noticed off to the right a large stone pond filled with ornamental carp. These huge orange, white, and black fish splashed in the water, bodies swirling back and forth.

"Come, See You Lai. First, take off your shoes." Once I had placed the soft slippers she handed me on my feet and was standing upright, Judy suddenly exclaimed, "Who's taller?" to everyone assembled.

Smiling at her, I said, "I don't know."

"Come here! Let's see!" Grabbing my arm, she said, "Turn around. Put your back to mine. Esther. Mong Fok [Janet's Chinese name], tell me. Which one of us is taller?"

Peering, both wavered for a moment and then the pronouncement was made. "I think See You Lai is taller. Just by a tiny bit."

"Hmph. Are you sure?"

"Yes . . . just by a little" was Janet's reply.

Laughing, Judy then said, "Okay. Well, I've always been tallest."

I'd been in my aunt Judy's home all of five minutes and could see what Daisy was talking about when she mentioned how competitive her sister could be. Judy was already living up to her Chinese name, Yau Gai, which means "The Best."

"Come, See You Lai. Everyone is waiting for you." With that, she bade me to follow her upstairs to the main living area.

"But what about my luggage?" I asked.

"Don't worry. One of the maids will bring it to your room."

Maids. As in plural?

I made my way up a steep staircase with a hairpin curve midway up the corridor. As I turned the corner, I saw a row of people lined up along the glass partition and bannister that peered over the last part of the stairs. Suddenly, everyone started clapping—a loud, steady sound that startled me. You'd think that they were greeting a dignitary with the thundering applause, but I learned that this is a common tradition when groups of Chinese meet new people. Unfamiliar with the practice, I nodded and dipped my head, bowing very slightly at the waist as I ascended each step. Later on I would read that the proper response would have been for me to clap back. I was glad I learned that afterward. This was already a weird enough experience, and clapping while entering a room would have made it even more surreal.

Very quickly I was introduced to the eldest people in the room. My poh poh, or maternal grandmother, first; then Judy's husband, Uncle Philip, and Esther's husband, Dave (referred to affectionately as Big D); then my mother's brother, Uncle Stephen, followed by his wife, Lisa. All of my mother's siblings were there except for my mother's sister, also named Lisa, who was an actress and away at a shoot. Next, I met Esther's children, my cousins

Phil and Dave; Phil's girlfriend, Samantha; and Dave's girlfriend, Karen. Finally, peeking out from behind their mother's legs, I spied two boys, Phil and Samantha's sons.

"What's your name?" I said to the sandy-haired one.

As he ducked back behind his mother, she said, "Come now, Oliver. Say hello to your cousin See You Lai."

Oliver wiggled back and forth, no words forthcoming, so I turned my attention to the dark-haired, taller boy, who announced, "I'm Thomas."

"Well, it's very nice to meet you, Thomas." It turned out my English cousins and their partners were also staying at Philip and Judy's home, while their mother, Esther, was staying at Poh Poh's apartment in Hong Kong.

We proceeded into a large sitting room, where we engaged in small talk while two of Judy's three Filipina maids bustled about to bring dinner out to the formal dining room. At one point, three of my aunts and uncles pronounced, "You look just like your mother. Even the way you move is like Daisy." This admittedly filled me with pride. I was glad that through me they could connect, at least emotionally, to their long-lost relative.

As I took in the surroundings, I noticed the beautiful framed artwork lining the walls, the smooth marble floors, and exquisite furnishings. Along one wall was a wide display of Buddhas of many shapes and sizes. Some appeared to be made of gold, while others were silver and jade. Lit from behind, they looked like an art exhibit. Which it turned out was not an accident, for Judy and Philip, in addition to being voracious collectors, were also owners of a high-end art gallery, and members of the flourishing international Hong Kong art scene.

"You know, Judy, I also collect Buddhas," I said. "Mine of course are not as beautiful or expensive as yours," which made her smile. My "collection" consisted of pieces I bought off the street in Chinatown, and a few that I had been given by friends over the years. There was nothing special about my Buddhas except for the one piece that was brought back from Dharamsala, Tibet, by a friend who visited the Dalai Lama. I don't remember what spurred me to start collecting them; I had done so even prior to reconnecting with Daisy.

After a half hour of chatting our dinner was finally ready, and we were all ushered into a large room whose central feature was an enormous circular table made of beautiful, hand-rubbed mahogany that seated twelve. In the center of the table was a large lazy Susan, which was built into the surface. This separate piece of raised, rotating wood allowed the various dishes to pass around the table when the diners moved its edge with their fingertips.

I was starved and sat salivating at the smorgasbord of vegetables, seafood, chicken, duck, and rice before me. This was the part of my fantasy that was like the opening dinner scene in *The Joy Luck Club*. But instead of there being raucous chatter, the energy in the room was slightly muted, which seemed appropriate given the elegant surroundings.

I picked up my chopsticks, noticing the mother-of-pearl inlay. Our porcelain dinner plates were exquisite, as was every piece of furniture and artwork in the room. Coming from my lower-middle-class background in America, I was silently pleased that someone in my family had done so well for herself. That the wealth in the family had not stopped with my maternal grandfather.

"I bet you never have real Chinese food before, have you, See You Lai?" Judy called out from across the table. "We don't eat like this every day, of course. But you coming here is special. We made this in your honor. You like?" she asked.

Dipping my chopsticks into a particularly tasty-looking dish made of crab, I enthusiastically nodded. "This is wonderful, Judy.

And to answer your question, no, I haven't had any real Chinese food before. At least, I don't think so."

"That food in America is not *real* Chinese food," she said proudly. "*This* is what real Chinese food tastes like."

And she was right. The food I was eating didn't taste like anything I'd had in the States. It was very light in consistency and the flavors delicately danced over my tongue. Not like the heavy, oil-saturated takeout food I had been accustomed to eating that my kids and I jokingly refer to as "Ghetto Chinese."

Seated immediately to my left was Poh Poh, and next to her my cousin Janet. A shriveled woman with short, black, wavy hair filled with silver strands, my grandmother's face was remarkably plain. Her mouth concealed a curiously pointed overbite, which surprised me given that her children all had perfect teeth. In fact, as I took in her face, I could not see any of her children's features, with the exception of Aunt Esther, who out of all her children was the only one who had inherited her short stature and bone structure. All of the children she had with my Gung Gung must have taken after his side of the family.

I wondered to myself, what about her had made her Gung Gung's favorite? She must have been very beautiful as a young woman. Either that, or very shrewd. Perhaps both.

Slowly chewing and staring into her rice bowl, Poh Poh muttered something low to Janet, who laughed out loud.

"What's so funny?" I asked.

"She says you don't know how to use chopsticks. You hold them funny."

Everyone at the table laughed, as did I. For the next five minutes, with Janet's assistance, Poh Poh tried to instruct me in the proper holding of chopsticks. No matter how many times I tried, I couldn't get the technique. To me, it didn't really matter because my way of holding them actually worked. Despite my rudimentary style, I could use them effectively enough to pick up one grain of rice, or a large piece of chicken. Although it didn't dawn on me at the time, my technique must have been as offensive to her as someone would be to me who gripped her knife and fork like daggers while attacking a steak. Just as you can tell a lot about people's breeding based upon the way they hold their cutlery in the West, the same is probably the case in the East.

As the family and I engaged in light conversation, I waited for the moment that I knew was coming. When the subject of my siblings would arise.

Grandma uttered a few words to Janet, who craned her neck to repeat Poh Poh's question to me.

"Grandma wants to know how your brother and sister are doing."

Eyeing Aunt Esther across the table, I did as I had been instructed.

"Daniel is good . . . He lives in Atlanta, Georgia, and is married. May Lai is fine. They both couldn't make it because of work," I lied.

"Tell us, what do they do?"

Rushing through the subject, I muttered something about May Lai's career in fashion and Dan's work for UPS. Not wanting to get caught up in offering up additional lies, I quickly changed the subject to my kids. With so much activity happening at once, nobody noticed my deflection. Aside from this blip, the rest of the dinner went smoothly. I told them about how I had made the transition from office secretary to now working as an independent event marketing consultant after working my way up from event coordinator at the legendary Roxy nightclub (not that they had heard of it) to eventually becoming the event director at several high-profile New York City venues. I wanted them to be proud of me and see that I had managed to carve out an actual career that required skills beyond filing and answering phones.

After dinner was finished, we retired to the living room, where the elder men, Big D and my uncles Philip and Stephen, sat off in a small group drinking scotch. In preparation for my trip, I had read a small primer on customs in Hong Kong and knew to bring gifts for everyone. Running up the stairs to their mahjong room, where a foldout bed had been placed and I was to stay for the duration of the trip, I pulled a bottle of Hennessy X.O. out of my luggage, along with a package of expensive petit fours I had picked up as an offering to all the others.

Placing the desserts on a side table, I presented the bottle to my Uncle Philip as a gift for allowing me to stay in his home.

"Thank you, See You Lai. This is very thoughtful of you. We will drink this another time. A special occasion," he said as he and the other men poured themselves glasses of Johnnie Walker Black.

Out of all my uncles, Philip was the one who spoke English the most fluently. He was an elegant, proud man very much like his wife. Due to his former profession in advertising, where he eventually became chairman of the advertising agency DDB Needham Asia, his English was exceptionally good. Turning their attention back to each other, they continued to converse in Cantonese, and I moved over to the middle seating area where my English cousins were sitting. I placed the petit fours out for everyone to eat, but no one except me ended up touching them because as I was to come to learn, the Chinese aren't big on sweets. At least not this group. Dessert for them was a plate of fresh-cut oranges.

My English cousins were delightful, and since we all lived in the Western hemisphere, we shared a common culture. Unlike me, however, my cousins Dave and Phil had been raised by their Chinese mother (their father, Esther's first husband, was English, so they too were biracial), who kept close ties to her family despite living halfway around the world. So they were familiar with Chinese customs and language, and seemed to straddle both Western and Eastern culture quite well. Unlike me, who felt completely out of my element. In that moment, I truly began to understand the term "culture shock."

As we chatted among ourselves, I noticed how the elder women continued to socialize, busying themselves between the kitchen and the dining area. My second cousins, Oliver and Thomas, were upstairs with their mother, who had put them to bed, so I was left with Dave, Phil, and Karen to try and begin to close the thirty-year gap of interaction between us. While I was present to our conversation, I was simultaneously observing the other groups dispersed around the house.

The Chinese culture is a Confucian one, largely influenced by the statesman and philosopher Confucius, who lived during the Zhou Dynasty. Confucian philosophy became the official backdrop of the Chinese people for many centuries, and his work is as influential in the East as Socrates is in the West. Confucius believed very strongly in filial loyalty, kinship, and righteousness. In a Confucian society people are extremely focused on social hierarchy, a respect for one's elders, and tradition. In Chinese culture, you give deference to the eldest family member out of respect. Tom Doctoroff, CEO of the advertising company JWT Worldwide in Shanghai and an expert on the consumer psychology of the Chinese, wrote, "In Chinese society, individuals have no identity apart from obligations to, and acknowledgment by, others. The clan and nation are the eternal pillars of identity. Western individualism—the idea of defining oneself independent of society—doesn't exist."

Chinese culture in the modern age is also an extremely materialistic one. Believe it or not, the Chinese are even more materialistic than their American counterparts. Gordon Gekko's infamous statement from the 1987 film *Wall Street*, "Greed is good," isn't just one of the most popular movie quotes in history. To the Chinese, it is a revered philosophy. It is for these reasons that among the men in my family, although my uncle Stephen was the oldest, Uncle Philip was the patriarch of the clan. As the most successful, his money and privilege trumped Stephen's birthright. Even as a materialistic American, I found it fascinating to watch this push-pull dynamic between tradition and materialism play itself out between my uncles. Philip held court with the men, who all behaved in a deferential manner toward him. I understood that the same dynamic would have probably played itself out in the States with Americans, but we aren't bound by their almost maniacal attachment to social order and familial hierarchy. I wondered how this made my uncle Stephen feel. If I were in his shoes I would be irritated, but then again, I'm not only a Westerner, but from America, home to the world's most individualistic society. To us, the needs of the individual are expected to trump that of the collective.

Uncle Stephen was a professional astrologer, of all things. In China, astrology has played an important role for centuries. While different from the Western zodiac, many believe very strongly in the predictions and influence that one's sign has on their choice of life partner and ultimate destiny. In what was another uncanny coincidence, I had informally begun studying astrology five years prior and was able to do cursory readings and chart interpretations under the tutelage of an evolutionary astrologer I had met when a friend gave me a reading for my birthday. Eventually, my friendship with the woman who had gifted me with the reading dissolved, but my relationship with the astrologer, a woman named Marian, flourished. While our modalities were very different, it was fascinating that there was another person in my family who was very serious about this ancient tool. It seemed that in the case of interests, nature was revealing itself in me through my shared interests with Judy and Stephen.

Big D was the outsider of the male trio. He and Esther owned a Chinese takeout store back in the small town in England in which they lived. From what I understand, they weren't technically married, but had been partnered in every way for over twenty years. Big D and Esther were comfortably middle-class expatriates who had managed to build a solid life together.

Out of all my aunts, the obvious HCIC (Head Chinese In Charge) was Judy. Not because she was the eldest—Esther was—but again because of her wealth. She, like my mother, was a very strong-willed woman, but it seemed that unlike my mother, Judy had been able to channel her ambition and intelligence into creating a life that, from a financial perspective, very few people in this world are blessed to enjoy. Philip and Judy weren't billionaires, but certainly multimillionaires whose net worth eclipsed the collective worth of every other person in the room.

Grandma was the matriarch and everyone treated her with the utmost respect, but Judy was given almost the same amount of deference. Esther was a very humble and kind woman who very comfortably stayed in the background while her more assertive younger sister took center stage. Esther didn't seem to mind. Out of all of the older generation, she was the one with whom I felt most comfortable. It could be because she was more open than the rest of the family due to having lived in England for so many years. Not that the English are known for being warm, but in contrast to the Chinese cultural tendency of not showing emotion or betraying their position by sharing their personal thoughts, she was positively effusive.

Janet, out of all of the nieces and nephews, seemed to be the family favorite, while Dave and Phil were also clearly adored. But their partners, Samantha and Karen, didn't seem to be accepted. They were lovely women, but they seemed to be tolerated more than accepted. Perhaps I was reading too much into it, but I surmised that being white Westerners is what kept a comfortable distance between them and the other women in the family. This isn't to say that they weren't liked, but given that they were outsiders by race and culture, it seemed that their place was firmly set just outside the confines of the close-knit group.

And now, within this curious family dynamic, there was me. Not only was I an outsider—literally, after not seeing the family for three decades—I was also an American, which was a definite strike against me. Combine that with the fact that I also culturally and racially identified as black, I was the equivalent of a cigar aficionado at an American Cancer Society event.

As our first night together wound down, everyone prepared to disperse to their respective rooms or homes. Uncle Philip pronounced to the entire group before retiring, "This is good! First, we find See You Lai. Now, Daisy!" His words struck me as odd, since I didn't see the correlation between me and my mother, especially since they all knew that I hadn't spoken to her in eight years. But as the days would unfold over my weeklong trip to my mother's homeland, their true, hidden intention behind this trip would become clear.

The next few days were a flurry of activities. First stop: to spend the day in Hong Kong at my grandmother's apartment, where she lived with my aunt Lisa in a simply appointed high-rise building in one of the nicer areas of the city. It was there that I met my *tai po*, or maternal great-grandmother. Tai Po looked like she stepped straight out of a *National Geographic* magazine. Dressed in a traditional mandarin-collared, dark-colored silk pantsuit, she sat on the couch next to Poh Poh's sister, my *ipo* (pronounced "ee-poh"), or great-aunt. Tai Po didn't speak

Cantonese—she spoke only Shanghainese. My poh poh and ipo spoke both Shanghainese and Mandarin dialects. My aunts and uncles spoke Mandarin, Cantonese, and English. My cousin Janet and the rest of us all spoke English and Cantonese (except for me), so to communicate between the generations literally required a family member to translate from one to the next. Janet didn't speak Shanghainese, so in order to speak to Tai Po, she would have to enlist the help of Poh Poh, or her mother, or any of her aunts and uncles. I found the entire situation very humorous in a Keystone Cops sort of way. If Janet were left alone with Tai Po, which I'm sure happened when she was a child, they would not be able to communicate because they spoke different dialects.

All around Poh Poh's apartment were photos of her children— I saw the ones she had of my mother in her curio cabinet and even one of May Lai and me from our visit back in 1973. My aunt Lisa, who had been unable to attend last night's dinner, made it back in time for us to briefly meet after an early-morning shoot. Lisa was a successful television actress who had at one time been married to Jackie Chan's martial arts teacher. Like me, she had ties into the entertainment industry, although mine were to black American music and hers were to Chinese film—another coincidence in interests that transcended time and space between my family and me.

Lisa was in her mid-fifties at this point and still a very beautiful woman. I had only a brief exchange with her that day—a quick hello, before she retired to her room to sleep. I found it odd that she wouldn't spend any time at all speaking to me, but I chalked her behavior up to being either very tired or self-absorbed. After all, she was an actress.

Once lunch was finished, my cousins and I ventured out into the streets of Hong Kong, where we were bombarded with a dizzying amount of sights, sounds, and smells. Everything was golden. Gold was sold in every other store in the area we traversed, each shop lit up with bright red neon signs. There were spice stores and fish markets. And everywhere were people, moving at a rapid pace that reminded me of how angry ants swarm around an anthill when you poke a stick in it. I found it funny that for the most part, this sea of people was at least a head shorter than me. I could pretty much walk down the street, especially in my high-heeled boots, and stare over the tops of their heads. Surprisingly, on a few occasions Chinese vendors spoke to me in Cantonese. This was I'm sure due to my wearing my hair straight for this trip and carefully flat-ironing it every morning and at night before we went out to dinner. Even with my darker skin, I was pleased that I could be mistaken for one of them.

Outside of the one meal at Judy's house, each night featured a different group dinner at a new restaurant, and a lot of sightseeing. We spent one day on Lantau Island to see the famed Tian Tian Buddha. Another afternoon Philip and Judy treated us to lunch at the historic Peninsula Hong Kong, which Judy drove us to in their Rolls-Royce (apparently Philip didn't know how to drive). Then of course there was the requisite dinner at the Hong Kong Club, after which we all made our way back to Philip and Judy's. We even had dinner one evening at a Korean barbecue restaurant, which Poh Poh loved. Each day's activities were carefully orchestrated and we all moved in a pack together. This was something very different from what I was accustomed to in my family, not only the one in which I was raised, but also the one I had created with my children.

By now I had been in Hong Kong for five days and had only two more left before I was to return home. In the time that I had spent with my family, I felt a tremendous sense of pride and wonder at their unity and loyalty. They in every way were the antithesis to the family in which I was raised. White collar. Upwardly mobile. Sophisticated.

But that evening my reunion bliss was interrupted by a request that was asked of me by the family. It was Uncle Philip and Aunt Judy who broached the subject that night after dinner.

As we were all chatting about the day, Philip veered the conversation into the direction of my mother. The entire group, sans Poh Poh, Tai Po, and Ipo, were there and standing in his living room when he boldly made his move.

"See You Lai. You know Grandma is very sick with cancer. It is very important for her to see Daisy before she dies. We want you to help us find her, so that Grandma can die in peace having seen her daughter."

I was stunned by the request. They had blatantly ignored the entire part of the story that I relayed to them about how Daisy had specifically requested that I not contact her.

Cautiously and slowly, so as to not reveal my discomfort, I replied, "I understand that it is very important and want to do anything I can do to help. But I'm not sure I'm the right person to do this. After all, Daisy told me that she didn't ever want to speak to me again. As you know, when Daisy sets her mind to things, you can't change it."

As calm as I was trying to remain, I was extremely agitated. This was an incredibly difficult position for me to be placed in, especially given the circumstances. Here I was, thousands of miles from home in a foreign land with a culture and language that I didn't understand. I had been welcomed into my hosts' home as their guest, which was a very kind gesture, but it also made me feel obligated to them, which I loathed.

"Yes, we understand, See You Lai," interjected Judy. "But she is your mother. We need you to help us bring her back to Hong Kong for Grandma."

After thirty years apart, I wanted nothing more than for us to get along and sail off into the sunset as one big, happy family, of which I would be a welcome member. But at the same time, I highly resented what they were asking me to do. It made me feel like my feelings and life experience were completely irrelevant to them. So I tried another approach.

"I'm not trying to be uncooperative, nor do I want you to feel that what you're asking is unfair," I responded, lying through my teeth. "But are you sure that you haven't exhausted every other option for finding her? There is only so much that I can do. I don't have the financial means to be able to pay for a private detective to find her."

This was the cue where Judy and Philip were supposed to jump in and say, "Not to worry . . . we'll take care of the costs. We just need you to be the emissary."

But they didn't offer anything. Instead, they simply reiterated their request. "You're in America and it will be much easier for you to find her than for us. We just need you to speak to her so she can come home."

I was trying in every way to smoothly slip out from their "ask" (which felt more like a demand), but Philip remained steadfast. My English cousins could tell that I was clearly uncomfortable, and the women, particularly Phil's girlfriend, Samantha, cast sympathetic glances in my direction.

"I will help in any way that I can, but you must understand that I can't do this on my own. I'll need your help."

"See You Lai, it can't be too hard to find her. You did it once. You can do it again," pronounced Philip.

At this point I was getting seriously pissed. Judy and Philip had enough money to retain a private investigator, and probably find Daisy within two weeks' time, if they really wanted to find her. Their behavior was contradictory. On the one hand, they were telling me how imperative it was for Grandma to find peace before dying and how committed they were to helping her do so. But they refused to spend a penny on making it happen and were asking me, after I told them Daisy didn't want to hear from me and that I didn't have the money to do what they could have done themselves.

The size of their request was nominal on the surface, but internally it churned up a tremendous amount of fear and confusion. The word that would best describe my feeling in that moment is *objectified*. My being there was nice, but incidental and a mere stepping-stone to their true goal, which was to bring Daisy back home.

Simmering with resentment, I bit my tongue. What I really wanted to say was that despite what she said, I didn't believe Judy really wanted that to happen. She had the means, intelligence, and aggressiveness that wouldn't allow something as insignificant as distance to impede her in the pursuit of a goal. And it wasn't as if she was unfamiliar with the States. When she and Philip married, they held two ceremonies: one in Hong Kong and another in New York City at the Plaza Hotel, with close to five hundred guests. If she could plan a wedding from Hong Kong, she could certainly organize a search for one human being.

As the elders continued to speak about the situation with Daisy as if I weren't in the room, my anger dangerously escalated. Over the years of my sobriety and time in therapy I had learned to control my temper, but I did have my triggers, and the family was pushing every button I had. My mind was racing as I sat there quietly trying to reconcile my feelings with their request of

me. The questions swirled in my mind: Why was I really there?
Didn't they care about how I felt? Did it matter at all to them
that Daisy had rejected me? Why couldn't they understand how
incredibly painful this request was? Not only painful, but in my
honest opinion, fruitless.

Not wanting to displease them, I caved in and said, "Yes,
Uncle Philip. I will help the family find Daisy. Just please understand that it isn't going to be as easy to do as you may think, and
she will probably hang up on me when she hears my voice."

I could tell the family was happy, but I was anything but. As
they continued to speak about how I should go about doing this
search, I became completely overwhelmed with emotion. This
was simply too much. And while I wanted to sit there quietly and
obediently, I was afraid that I was going to break down in tears
in front of them. Not wanting to "lose face," I jumped up from
my seat and said, "Excuse me. I can't do this right now." Running
up the stairs to my room, I flung myself on the bed and began
sobbing.

I was angry and humiliated by my lack of self-control and
worried that my reaction was going to cost me my relationship
with the family I had waited decades to meet. But at the same
time, I was upset at how they didn't see me as an individual, or
consider my thoughts or feelings as important at all. Their asking
me to do this was in my opinion not only in very poor taste, but
showing incredibly bad judgment. What they were doing was
the equivalent of recruiting a soldier for a Black Ops mission
without knowing if that soldier was psychologically fit for duty.
I knew I wasn't the right person for the job. I also knew what it
could potentially cost me. But I was also conflicted by my need
to make them happy and knowing the futility of the assignment.
They didn't know, nor did I have the heart to tell them, that Daisy

hated them. That in our time together she bitterly recalled stories of being beaten for no reason by her mother with a hairbrush. She talked of how she loathed their materialism. And she absolutely seethed with disgust whenever speaking of Judy. I don't know if it was a case of arrested development, of unresolved sibling rivalry gone amuck, but one thing I knew for sure: Daisy had intentionally cut her family off. She had their contact information and over the past eighteen years had made the conscious decision not to speak to them. She had my number, and didn't reach out to me either. She was done with all of us.

As I lay sobbing, I heard a tap on the door, and then I saw Samantha's face peek in the doorway. "May I come in?" she inquired, and I nodded yes. I was mortified for her to see me like this. Like my mother, I was a proud woman who didn't like public displays of vulnerability.

"I'm so sorry, See You Lai. They don't get it. That's just the way they are. Once they set their mind to something, you can't tell them anything." I reiterated all of my concerns and why I felt like I was being placed in a horrible predicament. She listened compassionately, assuring me that I wasn't crazy.

"I've been in the family for over ten years and still feel like an outsider. They don't mean to be cruel. They're just a little emotionally tone deaf," she said.

A little?

I then asked what happened after I left the room.

"Everyone started to talk about how much you were like your mother. How Daisy would react in the same emotional way. They said you are like her twin. Seeing you is like seeing Daisy." Which made sense, since I had inherited her emotional sensitivity and other psychological quirks as well.

After about a half hour, Samantha left once she felt assured that I was feeling better. Her small act of kindness was greatly appreciated, although I wasn't going to go back downstairs that evening. I was too embarrassed by my emotional display, and the fact that they knew I had cried.

The next day, I was greeted as if nothing had happened when we all gathered for breakfast. This time I appreciated their ability to pretend as if emotions didn't exist. I didn't want to try and explain to them why I was so upset the night before. Plus, I figured if anyone really wanted to know, they would ask.

As my trip wound to a close, there was still one conversation that I needed to have with my extended family: the identity of my biological father. Everyone had known what was going on at the time of Daisy's engagement, and my aunt Esther, and Judy in particular, shared stories about how wild Daisy had been as a teenager.

One story that stood out to me was how like me, Daisy was a runaway and a high school dropout who preferred drinking and partying to anything else. Esther shared how the family would go out on searches for Daisy's known associates on a regular basis in an effort to bring her home after she had been gone overnight. While the police were never involved, trying to curtail Daisy's out-of-control behavior was practically a full-time job for Poh Poh. Daisy never shared the extent of her unruly behavior as a teen, but the family was more than willing to recount how uncontrollable she was. During one of these storytelling sessions, I brought up the subject of her relationship with my dad and also of the man who was my biological father, the Air America pilot. They remembered him, but like Daisy, no one could recall his name.

I then told them the discrepancy between the stories given by Daisy and Dad about this man's racial background. It was Uncle Stephen who spoke up this time.

"He wasn't black black, See You Lai. You know, more like Puerto Rican."

Judy chimed in, "I think he was probably Brazilian . . ."

This was straight out of the 1993 film *Groundhog Day*.

"Dad swears he saw him one night and is absolutely certain that he was a light-skinned black man," I stated, continuing, "Do you think that it's at all possible that you're wrong?"

"Oh no, no. You not black. You Chinese and Brazilian. Maybe Puerto Rican or Cuban. Not black."

"But what if I *am* black?" I pressed. "Doesn't it matter?"

"Impossible," said Judy. "You not black."

As the topic was bandied back and forth, I couldn't even find it in me to bother to argue with them. My trip was almost over and I had no interest in getting into a potentially heated exchange with them over their ignorance.

If I wasn't black, then why was my skin tone so much darker?

If I wasn't black, then why was my hair so curly?

My questions, I realized, were irrelevant. Just as my parents had ignored my race in an effort to protect me from feeling different, my Chinese family was engaging in a similar ostrich-head-in-the-sand move. There was no point in trying to have a discussion on the diaspora of African people around the globe, as there was no way they were going to admit that one of their family members had black blood.

I realized that the bigger question to them wasn't *why* I looked the way that I did. It was *what* it would mean to them if in fact I actually was black. My coloring and features made me look more Filipina than Chinese. In Hong Kong society, most of the domestic workers were immigrants from the Philippines. That was embarrassing enough. But for me to be black? That was unconscionable. Of all the races, the African race is the most derided in China. This is partly because of their obsession with class and status and that for thousands of years, darker skin meant you were from the peasant class who worked in the fields. And thanks to Western media, those in the East had absorbed the false narrative of black people as dirty and bad, just like their Western counterparts.

I knew my family would continue to promote this polite lie to "save face," for the alternative would be they would have to admit having a black person in their family. Which, based upon their response to my question, was never going to happen. And while I understood why they took the position they did, it didn't tamp out my disgust at their behavior. It had taken me years to come to terms with my blackness. To view it as a symbol of strength and beauty. A connection to a race of people who were still here, in spite of the lash of slavery, institutional oppression, lynchings, dehumanizing laws, and social constructs that were designed to destroy our spirit while stripping away our physical, psychological, and intellectual capital for the benefit of a nation that deemed us three-fifths human. Many of us were lost along the way, but there is an indomitable fierceness and spirit of self-preservation that overshadowed the attempts of the many to subjugate and alienate the few. They did not understand how their "saving face" was a direct slap in my face for all that I held most dear about myself. A part of my identity that I was taught to hate but eventually learned to love, even revere. I didn't care what they thought about my blackness. It would not stop me from loving all of me. I would not place my Chinese ancestry above that of my African blood.

Did I tell them this? Of course not. But I knew that as they continued to get to know me, it would become very clear that I was a woman who was not going to change my identity in order to try to fit into their construct of who they thought I should be.

By the day of my flight to return home, I was both relieved and sad to go. In the end, nearly everyone came to the airport to send me off, including my poh poh. During my stay in Hong Kong, our communication was limited by the language barrier. But I could see her eyes always watching me, no matter where

I was in the room. I felt a true emotional connection to her, one that eluded me with all of the other family members. With my English cousins, I felt kinship. With the rest of my Chinese family I felt a distant, respectful connection. But Poh Poh and I clicked, despite our inability to communicate. In our interactions, I felt a faint sense of sadness, of longing, that we could not convey to each other with words. She loved me. That I knew. While the others may have viewed me as a curious oddity, I felt that universally transcendent emotion that knew neither distance, time, race, or class. I was her granddaughter. Her *ngoih syún néui*.

Standing next to her in the airport terminal, I had so many things I wanted to say. But neither of us could speak to each other without bringing another person into our conversation. I wanted to hug her, but knowing that the Chinese weren't affectionate made me keep a polite distance. Poh Poh stood stiffly upright while everyone else said their goodbyes. Finally, it was time for me to bid her farewell.

Knowing that a wave was a universal sign of greeting or good-bye, I smiled at her and waved, saying, "Goodbye, Poh Poh." As my hands were moving I saw her mask crumble and tears began to flow down her face. Stepping toward me, she threw her arms around my body and gave me a brief hug, stepping back quickly to compose herself. Tears began filling my eyes, too. For I knew in that moment that Poh Poh had allowed her emotions to override her decorum, and in our last moments together she allowed her true feelings to emerge from behind the respectability she wore like a mantle. I turned my head away so she couldn't see my face, embarrassed.

Judy bounded up and said, "Okay, See You Lai. You better go. You'll miss your flight! Travel safely!"

Composing myself, I grabbed my things and walked away from them. Sunlight flooded the entire airport wing like the in-

My son's high school graduation dinner.
(L to R) My daughter, Amanda, my best friend and "Mom,"
Carol Ingram, me, and my son, Christian, 2008.

side of an MRI cylinder. Walking slowly, every ten steps or so I turned around to see if they were still standing there. I saw Judy and Esther waving, along with my cousins. And Poh Poh standing in between them all, her tiny form still, arms hanging at her side. I hurried my pace and then turned around one final time as I was exiting the area to see if they were still standing there. Craning my neck, I looked. They were gone.

CHAPTER SIXTEEN

$\mathcal{D}$URING THE TIME I WAS AWAY, MY CHILDREN HAD STAYED OVER AT a friend's house in Westchester, and upon my return I went to pick them up and bring them home. While I had only been gone a week, it seemed like a lifetime. I had returned a changed woman. One more in touch with how important family ties were to the health and well-being of individuals and communities. More complete in some ways and wounded in others. Throwing my arms around my daughter Amanda, I gave her a big hug and handed her a gift I had brought back for her, Hello Kitty toys. My son greeted me with a gruff "Hi." Expressing his thanks when I handed him an abacus, he kept his distance. Christian wasn't a very touchy-feely person, and we rarely if ever hugged each other.

Once we got back home, I brought out the camcorder I had used to capture my trip and showed them the footage of my time in Hong Kong: the initial ride to Judy's home; the clapping as I climbed the stairs and was greeted by my family for the first time; the footage of Judy's home; our trip to Lantau Island to see the Big Buddha. Pointing out Poh Poh, I said, "That is your great-grandmother. Daisy's mother. And that woman there? She's your great-great-grandmother. My Tai Po. She's 103 years old!" With each change in scenery I would regale them with stories of what each situation was like. "We took a tram, like the one we have here in New York that takes you from the city to Roosevelt Island, to get to the top of Victoria Peak, where you can see all of Hong Kong from the mountaintop."

They shifted back and forth in their seats as I showed them the footage. I could tell they were not nearly as impressed as I was with the film. "Can we go now?" asked Amanda after ten minutes had gone by.

"Sure thing. Have fun," I said, as they both raced down the hall to the living room to watch television.

While I was very open with the sights and sounds of what it was like to see a foreign country with my friends, I kept the emotional aspect of the trip to myself. I didn't want to let them know my mixed feelings around my experience, for fear of tainting their thoughts about the family I had just reconnected with.

It felt good to be home. To be back in the city that had provided me the opportunity to create an entirely new life and racial identity. My children didn't seem too interested in my newfound connection to my Chinese family, for just as I had been brought up in a white home, with a white identity and white environment, they had been brought up in a black one. I believed it was my duty to protect them from the virulent racism that had poisoned my mind and spirit as a child. Which meant that unlike my parents, I made a point to discuss race and racism with them. To raise them in multicultural environments where their skin color was not a reason for shame. And to ensure that they would never feel the sting of the word *nigger* spat in their face. Not only did I actively teach them black history, but I shared what I had gone through as a child to make sure they understood that despite having been shielded from overt racism, they must admit its existence. I would not send my kids into the world as I had been. A harsh truth is better than the sweetest lie, and I made sure to inoculate them from the false belief that the safe and privileged space in which they were being raised in Park Slope was the only reality that existed.

My son swallowed my lessons the way a baby bird gulps food from its mother's gullet. When asked what his racial background was, he always answered "black." Despite not having a relationship with his biological father's family, his identity from the day he was born was intentionally shaped to be black and proud of that fact.

My daughter, on the other hand, despite being given the same messaging, elected to call herself multiracial. At the young age of six, she would correct me whenever I said the word *white* or *black* to describe a person. Rolling her eyes, she'd say, "Mom, it's not white, but Caucasian. And it's not black. It's African American." When I would ask her why she identified as multiracial, she would simply shrug her tiny light brown shoulders and say, "Because I am."

As she got older, she remained adamant in her self-identification. Her brother and I were lost as to how she had somehow managed to make herself color-blind. Was this some form of rebellion? I would look at her and wonder why she felt the need to select so many identities when I had fought so hard to be able to claim one. Where had she picked up on this message that she was "other"? Was it from her white friends at school? So I pressed her to explain to me why she couldn't just say she was black like Christian and me.

"Because I *am* multiracial, Mom, just like you and Chris! I'm a quarter Chinese. A quarter Dominican and half black. That makes me multiracial."

"Amanda, you're black. I don't know where you're getting these ideas, but trust me, girl. If it was 1960 your behind would be sitting in the back of the bus with the rest of us!"

She just stared at me blankly as I continued, "Just wait until you get out into the real world, Amanda. You'll see what I'm talking about. The world is not fair, and just because you say you're multiracial doesn't mean you aren't black in the eyes of society. I just want you to be prepared. We live in New York City, but once you get outside of here you'll see what I'm talking about. I'm not making this up!"

"Mom, the only reason why race is such a big issue is because *you* make it a big issue. This isn't Florida. We're not living in the sixties, or the eighties. Just because things were bad for you doesn't mean they have to be bad for me. This is *your* problem, not mine."

And in a huff she would storm away to her room to sulk.

Her words frightened me. How had I failed to give her a sense of black pride? She had a point—she was multiracial. But most black people in America are, unless they are Africans who have immigrated to the States. In time, I left the subject alone. For I knew that as she grew up, she would discover that as much as she wanted to pretend that we were living in a "post-racial" America, white supremacy was still alive and well. And as she grew older and saw how class intersected with race, I was confident that she would change her tune. Eventually she did.

❧

Not long after returning, I shared the photos I had received from my cousins through email with my brother, and told Julie about the reunion. Dan didn't have much to say when I called to tell him about the trip, and when I asked him if he wanted to go back to Hong Kong to meet the family, he declined.

"Why?" I asked. "They would love to meet you."

"I just don't have any interest, that's all," he replied.

As with the rest of us, once a subject was closed with my brother it was pointless to continue to engage in a conversation. Plus, I honestly couldn't blame him after his experience with Daisy. Mom was always a good listener, but I did feel somewhat uneasy speaking with her about my Chinese relatives since it was she who had picked up the slack when Daisy was taken from us. Although I was still very much on an emotional high, I didn't want her to feel marginalized because of my new relationship with my Chinese family. Mom and I had come a long way since the days of my youth and over the years I came to appreciate her more and more, despite my grievances with much of her parenting style. I had finally developed compassion and forgiveness for much of what happened between us.

By now, Dad and I were no longer speaking, so I didn't share the story with him. I had long since forgiven him for his well-intended lies about my racial identity, for I realized that the decisions he made as a twenty-something father were ones that he truly felt were in the best interest of our family—collectively. Sort of a Western version of "saving face," I guess. But at some point during the past three years, we both sort of just gave up on our relationship. For me, it was a gradual decision to not put the effort into staying in touch. For one thing, I was tired of being the initiator of communication with my family—all of them. Secondly, after he had come to visit me in New York a few years earlier and pulled his usual "raised in a barn" style of etiquette (like walking around my apartment in his bikini underwear despite my telling him I wasn't comfortable with this, especially in front of my children—and his tendency to eat the food I'd prepared and leave the plate for someone—meaning me—to pick it up), I had started to turn off emotionally again. His inappropriate actions at my sister's funeral, combined with his current boorish behavior, had brought back to the surface feelings of anger that I had pushed to the side seven years earlier. I had never forgiven him for enabling May Lai's addiction by trying to be the "cool dad" by going bar-hopping with her in South Beach. All of these unexpressed, silent resentments began to stretch the emotional tie between us to the breaking point.

I was beginning to believe his selfishness and lack of emotional intelligence weren't a thing of the past—they were who Dad was. To test my theory about him, one day I decided to perform an experiment to see how long it would take before he would pick up the phone and call me. Weeks turned into months, months into years, and it was now three years since we had last spoken. There was no final argument. No fireworks. Just an unspoken emotional current on which we drifted slowly away from each other.

A few months after I returned from Hong Kong, his mother, my Grandma Lou, died. This was the one and only time I picked up the phone to call him. His sister Doni had told me that he was not going to attend his mother's funeral because he was angry at his cousins for allegedly "stealing Grandma's money" (they didn't). In typical fashion, I took the initiative to try to talk some sense into him. I used a super-sized guilt trip to try to get him to change his mind, but in the end Dad opted to not go. If there was one thing that I loathed after my personal experiences with abandonment, it was a person who doesn't carry his weight, or do what's right. His decision to boycott his own mother's funeral was further confirmation that I had made the right decision by letting us drift apart.

I did, however, share my adventures in China with Doni, who expressed her dismay over the pressure my Chinese relatives put on me to try to find Daisy, given the fact that she had made it clear she wanted nothing more to do with me. "They're so insensitive, Sil Lai!" she exclaimed. "Why would they ask that of you?"

"I know, I know," I responded. "It's bullshit, but we'll figure it out." She felt that I was being too easy on them, but I disagreed. My newfound hope of finally having a proper family to belong to, a clan, drowned out the sound of her criticisms.

Now that I was back in the States, I had to at least make an attempt to honor my word to help them find my biological mother. There's nothing quite like a "Grandma is dying of cancer and this is her last request" guilt trip to spur a person into action. Truth be told, I only half-heartedly executed the search, and only for a very brief time. After running a report on one of the paid internet search engines, I downloaded it to my computer and sat on it. I wanted to see if they, especially Judy, would be as interested in maintaining a relationship with me as I was with them—without my constant initiating of contact. For the first year, I reached out to all of my family members and tried to keep in touch. I called Judy, Janet, and Poh Poh in Hong Kong a few times and we spoke, but due to the time difference and my work schedule it was hard to find a mutually agreeable time to chat.

I emailed Judy a few times, but she didn't seem particularly focused on trying to keep a connection to me. Eventually I did share the information I had found online about Daisy with her, but I was unwilling to go any further with "Operation Daisy" without any input from the woman who was insisting that I complete their mission. I was willing to keep my word, but they would have to participate in this search as well. It was too much responsibility to place on one person—especially one who wasn't equipped with the financial or emotional resources to handle it alone.

Aunt Esther was the main person I stayed in touch with for the first couple of years. Generally, we would speak every four months or so, with the exception of when she was in Hong Kong. As welcoming as she was of my calls, she was less enthusiastic about my desire to come back to Hong Kong to visit. By now it was 2008, and I was fully immersed in the publishing of my first book. While I had always struggled financially, thanks to a cash infusion from an angel investor, I finally had enough financial stability to take a short trip overseas to see Poh Poh, whose cancer had spread. I asked repeatedly if I could come and visit, but each time Esther demurred.

"The time isn't right. When Grandma stronger, you can come."

"But I really want to come and see her now, while she is in the hospital. I want to be there for support."

"See You Lai, it will be better when everything settle down. Grandma too weak right now. I will let you know when she is better."

Frustrated, I knew I had no choice but to defer to Esther's boundaries around my relationship with Poh Poh—again. On the one hand, I could have easily jumped on a plane and gone over to visit without her permission. But I felt it would be an incredibly inappropriate thing to do, considering my new status in the family. Plus, without their cooperation, it was unlikely I would even know which hospital my grandmother was in, let alone be granted access to her room. Instead of pushing the issue, I decided to let some time pass by and then repeat "The Ask." Always sensitive to a rebuff, I was secretly hurt that Esther didn't support my visiting Poh Poh. Of course, I wasn't going to tell her that, for fear of being cut off completely from the family that I had waited over three decades to find.

Esther typically spent three to four months per year in Hong Kong, arriving in October and departing just after Chinese New Year in February. This trip was going to be longer, since she was staying to support Poh Poh through her cancer treatment. While I wanted to call and check in on her and Poh Poh, I decided against it. She typically stayed with friends and I didn't want to bother them with my calls. Plus, I wasn't even sure if she had a cell phone while she was in China. Instead of worrying about Poh Poh's health and why Esther didn't want me to come and visit, I buried myself in my work, which kept my mind occupied around the clock.

My life as social entrepreneur left me very little free time to think much about what was happening with my family all the way around the globe. The grueling demands of my career had affected my interactions with even my closest friends, who lived only a couple of miles away from me in the States. Given all the complications around time zones and Poh Poh's health, my attempts to stay in touch with my Chinese family dissipated as well, another casualty of my crushing workload and the effort of sending my son off to college.

Part of me felt guilty, but I rationalized my lack of outreach with the fact that outside of Esther, for the first couple of years after my trip, no one in the family ever made an attempt to reach out to me. I had spent my whole life being the initiator of contact with everyone in my family. This pattern was one that had been going on for years, first with the members of my family of origin, and now with my Chinese family.

No, I told myself. *It's going to take two to tango here.*

And then one day I looked up and it had been over two years since I had spoken to Esther, and even longer to my other family members in Hong Kong. In spite of my self-imposed moratorium on outreach, I decided to pick up the phone and call her. It was now the spring of 2011, nearly six years after I had initially met my clan.

Esther answered the phone in her wheezy voice and, as always, was welcoming of my call. We spent the first few minutes catching up on her children, my cousins Dave and Phil, and her husband, Big D. The typical small talk you engage in after you haven't spoken to a distant family member in quite some time.

She wasn't going to bring up the family in China, so I turned the conversation toward Poh Poh's health.

"How is Grandma doing? Did her cancer go into remission?" I asked.

"Oh, See You Lai, Grandma died."

I was dumbstruck.

"When did this happen?" I half demanded.

"Let me think," she said, pausing for a moment before continuing. "I think Grandma died in September of 2008 and Tai Po died in 2009. February." She added, "It was so sad. Cousin Janet and Louie finally got married in November, I think 2008. At least Tai Po could attend the wedding."

Horrified, I asked, "Grandma and Tai Po are dead?" and without waiting for her response, I continued, "I wish someone would have told me she was so sick! I would've come to China. I would have come to the funeral!"

"See You Lai, we didn't want to upset you. It was a very busy time. First Grandma died. Then Janet get married. Then Tai Po died."

"But Esther . . . I would have preferred that someone tell me. It is bad news, but I would have come to support the family."

Our conversation continued for another fifteen minutes or so while I got the facts from her about the dates of Grandma's death, Janet's wedding, and Tai Po's passing. Grandma had passed away on September 7, 2008, from the stomach cancer that had spread throughout her entire body, a painful disease that had ravaged her small frame until she finally succumbed at the age of eighty. Tai Po had died on Valentine's Day 2009 from old age. She lived a long life, passing into the legacy of our ancestors at 106.

A sinking, hollow feeling spread throughout my gut as we spoke. A spreading sadness tinged with a hint of anger, which I successfully hid from her.

"Well, I'm very sorry for your loss, Esther. I will talk to you soon, okay?"

"Okay, See You Lai. I talk to you soon. Byeeee."

Click.

Large, fat tears began rolling down my cheeks. It was true that we hadn't spoken in two years, but that was only because I didn't call. Nothing stopped them from picking up the phone and sharing the news that my grandma had died. I understood the whole "collective before individual" thing, but this was ridiculous. How could the family have made the decision to take away my opportunity to say goodbye to my grandmother, a woman I loved? She was my poh poh as much as anyone else's. And while I wouldn't have been able to attend both funerals, I would have at least wanted the opportunity to send some sort of floral arrangement to Tai Po's. Once again, I felt utterly rejected.

And then there was the matter of my cousin Janet's wedding, the celebratory event of the decade in our family. Janet had gotten married in a lavish ceremony that everyone appeared to have attended—except for me. When I looked on her profile and saw the photos on Facebook, I witnessed an incredibly decadent series of large celebrations that had everyone in Hong Kong and some from abroad in attendance. How could she have a wedding and not invite me? I was family, too, wasn't I?

But for whatever reason, I was not welcome on her special day. This could not be an unintentional oversight. As the guest list was worked on for months, at some point Aunt Judy and Aunt Lisa made the decision to not include me. My eyes froze on a large group photograph with everyone on my mother's side of the family. It must have contained twenty people. All of my extended family was represented but my branch. It was at that point that my heart broke.

And that was when the words that Daisy said in 1997 came back to me.

"You know, See You Lai, those talk shows never share the reunion stories that don't have happy endings . . . Most family reunions after a long time apart end up with the families not staying together."

At the time I took her words for granted. But the reality was that they were a cruel prophecy, not only for my relationship with her, but now with her immediate family. Of course, they were much too polite to tell me that I was not one of them—I was an outsider who was never going to become a part of their clan. But their actions said it all. Naïvely, I thought that because we shared blood, I would not be relegated to outsider status like that of my cousin Phil's English now-wife and his brother Dave's ex-girlfriend (and now mother of his daughter Isabel). That I would not be doomed to the fate of Samantha and Karen— forever outsiders. But I obviously was, and in a way, my position was worse. Karen and Samantha did not share our blood. They were family through relationship only. The blood of our ancestors ran through my veins. I was one of them, yet despite their adherence to "filial loyalty," it was obvious there was a line of division between them and me.

Unlike when I was a child, as a woman, I had the wisdom and knowledge of self to know that their rejection had nothing to do with me per se, but was about their own amalgam of internal conflicts around race, class, and family dynamics.

The truth was that they didn't need me in order to feel a sense of completeness in the way I needed them. They did, however, need me to try and bring their "real" family home—my mother,

Daisy. But I had failed them by not wholeheartedly devoting myself to a quest that I deemed them capable of fulfilling. And my act of self-preservation and defiance, it seemed, had cost me dearly.

Yet my failure with "Operation Daisy" concealed larger issues that underscored their behavior toward me. From a values perspective, we shared nothing in common except for the need to belong. I was the family's metaphorical alley cat, feral and untamed, the one who had spent too much time clawing her way through the world, a Western one at that. Yet it was my fierce individualism that saved my life from ending up on the scrap heap due to my lack of formal education, money, or family support. I was free to redefine my story with values that ran counter to theirs, ensuring that I wouldn't become anyone's puppet. Our DNA linked us in many ways: physically, behaviorally, even our interests. But on a cultural level there was a complete disconnect.

In spite of my hyper-Westernized way of viewing and moving through the world, I felt their elitism and clannishness could be overcome. Class, even to the Chinese, is a very movable structure, particularly if you were wealthy. It didn't matter if your money was nouveau. A sizable bank account could overcome many barriers. But what was immovable was my self-identification as a black woman from the United States. While they never said it, my outspokenness about my racial pride and refusal to mute my voice for their comfort was symbolic of how our cultural and racial differences came together to build an unscalable wall between us.

China is primarily populated by people of Han (what are considered ethnically pure Chinese) descent—92 percent, in fact. The Chinese didn't have an inherently racist view on black people until they became more and more exposed to Western cinema and stereotypes. While it is wrong, when you take into account that there are fewer than 200,000 black people in China, a country made up of 1.3 *billion*, it isn't difficult to see how easy it would be for an entire race of people who in their lifetime would probably never see a black person (except through the stereotypes they saw in the media) to believe that we are inferior, violent, ugly, and subhuman. Hell, I was raised in the United States and I grew up being taught the same thing through the media I consumed, which served to reinforce the racist culture in which I was raised—despite personally knowing black people.

Barry Sautman is a sociology professor at the Hong Kong University of Science and Technology who focuses his work on the issue of racism against black people in China. He wrote, "It was imported as early as the 1880s by Chinese intellectuals exposed to the Western racist literature. In the media, Africa is portrayed as a house of horrors, with a huge number of people dying from diseases, wars and extremely high crime rates."

If I were in my Chinese relatives' shoes, would I be striving to reconnect with a woman whose identity and history made them "lose face"? No. Chance. At. All.

Epilogue

It is my belief that the things that can destroy you can also rebuild you. That our darkest experiences have the capacity to provide the greatest opportunities for growth and healing. Daisy's abandonment, my dad's refusal to acknowledge my racial identity or be a loving parent, Mom's clumsy attempts to discipline me or provide a strong female role model—all sent me out into the world seeking validation and worth wherever I could find it. Whether it was with the punks of my teenage years, or within the glittering, hollow world of fashion and celebrity, I repeatedly failed to create a healthy sense of self.

I was doomed from the start. By taking this approach, I placed responsibility for my healing and search for self-worth onto the shoulders of others, giving people with little or no investment in my well-being the power to define my value. Until I explored my own soul to discover the self-love and acceptance deeply buried within, I was condemned to wander the world in search of what had always been mine.

Through two of my greatest failures, I received my greatest gifts. The abandonment of Keith and the abuse of Nelson gave me two beautiful children who grounded me. It was my love for them that forced me to push through circumstances that, had I been alone, would have caused me to give up on life. Through grace, divine order, fate, or a perfectly imperfect sequence of events, I was able to pass through the darkness and into the light of a new world in which I had the freedom to *choose* my truth.

I fully recognize that not everyone has the capacity to do this. As flawed as my parents' treatment of me was, I realize that they were operating from their own brokenness. Much of what they did to me was done to them. For a variety of complex reasons, they simply did not have the ability or desire to break the patterns they inherited. Does this make them bad? I don't believe so. Did this make them ineffective in many ways? Absolutely.

Mom and I have since developed a close bond; however, I have not spoken to my dad since 2005 when I attempted and failed to convince him to attend his mother's funeral. As of today, it has been eighteen years since I have spoken to Daisy. I am still wounded by their abandonment, and I know that I most likely will never receive a full reprieve from the trauma of my past. However, free of the emotional discord and complexities of a relationship with Dad or Daisy, I have been gifted with the chance to alter the trajectory of my life, and the lives of my children.

My traumatic life experiences are what motivated me, in my own small way, to make the world a better place—beginning first with my children. My "outsider" status and repeated, traumatic rejections, while destructive, freed me from the filial sense of obligation and guilt that prohibits many adult children from ever feeling safe to challenge unhealthy family behaviors. My rage and dissatisfaction with myself spurred a lifelong quest to better myself. Although my addiction to alcohol nearly cost me my life, as of November 2015, one day at a time, I have not had a drink in twenty-one years. In spite of my lack of formal education, I have created a respected career as a domestic violence awareness advocate, writer, college lecturer, and media advocate, focused primarily on creating more diverse media representation of black and Afro-Latina women in an effort to reduce the disproportionately high rates of gender-based violence in the black community.

Even though I have made many mistakes, my children and I share a close bond. Our family dynamic isn't perfect, but both know unequivocally that I would lay my life down for them, something I never had. This innate sense of acceptance and unconditional love has allowed my children to soar in ways unimaginable to other members of my clan.

In my family, there is a history of broken dreams fueled by a lack of education and emotional neglect, an intergenerational curse that has skipped my children. Thanks to a significant scholarship through Prep for Prep (a nonprofit that trains and steers gifted minority children into elite private schools), Christian graduated from the prestigious Calhoun School on the Upper West Side of Manhattan, and attended Clark University in Worcester, Massachusetts. Amanda graduated from a revered all-girls college preparatory school, Saint Vincent Academy in Newark, New Jersey, and is attending a university within the SUNY system in New York. While both are still working on completing their degrees, educationally speaking, they have already gone farther than everyone else. By the grace of God, neither of my children seems to have inherited the trait of addiction that has ravaged my family for generations.

These are wonderful achievements, but on an emotional level, I too have fallen short. Despite my best efforts, my children have both expressed disappointment over my lack of emotional availability due to my work schedule, and other life choices. I desperately sought to create a nuclear family comprised of two parents, but like me, neither child has a relationship with their father. My son had to live through the final years of my addiction to alcohol, and both had to carry more responsibility than is fair when I struggled with major depression. In this way, I unwittingly repeated the sins of my parents. The hurt I have inflicted upon them was never intentional, but I managed to do it all the same.

That is a larger lesson of my story—we are all flawed. Whether we are all deserving of forgiveness is a topic for another book, but I can say that acknowledgment of one's shortcomings, open communication, and a commitment to righting the wrongs of the past can go a long way toward strengthening family bonds. I believe much of our identity is formed not only through traits passed down in our families, but also our personal temperament, and forces beyond our control. I may have had many privileges I was born into (like a loosely curled hair texture, light skin, consistent material sustenance, and conventional beauty), plus coincidences and fateful allies that helped propel me forward. No one can control the opportunities that we are blessed with, but those who are born or attain any form of privilege should endeavor to cultivate compassion for those who for whatever reason aren't able to be all that it seems they could.

Over the course of my life, including writing this book, I have come to understand that it is the norm and not the exception to be hungry for a sense of belonging in a world becoming increasingly devoid of true recognition and compassion for each other's humanity. This desperate need for emotional connection and healing isn't limited to those of us with mixed-race backgrounds or dysfunctional family histories. Far too often this vital attention is only paid when a person has experiences similar to mine. When there has been so much trauma that they are almost beyond the point of saving. Or it is never paid, and the tragically damaged are judged and pathologized by a society steeped in respectability politics.

The truth is that for every person who manages to do more than survive their oppressive childhoods, there are hundreds more who die directly or indirectly from the pain, or lead "lives of quiet desperation," just scraping by but never really thriving inside.

In order to break free from the chains that bind, one must take whatever action they can to disconnect internally from the larger systems of oppression, of which the family unit is merely a microcosm. True revolutionary change begins by first challenging yourself—not the world. Until you own your story and the complexities of your experience, no matter how much you may strain against it, you will still be enslaved—if not by your oppressor, by your past.

I spent the early part of my life furtively attempting to create a sense of healing by chasing celebrity and living a hedonistic, materialistic lifestyle. In popular culture today, this lifestyle is revered and held up as an aspirational goal that many young women with shaky self-esteem and few prospects for advancement seek to emulate. But, there are emotional wounds and deprivations no amount of money or notoriety can repair, and that many of us must heal before we can do more than just survive our past or present circumstances. To thrive requires us to actively struggle to find a greater sense of freedom, power, and meaning in the now.

My firsthand knowledge of the destructiveness of harmful conditioning is what drives me to shake up the status quo through my work around domestic violence awareness and media advocacy. Through my advocacy work to create more diverse representations of black women, I hope to demonstrate to the world that there is so much to our womanhood. That behind the stereotypes that proliferate media, we are *real people*. I know all too well that given a few different choices, the trajectory of my life would be very different, as well as how the media played a large role in shaping my personal views on the world and myself. For this reason, I believe that it is urgent that black women and girls be provided with more complex, nuanced, and balanced images that affirm their beauty instead of focusing on the deficits. Deficits that come from living in a world where our humanity is stripped from us on a daily basis through macroaggressions such as gendered violence, and microaggressions hidden as compliments, such as the ubiquitous "You're pretty for a black girl."

Though many would argue against this, being mixed race does not insulate you from the pain that comes with living in a country that dehumanizes and marginalizes black people—especially black women and girls. As a black woman of biracial descent whose family determined that it was in my best interest to ignore race, I know the damage that the fallacious "postracial" mindset can inflict on a black child. *Race matters.* Yes, it is purely a "social construct," but that doesn't minimize the impact of systemic racism. The solution to racism is not to avoid it, but to face it head on. Parents of children with black blood have a responsibility to push past their own idealistic notions around how things *should* be so their children are prepared for the way things actually are. True understanding of what it means to be black in America is developed by struggling with your child to forge an integrated identity that celebrates their blackness, as much as their other ethnicities. Through this one decision, we can take a small step toward eliminating the white supremacist mindset.

While my Chinese family remains elusive, I have myself and my children. And along the way, I have cultivated my own milieu, comprised of a patchwork quilt of souls that have loved me while I have been both whole and broken. Through their surrogacy, I have been able to do more with my life than I ever thought possible. In this small clan, I have ensured that my children will never live under the misguided premise that their skin color is defective, or that their lives have less value because they are black.

My racial identity is a point of extreme pride. I am a black woman. I live in a black world filled with black culture. I take comfort in knowing that as a black woman, I am a part of a people who, like myself, have been beaten down, and stripped of their ancestral heritage, but who remain unbowed. Acceptance and appreciation for one's identity, be it race, gender, or sexual orientation, is as vital to one's life as the very air we breathe. For my identity, no matter how it was denied or hidden by lies, is proof that while you cannot rewrite history, you can be the author of your life. I am a woman redefining her story in her own way, and for this reason, I am truly free, with all the joy, pain, and uncertainty that comes with it.

Postscript

N̄OT LONG AFTER LEARNING OF POH POH'S PASSING, I PITCHED AN
article to the then editor in chief of *EBONY* magazine, Amy
Barnett, about my strange experience with race and family, to
be featured in an upcoming issue titled "Multiracial in America." My article, published in May 2011 and entitled "Passing
Strangely," was the catalyst for this book. In 2012, my piece won
the "Salute to Excellence" award in the Magazine/Essay category at the prestigious National Association of Black Journalists
annual conference. Of course, I made sure to share it promi-
nently on my Facebook page.

As of today, no one on my Chinese side has "liked" it.

Acknowledgments

First and foremost, I would like to thank Amy DuBois Barnett for agreeing to publish the short-form version of my story in *EBONY* magazine. Without this opportunity, this book would not have been possible.

Thank you to my agent, Robert Guinsler, for taking me on as your client and advocating for me and my book. You are magnificent.

Thank you to Karen Hunter, for believing in me and my story enough to publish this book. Your willingness to tell *our* stories is an inspiration.

Thank you to my amazing editor, Alexis Garrett Stodghill. Your innate understanding of storytelling and wickedly sharp observations transformed this book. I am eternally grateful to you for the excellence of your craftsmanship.

Thank you, John Pasmore, for convincing me nearly ten years ago that my life story was worth sharing.

Thank you to my aunt, Shalina Lu, for your love and for helping to piece together the story of my life.

Thank you to my British kin: Aunt Esther, Big D, my cousins Philip, Samantha, and David Branagh, for embracing me as your family.

Thank you to everyone who has given me the opportunity to hone my writing craft on their platforms or promoted my work, especially Roy Johnson, Joy Reid, Alexis Garrett Stodghill, Kirsten West Savali, Terrell J. Starr, Roland S. Martin, Kierna Mayo, and Jamilah Lemieux.

Thank you to those who have touched my life in some way over the years and taught me the lessons of friendship and family: my mom, Julie Emmons; my brother, Daniel Baber; Carol Ingram; Wilson Christopher; Julio Castaing; Renau Daniels; Jeff Kaplan; Angela Lyons; Madeline and Tom Burrell; and Matthew Jordan Smith.

Last but certainly not least, thank you, my dearest Christian and Amanda, for loving me and giving me the privilege of being your mother.